Performance Measurement and Management for Engineers

Performance Measurement and Management for Engineers

Michela Arnaboldi, Giovanni Azzone & Marco Giorgino
Politecnico di Milano,
Department of Management,
Economics & Industrial Engineering
32 Piazza Leonardo da Vinci Milano

AMSTERDAM • BOSTON • HEIDELBERG • LONDON
NEW YORK • OXFORD • PARIS • SAN DIEGO
SAN FRANCISCO • SINGAPORE • SYDNEY • TOKYO

Academic Press is an imprint of Elsevier

Academic Press is an imprint of Elsevier
32 Jamestown Road, London NW1 7BY, UK
525 B Street, Suite 1800, San Diego, CA 92101-4495, USA
225 Wyman Street, Waltham, MA 02451, USA
The Boulevard, Langford Lane, Kidlington, Oxford OX5 1GB, UK

Library of Congress Cataloging-in-Publication Data
A catalog record for this book is available from the Library of Congress

British Library Cataloguing in Publication Data
A catalogue record for this book is available from the British Library

ISBN: 978-0-12-801902-3

For Information on all Academic Press publications
visit our website at http://store.elsevier.com/

This book has been manufactured using Print On Demand technology. Each copy is produced to
order and is limited to black ink. The online version of this book will show color figures where
appropriate.

CONTENTS

For additional information on the topics covered in the book, visit the
companion site: http://booksite.elsevier.com/9780128019023/.

ACKNOWLEDGMENTS

The idea of this book was developed at Politecnico di Milano by interacting with our students, alumni, and colleagues. We saw the importance that performance measurement and management has for engineers and, more generally, people with a technical background, such as architects and designers.

These professionals and managers are not meant to become specialists in finance or accounting, but they do make decisions that affect enterprises' value and performance. Engineers, architects, and designers are extremely interested in this field and want to learn more, but information about this field is often spread across many books, vertically analyzing techniques.

This book has a different perspective and is for students, managers, and professionals with a technical background who want to understand what enterprise value is, how to measure it, and how and why to manage it.

To achieve this goal, we assembled topics from financial accounting, management accounting, and finance; this was a challenge that we pursued with the support of our research group.

In particular, we acknowledge the help of Deborah Agostino, Marika Arena, and Tommaso Buganza, who are coauthors of chapters in this book. We are also grateful to Antonio Conte, Laura Grassi, and Yulia Sidorova, who wrote the cases that are available online. Finally, we would also like to thank Emanuele Lettieri, Lucio Lamberti, Paolo Maccarrone, and Martina Santandrea for their valuable comments on the preliminary versions of the book.

ACKNOWLEDGMENTS

CHAPTER 1

Introduction

Large infrastructural projects, technology and product development, manufacturing reconfiguration, and cloud computing conversion are just a few examples of activities that are now carried out in enterprises with increasing frequency. These activities are usually managed by engineers from various disciplines, yet they widely impact overall financial performance, exposure, and company value. In this context, it is mandatory to have managers who are capable of measuring weak signals from operations and projects; understanding their wider financial impact considering internal and external stakeholders; and then knowing, as a consequence, the impact on the enterprise value.

Enterprise value is the backbone of this book and the focus of this introductory chapter. In the first section, we illustrate what enterprise value is, how to measure it and, finally, how value can be managed in a coordinated but delegated manner.

1.1 WHAT IS ENTERPRISE VALUE?

To address the question "What is enterprise value?" it is first useful to understand what an enterprise is.[1] Instead of quoting the formal definition, we can conceptualize companies as *input—output systems* (Figure 1.1).

Enterprises aim to provide outputs (products and services) to customers and to add value to employed inputs, which include human, financial, and technological resources. To simplify: Enterprises want to maximize their output against their inputs. This simple logical thinking clashes with a fundamental computational problem: There are different types of inputs (people, machines, and patents) and outputs (various products and multiple services), each of them with diverse measurement units; hence, we simply cannot list all of them. To solve this problem and analyze the enterprise capability of creating value, money is used as a reference measurement unit. Inputs and outputs can then be expressed in *cash* equivalents, measuring inputs in term of the cash outflows needed to get them and outputs in terms of cash inflows deriving from their sale. From an economic point of view, we can further distinguish between:

- *Investments (I)*: Investments refer to cash outflows related to the purchase of assets that a company is going to use for more than 1 year; examples of assets are machinery, patents, equity investments, and land.
- *Cash flows (CF)*: Cash flows refer to cash exchanges related to transactions that have an impact on the short-term operating cycle of the company. Some examples include cash inflows originated by the sales of products or services and cash outflows for personnel wages, material purchases, or rent.

---

[1]In this book, we refer to profit organizations.

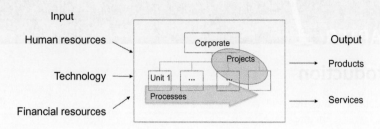

Input

Human resources

Technology

Financial resources

Output

Products

Services

Corporate

Projects

Unit 1   ...

Processes

Figure 1.1 A company as an input–output system.

Starting from this assertion, considering a single year, the contribution of company activities to the value of a company can be expressed as net cash flow (NCF) originated for Year 0:

$$V = \text{NCF}(0) = \text{CF}(0) - I(0)$$

However, companies are founded and then are supposed to have an infinite lifecycle; hence, to understand the overall value, the time horizon must be lengthened, considering not only the NCF originated at Year 0 but also all the NCFs that the enterprise is going to generate in future years, with an infinite (∞) horizon of time (Figure 1.2).

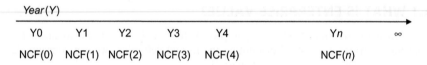

Year(Y)

Y0	Y1	Y2	Y3	Y4	Yn	∞
NCF(0)	NCF(1)	NCF(2)	NCF(3)	NCF(4)	NCF(n)	

Figure 1.2 Time horizon for enterprise value and NCF analysis.

The sum of NCFs originated in different years can appear to be the simpler solution to calculate the overall value, yet this solution overlooks a crucial issue. The value of money changes over time. To test this issue yourself, think about this: Would you agree to give a company 10,000€ this year (Y0) in exchange for 10,000€ next year (Y1)? The answer would be no because you could invest your 10,000€ in other risk-free activities—such as government bonds—to obtain a greater amount of money. For example, if the annual interest rate of government bonds (the so-called risk-free rate) is 3%, by investing 10,000€ now (Year 0), you will get back 10,300€ in 1 year. To explain these calculations:

$$V(0) = 10,000 \quad [\text{Value at } Y0]$$

$$V(1) = 10,000 * 0.03 = 10,300 \quad [\text{Value projected at } Y1 \text{ with the annual risk-free rate of 3\%}]$$

This future projection of cash flows is generalized with the compounding formula, where r_f is the risk-free rate, n is a generic year, and FV stands for future value.

$$\text{FV}(n) = V(0) \times (1 + r_f)^n \quad [\text{compounding formula}]$$

Going back to our problem of summing NCFs originated in different future years (Figure 1.2), we have the opposite problem: to calculate the *present value (PV)* of future cash flows. In this case, we use the discounting formula that can be easily obtained by the previous one:

$$PV(0) = \frac{FV(n)}{(1 + r_f)^n} \quad \text{[discounting formula]}$$

The discounting formula allows us to solve the computational problem of summing expected cash flows over different years. Using the risk-free rate and considering an infinite horizon, the present value of future NCFs can be obtained as follows:

$$PV(0) = \frac{NCF_1}{(1 + r_f)^1} + \frac{NCF_2}{(1 + r_f)^2} + \frac{NCF_3}{(1 + r_f)^3} + \cdots + \frac{NCF_N}{(1 + r_f)^N}$$

$$PV(0) = \sum_{t=0}^{+\infty} \frac{NCF_t}{(1 + r_f)^t} \quad \text{[present value in risk-free conditions]}$$

The calculation of the present value using the risk-free rate does not take into account another element of business activities: Enterprises operate in uncertain conditions; hence, they are not considered by investors as risk-free activities. This uncertainty is compensated by a risk premium for shareholders, who are individuals or entities buying and owning shares of equity[2] in a corporation. Considering risk from the shareholders' perspective, the present value formulation changes by including the risk premium at the denominator in the discounting factor, which is called cost of equity capital (k_E). Here, the generic term NCF is substituted by the term free cash flow to equity (FCFE) to clarify that we assume that cash flows pertain to shareholders.[3]

The value formulated in this perspective is called the equity value (E) and is analytically expressed by

$$E(0) = \sum_{t=0}^{+\infty} \frac{FCFE(t)}{(1 + k_E)^t} \quad \text{[Equity present value]}$$

Finally, it is important to consider that enterprises are financed not only by equity capital (E) but also by debt capital (D), which may be referred to two main investors: financial institutions and bondholders. In this case, we can still refer to the formulation of equity present value, but another perspective can be adopted wherein the value is calculated with reference to all capital investors (equity and debt). In particular:

- Cash flows at the numerator pertain to both equity and debtholders and are called free cash flow to firm (FCFF).
- The discounting rate is the weighted average cost of capital (WACC), including the required rate of return of shareholder capital (k_E) and the average interest rate of debt (k_D) after tax $(1 - t)$, where t is the tax rate:

$$WACC(t) = \frac{D}{D + E} \times k_D \times (1 - t) + \frac{E}{D + E} \times k_E$$

---

[2] Refer to Annex 1 for an illustration of equity and financial accounting basics.
[3] Chapter 2 illustrates the calculation in detail for both k_E and FCFE.

The formulation using the investors' perspective is called the enterprise value (EV) and is expressed as follows:

$$EV(0) = \sum_{t=0}^{+\infty} \frac{FCFF(t)}{(1+WACC)^t} \quad \text{[Enterprise present value]}$$

1.2 HOW TO MANAGE ENTERPRISE VALUE: ENLARGING THE PERFORMANCE MEASUREMENT TOOLKIT

Having defined present value as a measure of a company's objective, the next stage is to understand how to use this metric for performance management. Although present value has the advantage of being synthetic and unique, its operational use is not straightforward, as we cannot measure value in an objective way—we can only estimate it, and any estimation depends on the expectations and information of the single investor looking at the firm. The difficulty in measuring the value of a company is even worse in the present competitive environment for several reasons:

- *Increasing pressures for enterprise sustainable corporate behavior*: Enterprises are nowadays required to show their capability to pursue not only economic but also environmental and societal sustainable behaviors (often referred to as the *triple bottom line*). This broadens the factors to be considered as value drivers, although their impact on NCFs is sometimes uncertain. Think, for example, of environmental damages: forecasting their impact on present value is not easy due to the interconnectedness between effects on a company's reputation, the financial market reaction, and actual damages and costs to be sustained, but each of these can be measured and managed as drivers of $V(0)$.
- *Tradeoff between completeness and timeliness*: The present value is indeed a complete and long-term-oriented measure, which theoretically takes into account all the factors affecting the company cash flows with an infinite time horizon. However, even if we assumed that a company were able to assess all relevant factors across time (e.g., quality, environmental changes, financial market reaction), the time required to translate them into NCF and then to compute present value wouldn't be compatible with the short time frame required for the many decisions that are made every day in companies.
- *Misalignment with managers' responsibility*: Present value is the reference for everyone in the organization, yet only top executives have wider visibility (and responsibility) over all the variables affecting present value; other managers across the organization are in charge of specific projects, processes, and functions in which there is a need to have more specific measures aligned with their responsibilities and their area of authority.
- *Interconnection between enterprise and global risks*: Risk is inbound in every business activity and is considered formally in the present value formulation with the cost of capital (k); the higher the risk, the higher the required rate of return for stakeholders. Yet the repeated financial crises have shown how excessive enterprise risks (and failures) have repercussions that go beyond the specific context in which they originate due to the globalization of financial and competitive markets. This situation has posed risk and "risk appetite" as significant factors, pressuring companies—more so than in the past—to measure not only present value but its variability and potential loss and to monitor frequently weak signals to anticipate change

in performance and in the risk profile. Again, in theory, present value could be used, but the time required for its operational use would not be useful for decision making.

As a result, present value is more a conceptual reference than an operational measure for managerial needs. A wider set of indicators (our performance measurement toolkit) is required to drive value and to warn of possible loss and variances that might impact the company results and risk profile. In particular, the indicators in this book are organized into three categories:

- *Value-based measures*: These indicators aim at measuring more holistically value. They include the direct measurement of value and its components: NCF, the cost of capital (k), and the terminal value of the company. In addition, value-based measures include other indicators that aim to measure the value and its potential loss through proxies.
- *Accounting-based indicators*: These are indicators based on financial statements. These include traditional (but still diffuse) ratio indicators such as return on investment (ROI) and return on equity (ROE).
- *Value drivers*: These encompass nonfinancial performance indicators (e.g., delivery time), resource indicators (e.g., human resource turnover), and key risk indicators (e.g., supplier failure). These indicators are called value drivers because they provide early signals about the future achievement or loss of present value, and they have become crucial in turbulent contexts in order for companies to decide and act timely.

1.3 WHY TO MANAGE ENTERPRISE VALUE: A MULTISTAKEHOLDER PERSPECTIVE

The previous section showed the opportunity to have a wider set of indicators in order to better measure and then operationally manage value. To fully understand how we can manage performances, a crucial final stage is analyzing why we need to measure and manage performances.

In general terms, we need a performance measurement and management system to serve different stakeholders that can be divided into two realms:

- *External*, including individuals and entities who have direct or indirect interests in enterprises and therefore in monitoring and controlling enterprises' performances; they are addressed as stakeholders and include shareholders, debtholders, and other societal actors more broadly.
- *Internal*, which refers to managers operating at different levels of the enterprise.

Figure 1.3 (adapted from Damodaran, 2011) visualizes all these actors introducing the concept of *internal accountability*, which is the use of indicators by and for managers and *external accountability*, which is the use of indicators to account for results externally.

The following sections illustrate in detail who these actors are, their needs, their influence on companies, and the role of performance in the two realms of internal and external accountability. In particular, we start with the analysis of different categories of stakeholders and their influence on managers; then, we illustrate instruments to account and control behaviors from the outside (external accountability); and, finally, attention is moved toward managers and the use of performance measures to support their decisions and guide their behavior (internal accountability).

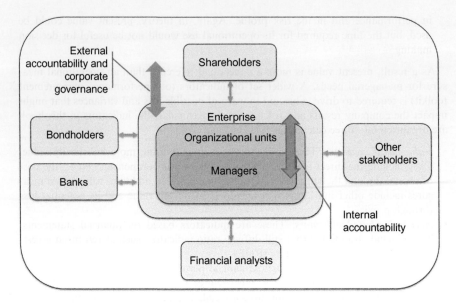

Figure 1.3 Internal and external accountability. Adapted from Damodaran, 2011.

1.3.1 Enterprise Stakeholders

The actions of enterprises and, in particular, managers' behaviors and decisions are affected by a large set of actors—understanding who they are, their interests, and their potential influence is the first step in comprehending accountability requirements outside and inside enterprises.

1.3.1.1 Shareholders

Shareholders are the main investors in risk capital for enterprises. Managers are asked by shareholders to increase the company value. More precisely, shareholders ask managers to increase the company equity value. In the case of a public company, it is possible to know the exact current value of the share (i.e., the so-called market value), which is the stock price at that moment. In general terms, this value changes continuously (even more than once per second), reflecting the information that circulates about the company and during trading activities in real time.

The current share market value is hence the central element of analysis for shareholders, who have an influence on the decisions managers make. This goal might be short-term oriented, and it might not be aligned with the maximization of the present value. To clarify this potential misalignment, consider the possibility for an enterprise to invest in a valuable project with a positive present value; it is quite reasonable that managers should decide to invest. However, there could be some consequences, such as:

- *Uncertainty*: The value of a project is an *expected* value, which means that both cash flows and the cost of capital are probabilistic, not certain. Thus, a project that seems to be a great opportunity right now could turn out to be unattractive due to unexpected events that could affect the company—e.g., revenues could be lower, costs could become higher, or the company's level of risk (i e., its cost of capital) could increase.

- *Opportunism*: Managers could present opportunistic behavior due to misguided information. They could enter into low-value projects, making them appear to be great opportunities, persuading the financial market of their positive value, causing the projects to have an enhanced current value. This could especially happen if managers have personal interests—for example, if their remuneration is linked to the current stock value, which makes them adopt a short-term view.
- *Alternative opportunity*: Due to financial constraints, the choice to enter into a project means that a manager must choose not to enter into another one, especially in the case of relevant projects. Thus, present decisions could restrict future ones, even though that is not always apparent.

The consequences of misalignment between managerial decisions and shareholders' perspectives can be serious. If shareholders do not agree with managers' choices, according to company bylaws and national laws, they could:

- Replace the board of directors: In fact, shareholders have the right to ask some directors to be replaced. In some cases, this request could result in the renewal of the whole board. In such an event, there is typically a call for an unexpected shareholders meeting.
- Sell their stocks in private transactions or on the stock exchange if the company is listed. The probability and the success of this latter action are related to the liquidity of the stock. A share is said to be liquid if there is a consistent volume of outstanding shares traded every day, which is a proxy of the probability to sell owned shares soon, and if the bid-ask spread[4] is quite narrow, which reflects the probability of selling shares at a price that is not too disadvantageous.

The influence of shareholders over managerial decisions varies from company to company. The term *shareholder* actually refers to a plurality of subjects, sometimes with different information and rights. In particular, there is a major difference between controlled and noncontrolled[5] companies. *Controlled companies* are those where there is either:

- A major shareholder who owns more than half of the ordinary shares
- A minor shareholder who owns either more than 30% of the ordinary shares or more than 20% of the ordinary shares and more than the 50% of the quota owned by all shareholders whose participation is higher than 2% of the ordinary shares
- A shareholders' agreement on more than 20% of the ordinary shares or the company is controlled by a noncontrolled unlisted company on which there is a shareholders' agreement in force about the majority of the shares.

Noncontrolled companies are either those companies not included in the previous description (referred to also as *public companies*) or *cooperative companies*.

If a company has a major shareholder, managers will tend to follow his or her objectives, which turns out to be more difficult in the case of a public company. This possible difference between major and residual shareholders (i.e., all nonmajor shareholders), which typically arises outside the Anglo-Saxon context, is relevant to company operations. These shareholders are the focus of the Corporate Governance Code, which is introduced later in this chapter.

---

[4]The bid-ask spread is the difference between the price of the best selling proposal and the best buying proposal, as reported by the stock exchange.
[5]The definition is based on the Consob *2013 Report on Corporate Governance of Italian Listed Companies*, which relies on international principles and practice.

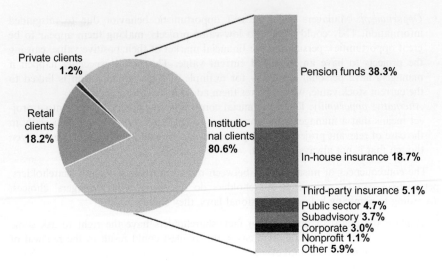

Figure 1.4 Assets managed in the United Kingdom by client type. IMA, Asset Management in the UK 2011–2012, The IMA Annual Survey, 2012.

Finally, to understand the link between managers and shareholders and the influence of the latter on enterprises, another relevant element to be considered is who the shareholders of a company are. Figure 1.4 demonstrates quite well the incredible presence of institutional investors (i.e., pension funds, mutual funds, insurance companies, investment trusts, and other collective investment vehicles) in the shareholders' room of UK companies. Afterward, they have a remarkable influence on both companies operations and managerial decisions. Institutional investors could have the same interests of individual investors in the way they manage the shares on behalf of their clients, but they are also more skilled and better-informed.

1.3.1.2 Debtholders

The debtholders of a company could be divided into banks (or financial institutions) and bondholders. Their attitude might differ from shareholders. In fact, in the case of an increase of leverage (i.e., the ratio between the amount of debt and equity) of the company or an increase of the dividend payout, creditors are damaged in favor of shareholders.

Banks and, more broadly, financial institutions are extremely relevant in supporting the development of a company and granting it loans. The loans provided could be different in terms of:

- The amount granted
- The maturity
- The interest rate—i.e., fixed, floating during the duration, mixed or capped rate, with a cap or with a floor
- The type of the amortization schedule—i.e., how the initial lending will be repaid
- Other features—e.g., prepayments, collateral required, late payment interest.

The main characteristic of a loan is, however, its seniority. The seniority of a debt indicates the priority of its reimbursement in case of bankruptcy. Generally, mortgage loans have the highest seniority, while lines of credit have the lowest.

Thus, each debtholder has the objective to ensure his or her loan with the highest security in order to be more confident of its repayment and hence limit the counterparty risk he or she suffers. In addition, a shrewd lender will require the company to fulfill some covenants[6] to limit the amount of dividends a company could pay out. However, things are changing.[7] If the proportion of covenant-lite debt increases, the company could become more risky and have higher leverage. Shareholders could take advantage of that, while creditors could not be compensated with a yield, which really reflects the company fundamentals.

Bondholders' relevance in company operations is strengthened if they are institutional investors, while small-scale savers have less influence. Small-scale creditors are more interested in the features of the corporate bond, such as the amount and frequency of the coupon and its maturity, rather than company operations. This will result in less micromanaging, which could result in less pressure to improve the management of the company.

1.3.1.3 Other Stakeholders

The environment in which the company operates causes it to come into contact with a plurality of actors who could influence the company's choices. These actors include:

- Employees, who are interested in gaining benefits such as insurance policies or medical expense reimbursement, compensations and rewards, and continuous training and development and career opportunities. They also require nondiscrimination and the opportunity for part-time work if their circumstances change.
- Customers and suppliers, who consider the company's general policy and its reputation. In addition, the former are interested in product safety and in the company's awareness of their needs, while the latter guard their relative power.
- The local community aims to increase job placement within the community and to improve the services and opportunities it offers to citizens. In addition, environmental conservation and contamination control are among their primary issues.
- State and local authorities are responsible for public health, safety, and protection and are interested in boosting community relations. They guard company development also because they collect taxes and act as arbitrators to avoid the offshoring of production in case the company is ready to drop. They also try to attract companies, providing incentives and granting services.

Some companies have started to release corporate social responsibility reports whose main aim is to disclose how the interests of stakeholders are considered. Nowadays, it is quite common for listed companies to provide this document. It is a good omen that an increasing number of nonlisted companies' managers are also considering this issue to be more relevant.

In addition, stakeholders could be included in an effective way as directors. Generally, this opportunity is presented only to a particular category of stakeholders—i.e., employees. It is typical in Germany for an employee representative to be on the supervisory board. In fact, large companies with more than 500 employees are required to have at least one-third of the supervisory board be represented by

---

[6]Covenants are clauses that dictate how the company has to perform during that time (i.e., NFD/equity not higher than a cap or EBITDA/financial interests not lower than a floor...).
[7]For example, refer to "Cov-lite loans soar in dash for yield" by Stephen Foley (2013) available at ft.com.

employees. In addition, German companies with at least five employees also form a work council whose objective is to represent the interests of employees within the company.

1.3.1.4 Financial Analysts

A financial analyst is a professional who is responsible for investigating companies that belong to the same industry, the same country, or the same market (e.g., large, mid, small caps). In fact, he or she is tasked with performing a deep analysis of the company, focusing not only on the financial aspect but also on the overall business. The final report to be released on the stock exchange will contain the stock target price and a rating (e.g., buy, neutral/hold, or sell), which will drive investment decisions, the analyses carried out, and investment ideas.

Generally, it is possible to divide financial analysts into sell-side and buy-side analysts. A sell-side analyst works for a brokerage or firm (e.g., investment bank, independent research company) that gives blanket recommendations to the firm's clients. A buy-side analyst works for a pension fund or mutual fund company, focusing only on those investments that could fit fund clients' characteristics. Its research and recommendations are only available directly to the portfolio managers of the fund and are not available to anyone outside the fund. The analyst should determine how promising an investment seems and how well it coincides with the fund investment strategy.

Usually, the typical equity research report includes:

- Investment summary
- Business description
- Industry overview and competitive positioning
- Financial analysis
- Valuation (generally value-based and relative valuation)
- Sensitivity analysis
- Investment risks
- Additional information, such as strategy, company history, top management, compensation and ownership, human resources, or corporate governance
- Disclaimer.

The report is called *Initial Coverage* if it is the first report the brokerage firm writes on that company—e.g., in the case of an initial public offering (IPO), breakup, equity carveout, or if it is the first report in many years. The report is called a *Company Update* if it is a periodical update of information—for example, after the quarterly results or a supplement due to new information becoming available.

Financial analysts' research reports on listed companies are an additional hard source of information and a description of the company itself. Furthermore, analysts provide a complete evaluation of the company value: providing the target price is similar to or better than providing the market capitalization and thus the value. The relevance of their evaluation, based on deep expertise in the financial market, also relies on the independence and fairness of the judgment they provide.

1.3.2 External Accountability

Having defined actors influencing companies' performances, we now illustrate the instruments that companies adopt to be accountable outside—that is, external accountability. There are two central instruments in particular: disclosure and corporate governance.

1.3.2.1 Disclosure

All stakeholders are interested in enterprises' performances and risks. While in the past the main reporting line was financial statements, nowadays there is more information provided externally, and the way of communicating this information influences these actors. If, for example, there is a perception that an enterprise is not environmentally friendly, investors may become more skeptical, and the government can enact more restrictive laws. This information (published outside the company) may be called disclosure.

To be disclosed externally, performance indicators have to be relevant and trustworthy. For financial reporting, there are national and international reference standards that are followed by companies in drafting their reports. However, nonmandatory reports, such as social, environmental, and sustainability reports, do not follow predefined standards, and companies have the freedom to choose the type of indicators and information to be published. This freedom might cause stakeholders to doubt the company if the company publishes information that is more favorable to its image. To avoid this situation, disclosure should be:

- Complete with reference to international or national standards; although nonfinancial reports are not mandatory by law, there are international independent bodies that have developed recognized standards for sustainability, environmental, and social reports. An example of this standard is the Global Reporting Initiative (GRI).
- Stable across time; changes in reporting initiatives have to be justified.
- Transparent and understandable for readers; this implies that performance indicators included in these reports have to be measurable and clear.

1.3.2.2 Corporate Governance

The Corporate Governance Code is a regulatory framework regarding how companies are governed, the interests companies serve, and the types of objectives they are pursuing.

The relevance of corporate governance issues has been addressed by the European Commission (among others), whose Green Papers aim is to stimulate the discussion about specific topics in order to gather opinions of and comments on relevant subjects before the issuance of EU dispositions. Furthermore, following the financial crisis, the European Commission has stated[8] that weakness in corporate governance played an important role in the development of the financial crisis, even though corporate governance could not be identified as the primary cause of the crisis. In addition, it will examine corporate governance rules and practice within financial institutions, particularly banks, and make recommendations or propose regulatory measures.

Earlier, the Organisation for Economic Co-operation and Development (OECD) released its 1999 "OECD Principles of Corporate Governance," which is now undergoing its second revision after the 2004 one. This has been indicated as the milestone for the subsequent diffusion and adoption of the Corporate Governance Code.

Nowadays, more than 90 countries in the world have at least one Corporate Governance Code in force. Corporate governance provisions are inserted in both national laws and regulations and in the National Codes of Corporate Governance.

---

[8]European Commission, Green Paper 2010.

In general terms, these codes contain best practices in terms of corporate governance, adapted at a national level to take into consideration the peculiarities of each system. These provisions are related to some core governance issues, such as board, director, and manager compensations; internal control systems; risk management; and shareholders' and stakeholders' rights.

Although the code could be useful for any company, it is generally addressed to listed ones, which could autonomously decide whether to adopt it. Nevertheless, the stock exchange requires companies to disclose their choices. In addition, even if the company adopts the code, it is possible that it will not fulfill all the included provisions. This possibility is called the "comply or explain approach," which makes each company disclose the provisions it does not comply with, illustrating its motivations. This approach gives flexibility to companies that could adapt any dispositions to their specific size, shareholding structure, and departmental specifications.

The structure of the codes is quite standardized, following the Anglo-Saxon guidelines and format. This uniformity lets institutional investors lower their effort in terms of costs and time spent to analyze all the provisions, thus concentrating only on those country-specific provisions that differentiate each code.

In addition, these Codes are continuously revised in order to (i) promptly respond to the market and society's innovations, developments, and changes; (ii) consider concrete problems that have recently occurred; and (iii) be in line with the adoption of some provisions into the national laws, resolutions, or codes (e.g., the 2011 Italian Corporate Governance Code does not include provisions regarding transactions with related parties anymore, as Consob provided a resolution in 2010).

To better take into consideration the feature of particular companies, some specific codes were released. The United Kingdom is considered to be the birthplace of Corporate Governance Code, and its leadership position is reiterated in its forward-looking view. For example, the United Kingdom published the "Corporate Governance Guidance and Principles for Unlisted Companies in Europe," which were a restricted set of provisions whose adoption should increase with the complexity of the company, and the "Good Governance Code," which was directed at voluntary community organizations whose traits reflect their peculiarities, such as the presence of a trustee in place of the board, and the "Code of Good Practice" through which the HM Treasury aims to guide central government departments.

So far, there have been some open questions about the possibility of diversifying the governance provisions according to the company size and type and about how to effectively encourage unlisted companies to adopt best practices.

1.3.3 Internal Accountability

Internal accountability refers to the use of performance and risk indicators to guide management in pursuing their goals of maintaining viable patterns of behavior. Changing our perspective from the outside to the inside, we introduce the concept of a performance measurement system (PMS), which is intended to guide the decisions and behavior of managers by providing performance and risk indicators. Hence, PMS has two main intertwined functions:

- Decision making—that is, the use of indicators to support managers' decisions
- Motivation—that is, the use of indicators to align behaviors and motivate individuals to work toward enterprise goals.

1.3.3.1 Decision Making and Indicators

To illustrate the role of PMS for decision making, we can think of these functions as satellite navigators applied to managerial decisions in order to:

*   Understand if objectives are in line with available resources
*   Compare different ways to achieve objectives
*   Determine if actions carried out across the organization contribute to the company's overall objectives.

The role of PMS becomes clearer when one analyzes the four logical phases of a decision process: planning, measurement, variance analysis between planned and achieved results, and corrective action introduction. Figure 1.5 illustrates the phases in the control cycle positioned around a box, which represent the object to control (the overall enterprise, an organizational unit, a product, or a project).

The first phase is *planning*. This phase defines a set of objectives to achieve, risk factors that can identify their achievement, resources needed, and a plan of action through which available resources are used for the different goals.

The role of PMS in this phase is to help decision makers estimate the compatibility between resources, objectives, and actions—similar to the support offered by a satellite navigator in assessing if our destination can be reached within the time available. To this purpose, PMSs are based on a model of the enterprise functioning. To clarify this need, an analogy can be made to another individual decision: studying abroad. The period abroad becomes the object to control. In the programming phase, the study options are assessed in terms of resources available (time and costs); goals (university, destination); and possible sources of risk (political turmoil, diseases). To verify if options are compatible with available resources, a model is required, such as:

$$C(\text{study abroad}) = T + m \times (R + F + LT + X)$$

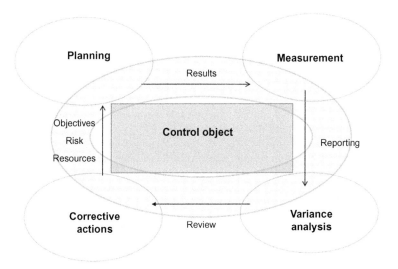

Figure 1.5 The management control cycle.

T, travel cost (return journey)

m, number of months

R, rent fee per month

F, food cost per month

LT, local transportation cost per month

X, percentage charge for extra expenses (e.g., pub, concerts, sports).

This simple example shows that the quality of the underlying model influences the quality of programming. Because the cost of accommodation is usually underestimated for studying abroad, students can find themselves lacking money in a foreign country.

If PMSs were complete and precise with respect to the enterprise functioning and all the variable values were known, the second phase, *measurement*, would be useless. Forecasts would be equal to actual results. In real contexts, actual values usually diverge from forecasts. First, some variables are *exogenous*; hence, they cannot be directly controlled by companies (for instance, the level of demand for predicting sales and then profitability). Second, other variables (*endogenous*) (although more directly controlled) can assume values that are different from what was expected. For example, if the labor force was less efficient than expected, the quantity of input required to produce the same output would be different from what was planned.

In summary, there is a certain degree of uncertainty to control by developing a measurement system capable of capturing:

- The trend of actual results in order to check intermediate steps in carrying out activities and projects
- The evolution of risks that can require early corrective actions.

Results measurement is the basis for the third phase: variance analysis between forecasted values and actual results. In particular, variances can be articulated according to the source of change: exogenous variances (when changes are due to external variables) and endogenous variances (when changes are due to a misalignment between the control model adopted and the enterprise). In this phase, the quality of the model is also important (refer to Box 1 for an example).

Even the most precise control models are unable to find a clear divide between exogenous and endogenous causes in variance analysis. There are factors that are in the middle, such as employee strikes and machine failures. These events are influenced by both external and internal action/elements. For example, enterprises can provide preventive maintenance to reduce the risks of failures to machines and equipment (hence seeing them as endogenous factors); sometimes, however, machine failure can be incidental and unpredictable (and thus exogenous).

The final phase of the control cycle is the introduction of *corrective actions* based on the analysis of variances. Interventions can affect both plans and objectives according to the type of control held by the enterprise over variances.

If variances are due to external causes, the reference context in which the enterprise planned its decision has changed; in this situation, it is unlikely that initial planned goals are still achievable. Think of automotive suppliers using rare earth in their components; when prices go up unpredictably, the planned target costs become unattainable. In such a context, the overall target profitability is likely to change, although some actions can be made to save material or other costs (e.g., reducing scrapes; higher efficiency in labor).

When variance causes are instead controllable, the priority is the definition of an alternative plan of action capable of maintaining the initial objectives. If, for example, there is a decrease of material use efficiency without any change in material supply, an analysis of the manufacturing cycle is suggested to uncover problems and define intervention priority. Even in this situation, initial objectives can be highlighted as too ambitious and thus can be modified, yet this is the final option when alternative plans are not feasible.

1.3.3.2 Motivation

PMSs provide information to managers about the results achieved by diverse organizational units across the company. This control function has a behavioral implication, particularly when results are linked to incentives. Enterprises are, in fact, composed of individuals who are not neutral to control mechanisms. To clarify, think, for example, of the head of a manufacturing plant who can be assessed both on delivery time or quality of output. According to the measure inserted in the rewarding system, the manufacturing head would devote more attention to one factor or another. Hence, associating performance measures with individuals offers the possibility to drive their behaviors, favoring coordination, delegation, and actions aligned with the company objectives.

To understand the behavioral implications of performance measurement, a brief analysis of the broader issue of motivation is analyzed in the following. The term motivation is used here to denote the possibility of helping individuals to achieve better performances aligned with company goals. Figure 1.6 illustrates a reference framework for the motivation process.

The results achieved by individuals depend on their *efforts*; the *coherence* between their capabilities and tasks assigned; and their *fate*, which comprises phenomena that are not directly controllable. The alignment between individuals' results and enterprise objectives determines their performance. The framework illustrated in Figure 1.6 shows problems related to the motivation process. The first problem (and opportunity) is how to increase individual efforts in organizational activities. Assuming that he or

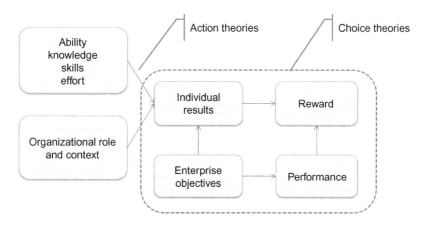

Figure 1.6 Motivation and performance: a reference process.

she is capable of performing his or her tasks (excluding external, uncontrollable circumstances), this increase in effort should lead to improved performance. These considerations are encompassed by the action theory. A second problem is how to direct effort in the right direction in order to improve the company's performance.

A seminal contribution to the subject of action theories is Maslow's hierarchy of needs (1954), which introduced the following needs: physiological (including hunger and other bodily needs); safety (linked to security and physical protection); social (acceptance and friendship); ego, which includes both internal and external esteem (self-respect, autonomy, status, recognition, and attention); and self-actualization (e.g., growth and self-fulfillment). These needs form a hierarchy of priority for actions: the individual must first act to satisfy the lower-level needs (physiological) and then move to the higher level needs. This traditional theory is important for managerial strategy; even when there is not explicit remuneration, negative performance can potentially impact an individual's self-realization and esteem (his or her secondary needs). Yet this problem arises and only has an impact when primary needs are satisfied.

More recently, higher emphasis has been placed on social relationships and capital within organizations (with both superior and other employees) as leverage for individual action. Individuals are motivated to intensify their efforts when they are part of a hardworking team (and therefore socialize more with coworkers) and when they receive feedback on their behavior from superiors (this can alleviate assessment anxiety). This latter issue in particular points out the need for a timely managerial control system that is capable of providing quick feedback to employees regarding their behavior and performance.

Once individuals have decided to put forth more effort at work, their behavior should be consistent with the enterprise's objectives. Three theories (*choice theories*) are valuable in understanding this motivation process: the expectancy theory, equity theory, and goal-setting theory. Theories focused on external factors are not considered here because they are not directly relevant to managerial strategies.

Expectancy theory is suggested as the dominant logic in motivation. According to this theory, individuals are rational; they act and exert effort based on the expectation of a reward associated with their performance. This theory views the attractiveness of the potential reward as crucial, but it highlights two relationships that are important for management: (i) performance and rewards and (ii) effort and performance.

The relationship between performance and reward emphasizes that individuals' choices are instrumental to the achievement of performances associated with rewards. This stresses the need to adopt a *complete* management control system in order to prevent individuals focusing only on some behaviors and neglecting others.

To clarify, think of customer service and the decision whether to decrease the number of employees to save money. A reduction in personnel will lower costs, but it could potentially increase customers' wait time. This decision can be influenced by management's strategy. If measured (and rewarded) performances include only the cost, according to the expectancy theory, the decision maker will choose to reduce personnel (saving cost), although this would cause a decline in customer service.

A second consequence of the expectancy theory is linked to the attitude of individuals in maximizing the expected outcome. To avoid demotivation, management control systems have to measure only performance that individuals can influence in line with their *specific responsibilities*. On the contrary, if employees feel that they are not able to influence the way in which their performance is measured, they will not put forth much effort. This second issue opens up a critical area for management control: on one hand, people work in teams more and more often, and job outcomes can be divided into subelements to be associated with individuals; on the other hand, assessing individuals by the overall team performance violates the specific responsibility principle.

The second process theory useful for understanding the link between motivation and performance is the *equity theory* (Adams, 1963). According to this theory, individuals provide inputs (effort, training, experience) to enterprises in consideration of the expected and obtained results, including both tangible benefits (wages, promotions, fringe benefits) and intangible benefits (autonomy, responsibilities). There is an equilibrium that needs to be considered when individuals are doing similar work. When disequilibrium occurs, an individual acts in order to rebalance the situation. In practice, usually individuals who are perceived to be underevaluated reduce their efforts; individuals who are overevaluated tend to rebalance their situation by adjusting their perception: They convince themselves that they have wrongly underestimated the contribution they can make to the company's goals.

Equity theory suggests having a holistic approach to management control design. Performances of individuals and then organizational units have to be seen globally with an enterprise-wide vision. Furthermore, it warns of overestimating employees' contributions, which is often considered less dangerous than underestimation. First of all, these errors are irreparable; over-rated employees tend to realign quickly to the ratio between expected reward and the effort put forth; thus, a possible future realignment, decreasing rewards with the same input, would be perceived by evaluated employees as an underevaluation. Second, employees who contend with the overevaluated colleague are affected. They are demotivated by seeing unequal treatment and tend to realign the ratio between reward and effort by reducing their efforts.

The last theory—the goal-setting theory—points out that an individual decision to direct efforts toward a specific goal is determined by the interest that he/she has in the goal itself. The theory suggests that an individual's motivation increases when targets are (i) precisely defined and (ii) challenging but hard to attain. This suggestion is in contrast with the use of the management control system as a decision making tool. If all organizational units are assigned unattainable targets, there is a risk of creating an unrealistic plan.

The relationship between motivation and the involvement of employees in the target-setting process is less straightforward. It is suggested that reduced participation leads to increased tensions among departments, negatively impacting motivation, whereas higher participation has a positive impact. Furthermore, the impact from participation on motivation is higher for managerial roles. The need suggested by the goal-setting theory to set well-defined objectives to motivate employees requires the adoption of measurable indicators.

The aforementioned three theories provide complementary indications for designing management control systems. Expectancy theory highlights the need to link rewards to individual behaviors; equity theory points out that this relationship cannot be set for single individuals, but with a broad organizational vision; finally, the goal-setting theory emphasizes the need to set difficult but precise goals.

Finally, it is useful to summarize the requirements of PMS in relation to motivation. The system must be *complete* to avoid opportunistic behaviors, *timely* to give individuals prompt feedback on their behavior, built around individuals' *specific responsibilities*, and based on measurable indicators.

1.4 CONCLUDING REMARKS

This chapter has introduced the present value as a reference goal for enterprises and has illustrated its formulation and the need to enlarge the performance indicator toolkit to better control it for different stakeholders' needs.

Now, before going into detail about the different types of indicators and their use, it is useful to summarize the requirements that stemmed from the analysis of different stakeholder needs. Specifically, six central requirements have emerged and can be taken as a reference for PMS and indicators:

- *Measurability*, which is the ability to associate performance and risk with indicators that can be clearly and univocally measured; the definition of measurement protocols is central in this, but the following chapters illustrate that some indicators are more consolidated and are more easily measured.
- *Completeness*, intended as the capability of PMS to control all the factors relevant for enterprises.
- *Precision*, which is the correlation between the diverse indicators and the present value as the ultimate reference goal for companies.
- *Long-term orientation*, which is the capability to measure and manage long-term implications.
- *Timeliness*, focusing on the need for indicators to enable prompt managerial action.
- *Specific responsibility*, which is the capability of PMS to give organizational units (and managers) responsibilities on which they can act.

These six criteria are used in the rest of the book to discuss the advantages and disadvantages of indicators. The first part of the book is devoted to performance measurement; the second part focuses on performance management.

CHAPTER 2

Value-Based Management Indicators

2.1 VALUE-BASED INDICATORS

Value-based (VB) indicators aim to control enterprises (or their organizational units), measuring the creation of value and its risks in a more or less direct way. This chapter specifically illustrates four types of measures:

- *Direct measurement of present value*, which is based on the estimation of cash flows exchanged between companies and shareholders or between companies and all their investors in the long term
- *Relative valuation*, which estimates the company's value by comparing the (target) company with other similar listed ones
- *VB proxies*, which try to approximate value using other variables that are more easily quantifiable
- *Risk value indicators*, which attempt to measure the risk attached to value.

2.1.1 Direct Measurement of Economic Value

The principle underlying the direct measurement of present value is that company performances must be measured by the value created for shareholders, which can be expressed by:

$$PV(0) = \sum_{t=0}^{+\infty} \frac{NCF_t}{(1 + k)^t} \tag{2.1}$$

where

PV(0), economic value (or present value) at year 0
NCF_t, net cash flow generated by the company available at period t
k, required rate of return.

PV can be formulated differently, dividing the planning horizon into two parts: the first one between time 0 and time T, the second one between T and infinite. This leads to:

$$PV(0) = \sum_{t=0}^{T} \frac{NCF_t}{(1 + k)^t} + \frac{TV}{(1 + k)^T} \tag{2.2}$$

where TV is the discounted sum of net cash flows from $T + 1$ to infinite.

At the theoretical level, Eqs. (2.1) and (2.2) are the same, yet Eq. (2.2) can be used to highlight two different components of the value creation. The first part refers to the time horizon in which cash flows can be calculated more precisely; this period varies in terms of years according to the turbulence of markets in which companies operate. The second part of Eq. (2.2)—terminal value—refers to the subsequent period in which cash flows are more difficult to forecast and/or the company could reach a steadier state.

Indeed, when enterprises are able to precisely forecast cash flows generated by projects and activities, even after year T, a detailed calculation is favored in order to increase the precision of the evaluation and its control. If, instead, forecasts of periodic cash flows become unrealistic, an alternative aggregate measure is preferable, although less precise.

A central characteristic of PV is the need to forecast now (Year 0) how the company will perform in the long term. To accomplish this task, three stages have to be carried out (Figure 2.1):

- Strategic planning and competitive analysis, by which the enterprise's position can be planned for future years.
- Financial analysis, which translates strategic plans into future financial statements. Here, two different logical approaches are presented:
  - The asset-side approach (or invested capital logic)
  - The equity-side approach (or shareholders capital logic).
- Present value computation, which can provide two different measures according to the type of logic adopted in the financial analysis:
  - With the asset-side approach (or invested capital logic), the value estimated is called enterprise value (EV).
  - With the equity-side approach (or the shareholders capital logic), the equity value (E) is obtained.

There is a strict relation between the strategic planning and the competitive analysis on one side and the PV computation on the other side. It is obvious that companies generate positive financial results in the long term only if they outperform their competitors. For this reason, companies must first analyze their competitive advantages and only estimate financial implications after completing this step.

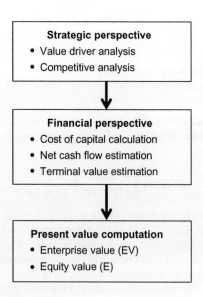

Figure 2.1 Steps for calculating present value.

2.1.1.1 Strategic Perspective

The first perspective aims to set the strategic boundary for then calculating cash flows in the long run. Two stages are useful:

- The *value driver analysis*, which identifies success factors critical to generate value for the company shareholders and to define the relationships between critical success factors and the NCF components of the company
- The *strategic analysis*, which is important to understand the expected trend of critical performances for the forecasting horizon in relation to different possible competitive positions.

The value driver analysis can be carried out using several methods; here, we present a tool that directly relates value drivers to cash flow generation: the value tree. The value tree approach was initially proposed by Stern and Stewart (http://www.sternstewart.com) and is a hierarchical scheme that allows one to first systematically analyze the financial elements contributing to the value generation, then examine and consider the driver of financial performance. Figure 2.2 shows the value tree readapted by Stern and Stewart. The structure of the tree can be analyzed from top to bottom. The first four levels of the tree are common to all companies, as they are the division of enterprise value in subcomponents. The leaves of the tree (in gray in the picture) are company-specific; they report the critical success factors of the company that generate value for its shareholders. As shown in Figure 2.2, improving delivery time is critical for the sales increase of existing products; an improvement of internal quality is key for reducing product costs.

The tree can be used during the planning or the review of actual results. In the planning phase, the analysis usually starts from critical success factors, from which the impact on financial measures and then on cash flows is drawn (moving across the tree from right to left). During the review of results, first, new estimates of cash flows are

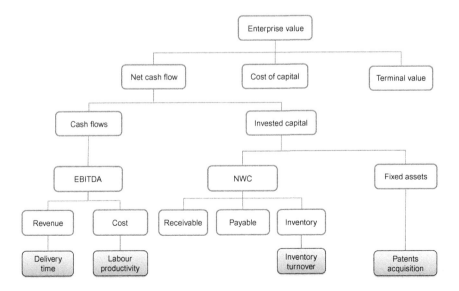

Figure 2.2 The value tree. Adapted from Stern and Stewart (http://www.sternstewart.com).

carried out using new information available to the company; then, the variation between new and previous cash flows is reviewed following the tree from top to bottom.

Once the value tree is defined, a strategic analysis of the future competitive position of the company must be carried out. Again, several strategic models and tools can be employed in this phase. Among these tools, the Pentagon of Value, developed by McKinsey, has been extensively adopted. The Pentagon of Value identifies the opportunities for an enterprise to create economic value with a five-step analysis, starting from the present market value.

The second step after the definition of the market value is the analysis of the "as-is" value, developing the hypothesis that the company will maintain its present strategy in terms of products/services delivered and the market served—the same competitive position against competitors in each product market.

Step 3 analyzes business opportunities stemming from operating improvements, which can be obtained by modifying strategies at the business unit level. Examples of actions are: plans modifying the competitive position of single product lines of the enterprise on the market in terms of the product range (by launching new products), service, time, or product quality; and interventions to improve the internal efficiency of the enterprise, reducing the entity of costs. Step 3 allows for a more complete analysis, given that a larger set of opportunities is included compared to Step 2 (the "as-is" strategy). Yet this more refined analysis has higher examination costs and less precision because the consequences of a strategic repositioning cannot be easily forecasted.

The fourth step is the analysis of opportunities to add external improvements, linked to acquisitions, mergers, and liquidations of businesses or parts of them; in this case, the completeness of the analysis is counterbalanced by a decrease in precision. The performance of acquired businesses is, in particular, highly dependent on becoming integrated with the buying company. It can also be problematic when certain departments are dissolved; power relationships at the top levels are modified, creating tension and internal negotiations during and after the change. This transition phase should be carefully considered because it can potentially impact decisions and the company's activities. The financial ramifications of this change are also difficult to forecast.

Finally, the last phase (Step 5) encompasses the analysis of the effects stemming from financial restructuring. Debt exposure—more specifically, the overall cost of capital of the company—can change due to a different capital composition (equity and debt) and the risk perceived by shareholders.[1]

2.1.1.2 Financial Analysis

Once the strategic and competitive analysis is carried out, the estimation of financials can begin. In this section, we separately analyze the components of Eq. (2.2):

- The cost of capital (k), considering the most complex case in which k varies across time (k_t)
- NCF_t
- TV.

---

[1] In perfect markets, the Modigliani-Miller (1958) theorem ensures that variations in the financial structure do not modify the economic value of the enterprise; however, the presence of failure costs and, more broadly, market imperfections may lead to the increase of the economic value through financial restructuring.

2.1.1.2.1 Cost of Capital

As previously discussed in the Introduction, the cost of capital calculation depends on the financial structure of the company, which may be financed by capital provided by shareholders (equity capital) and capital provided by banks and bondholders (debt). Shareholders and debtholders have different required rates of return. In this chapter, we illustrate the calculation of the equity cost of capital (referring only to shareholders) and the WACC (referring to both shareholders and debtholders).

2.1.1.2.1.1 The Equity Cost of Capital

To estimate the equity cost of capital, several approaches have been introduced. The key point to understand is that the cost of equity is what the company has to remunerate to the equity holders. As a consequence, this is what equity holders expect for their investment in the company. A rational investor would expect a remuneration that is a function of the taken and perceived risk. Most of the models are based on a structure where the equity cost of capital is a function of a risk premium. The capital asset pricing model (CAPM, Sharpe 1964), the arbitrage price theory (APT, Ross 1976), and the Fama and French model are discussed in this section.

In particular, the CAPM is taken as a reference, and the other two models are introduced by comparison.

The CAPM determines the cost of equity (k_e) considering two elements:

- The expected return on investment (risk-free rate r_f)
- The equity risk premium (market premium).

In analytical terms:

$$k_e = r_f + \beta \,(\text{market premium})$$

The r_f is the risk-free rate whose actual return is exactly equal to the expected return—i.e., there is no uncertainty around the expected return. A risk-free investment should have no default risk and no reinvestment risk. These two conditions make the government bonds of very stable and well-consolidated countries or areas ideal risk-free securities that let analysts assess the risk-free rate. However, it should be clear that not all government bonds are riskless, and there are some companies that could be thought to be.

For EUR-denominated cash flows, the German 10-Year Bond can be considered a reference for the risk-free rate.

The risk premium is instead the premium investors' demand for investing in a riskier investment relative to the risk-free rate. It should be computed as the difference between the riskier returns and the risk-free rate.

The risk premium considers an equity market risk premium calculation and a systematic risk coefficient that can explain how the single equity investment is related to the equity market. The equity market risk premium is given by the difference between stock market returns and risk-free rates. Usually, the stock market return is proxied by a stock exchange index. A stock exchange index measures the value of the stock market and how it changes over time. It is representative of different stocks included in the index and their changes[2] (e.g., the S&P 500 index in the United States or the FTSE index in Italy).

---

[2]Each price change on the index can be weighted in different ways (value-weighted, price-weighted, equally weighted).

Furthermore, it is necessary to introduce a basic element, β, as the systematic risk coefficient. In September 1964, in his paper on the *Journal of Finance*, William Sharpe introduces what nowadays is commonly indicated β: "a consistent relationship between the equity expected returns and the market returns. By definition the market returns are representative of the systematic risk." Furthermore, Sharpe (1964) believes that the β "is the part of an asset's risk which is due to its correlation with the return on a combination cannot be diversified away when the asset is added to the combination."

Accordingly, the company beta (β) is the ratio between the covariance of the asset with the market portfolio and the variance of the market portfolio (i.e., an ideal portfolio composed of all the stocks present in the market).

The beta could assume a different value; in particular:

- $\beta < 1$ means that the security has been less volatile than the market, and the security is said to be "defensive." It includes the case $\beta < 0$, which means that the security has moved against the market.
- $\beta = 1$ means that the security has moved with the market.
- $\beta > 1$ means that the security has been more volatile than the market, and the security is said to be "aggressive."

In fact, Sharpe (1964) reports that "it is common practice for investment advisors to accept a lower expected return from defensive securities [$\beta < 1$] (those which respond little to changes in the economy) than they require from aggressive securities [$\beta > 1$] (which exhibit significant response)."

There are some determinants for the beta:

- The industry effect
- The operating leverage
- The financial leverage.

The industry effect is related to the beta sensitivity of the demand and costs the company faces against macroeconomic factors. Generally, companies with cyclical business have higher betas.

The operating leverage measures the mix between the firm fixed and variable costs. Generally, companies with higher operating leverage have higher betas. The degree of operating leverage of a company is proxied by analyzing how much the earnings before interest and tax (EBIT) changes in the case of an increase of 1% in sales.

$$\text{Degree of operating leverage (DOL)} = \frac{\text{percentage change in EBIT}}{\text{percentage change in sales}}$$

Financial leverage, as a ratio between debt and equity, is proxied by analyzing how much the earnings per share (EPS) (i.e., the ratio between the earnings and the outstanding shares) changes in the case of an increase of 1% in EBIT. Similarly to the previous case, it measures the mix between the firm fixed and variable financial expenses. Companies with higher interest payments are those with higher betas.

The beta of a listed company can be computed by regressing the stock returns against market returns. Generally, weekly data are used on a long time horizon (i.e., 5 or 10 years).

What happens if the company is not listed? A common way to proceed is to find some comparable listed companies and estimate their beta. Yet the available beta is levered (β^L), which means that it is affected by the company debt-to-equity ratio and tax rate diminishing comparability. Once comparable companies have been identified, there are two possible ways to estimate the beta of the unlisted (target) company.

Following the first way, after having identified some comparable companies, for each comparable company, compute its unlevered beta (β^U) considering its debt-to-equity ratio and its tax rate.

$$\beta^U_{\text{comparable nr.1}} = \frac{\beta^L_{\text{comparable nr.1}}}{1 + (1 - t_{c,\text{comparable nr.1}}) \times (D/E)_{\text{comparable nr.1}}}$$

Then, compute the average unlevered beta.

It is then possible to use the average unlevered beta and releverage it, considering the target company data:

$$\beta^L_{\text{target}} = \beta^U \times \left[1 + (1 - t_{c,\text{target}}) \times \left(\frac{D}{E}\right)_{\text{target}} \right]$$

Instead, according to the second possibility, after having identified some comparable companies, compute the average levered betas of the comparable companies, their debt-to-equity ratios, and their average tax rates. Then, compute the comparable companies average unlevered beta:

$$\beta^U = \frac{\text{avg } \beta^L_{\text{comparable}}}{1 + (1 - \text{avg } t_{c,\text{comparable}}) \times (\text{avg}(D/E))_{\text{comparable}}}$$

It is then possible to use the average unlevered beta and releverage it, considering the target company data:

$$\beta^L_{\text{target}} = \beta^U \times \left[1 + (1 - t_{c,\text{target}}) \times \left(\frac{D}{E}\right)_{\text{target}} \right]$$

Damodaran (2010) suggests using the latter method.

The next example shows the difference between the two beta-estimating methods (Box 2.1).

Box 2.1

Suppose we have identified the following comparable companies of Alpha, an unlisted company of which we are interested in estimating the beta. Alpha is then our target company, which has a 0.4 debt-to-equity ratio and a tax rate of 30%. The following table reports the data for Alpha comparable companies (Gamma, Delta, and Omega).

	Beta (Levered)	Debt-to-Equity Ratio	Tax Rate
Gamma	1.331	0.3	30%
Delta	1.620	0.5	30%
Omega	1.846	0.6	30%

According to the first method, we should compute the unlevered beta for each of the comparable companies as follows:

$$\beta_{gamma}^{U} = \frac{\beta_{gamma}^{L}}{1 + (1 - t_{c,gamma}) \times (D/E)_{gamma}} = \frac{1.331}{1 + (1 - 0.3) \times 0.3} = 1.1$$

$$\beta_{delta}^{U} = \frac{\beta_{delta}^{L}}{1 + (1 - t_{c,delta}) \times (D/E)_{delta}} = \frac{1.620}{1 + (1 - 0.3) \times 0.5} = 1.2$$

$$\beta_{omega}^{U} = \frac{\beta_{omega}^{L}}{1 + (1 - t_{c,omega}) \times (D/E)_{omega}} = \frac{1.846}{1 + (1 - 0.3) \times 0.6} = 1.3$$

The average unlevered beta is:

$$avg\ \beta^{U} = \frac{1.1 + 1.2 + 1.3}{3} = 1.2$$

It is now possible to estimate the beta for Alpha:

$$\beta_{alpha}^{L} = \beta^{U} \times \left[1 + (1 - t_{c,alpha}) \times \left(\frac{D}{E}\right)_{alpha}\right] = 1.2 \times [1 + (1 - 0.3) \times 0.4] = 1.536$$

The second approach instead begins with the estimation of a comparable average levered beta, the average debt-to-equity ratio, and the average tax rate:

$$avg\ \beta^{L} = \frac{1.331 + 1.620 + 1.846}{3} = 1.599$$

$$avg\ debt\text{-}to\text{-}equity\ ratio = \frac{0.3 + 0.5 + 0.6}{3} = 0.466$$

$$avg\ tax\ rate = 0.3$$

Then, it computes the comparable companies' unlevered betas:

$$\beta^{U} = \frac{avg\ \beta_{comparable}^{L}}{1 + (1 - avg\ t_{c,comparable}) \times (avg(D/E))_{comparable}} = \frac{1.599}{1 + (1 - 0.3) \times 0.466} = 1.205$$

It is now possible to estimate the beta for Alpha:

$$\beta_{alpha}^{L} = \beta^{U} \times \left[1 + (1 - t_{c,alpha}) \times \left(\frac{D}{E}\right)_{alpha}\right] = 1.205 \times [1 + (1 - 0.3) \times 0.4] = 1.543$$

However, the CAPM employs only one factor (i.e., the beta) on which the equity cost of capital depends.

A second model that tries to improve this disadvantage is the arbitrage price theory (APT), which focuses on more than one factor to explain expected returns.

It is related to arbitrage opportunities. An arbitrage opportunity is the opportunity to buy an asset at a low price, then immediately sell it on a different market for a higher price.

To clarify, suppose there are two portfolios with the same exposure to risk but different expected returns. Investors can buy the portfolio with the higher expected returns and sell the other one, taking advantage of the arbitrage opportunity. In the absence of arbitrage opportunities, the market risk should be explained by the betas of different factors, determined with a factor analysis. Now betas are an expression of the correlation with the different factors.

$$r = r_f + \beta_1(r_{factor1} - r_f) + \beta_2(r_{factor2} - r_f) + \cdots$$

where the factors could be GDP, interest rate, and inflation. The CAPM could be thought of as a particular case of the APT with only one economic factor.

Fama and French (1996) proposed a three-factor model. The three factors are:

- *Market factor*: Return on market index minus risk-free interest rate.
- *Size factor*: Return on small-firm stocks less return on large-firm stocks.
- *Book-to-market factor*: Return on high book-to-market-ratio stocks less return on low book-to-market-ratio stocks.

$$r = r_f + \beta_{market} \times (r_{market\ factor}) + \beta_{size} \times (r_{size}) + \beta_{book\text{-}to\text{-}market\ factor} \times (r_{book\text{-}to\text{-}market\ factor})$$

In these models, the beta is computed using historical data; therefore, we are unable to capture future trends. For an example of how to solve this problem, some authors (McNulty et al., 2002) have proposed the market-derived capital pricing model (MCPM), which is a forward-looking method to estimate the company cost of capital, considering the future volatility derived from the option market.

2.1.1.2.1.2 The Firm Cost of Capital

While the equity cost of capital refers to the firm shareholders, the weighted average cost of capital (WACC) also considers debtholders. In fact, it is an average of the equity cost of capital and the debt cost weighted on the ratio between debt and equity.

$$WACC = \frac{D}{D + E} \times k_D \times (1 - t_c) + \frac{E}{D + E} \times k_e$$

D stands for both the long-term and short-term debt of the company, while E is the company equity. Some analysts use the net financial position (debt minus cash) instead of the debt, which could be correct just when the company debt is supposed to be risk-less (i.e., with the highest rating) or it pays a debt cost very close to the risk-free rate (because it is significantly less risky).

The k_D is the company cost of debt that can be computed as:

- A weighted average of the cost of the different loans the company has
- The risk-free rate plus the credit default spread associated with the company credit rating.

The t_c is the tax rate, which can be:

- The marginal tax rate
- The tax rate computed as the ratio between the profit & loss (P&L) account tax item and the earnings before taxes (EBT).

The reason for the inclusion of the cost of debt net of taxes relies on the tax shield that financial interest payables give to the company.

Finally, the k_e is the equity cost of capital, which could be computed according to the different methodologies described previously.

2.1.1.2.2 Net Cash Flow Estimation

Net cash flow can be calculated according to two different logical approaches, which takes into account that companies are financed by both equity and debt capital and that the value can be calculated referring only to shareholders of all finance actors. Two different approaches can be followed: the *invested capital logic* and the *shareholders capital logic*.

According to the *invested capital logic* approach, also called the asset-side approach, the enterprise value is measured with the view to remunerate all financers, including both shareholders and debtholders. As a result, cash flows, referred to as *FCFF*, are estimated gross of financial charges, which are accounted for in the remuneration rate (denominator of Eq. (2.1)).

FCFF is defined as the net cash flow available for both debt and equity holders of the company. The starting point to calculate FCFF is the estimation of expected EBIT, which is then adjusted to arrive to cash values. Table 2.1 illustrates how to compute FCFF for each forecast year needed.

Taxes are generally computed as the ratio between the P&L tax item and EBT, which should then be applied to the EBIT. This refers to the amount of taxes on EBIT. *D&A* is the P&L item exactly. D&A is deducted before reaching the EBIT. In fact, sales less operating expenses (OPEX) leads to earnings before interest, taxes, depreciation, and amortization (EBITDA). After D&A deduction, it is possible to obtain the EBIT. The underlying reason for why it should be added on again is that the EBIT we consider is net of D&A, which, however, is not a cash outflow or inflow. In this sense, adding the item means to correct for it. It is necessary to do this in order to express the tax savings coming from D&A.

Net working capital comprises accounts receivable, inventory, and accounts payable. In analytical terms, it is:

Net working capital = accounts receivable + inventories − accounts payable

Could a firm have a negative working capital? Yes, definitely. A negative net working capital means that the company is relying on supplier credit as a source of capital.

However, be careful. In valuating a company's cash flows, what matters is not the absolute value of the net working capital but its change across years. In this way, an increase in net working capital will affect the company cash flows, reducing them while a decrease in net working capital will improve the company cash flows.

Analyzing each item separately, it should be clear that an increase in both accounts receivable and inventories should negatively affect the company cash generation, contrary to an increase in accounts payable.

Table 2.1 FCFF Calculation
EBIT
− Taxes
+ Depreciation & Amortization (D&A)
+/ − ΔNet Working Capital
+ / − ΔCapital Expenditures (CapEx)
= FCFF

Finally, *capital expenditure* comprises the fixed capital investments, both for maintenance and new investments (expansion, acquisition, and so forth). It must be computed as the variation between two subsequent years of fixed assets (pay attention to the fact that a positive variation negatively affects cash flows) plus an amount equal to the D&A item value, which is the minimum investment that the company must make. Therefore, divestitures positively affect cash flows and have to be subtracted from capital expenditures.

Adopting the *invested capital logic* (hence *FCFF as NCF*) implies accounting for financial charges in the remuneration rate (denominator). In particular, the year by year discounting rate for this calculation is the WACC, which includes the required rate of return of shareholder capital (k_E) and the average interest rate of debt (k_D) after tax ($1 - t$), where *t* is the tax rate:

$$\text{WACC} = \frac{D}{D+E} \times k_D \times (1 - t) + \frac{E}{D+E} \times k_E$$

In order to obtain the equity value, the enterprise value calculated through the asset-side approach will be reduced by the net financial debts.

The second logical approach that can be used is *shareholders capital logic*, also called the equity-side approach. The equity value of the enterprise will be reached through a calculation with reference only to shareholders; hence, cash flows, referred to as FCFE, are assessed net of financial charges, and the cost of capital refers only to the required rate of return of shareholder capital (k_E).

FCFE is defined as the net cash flow available only to the equity holders. Table 2.2 shows how FCFE can be computed.

Beginning with the FCFF computed as previously described, *net financial revenues and expenses* should be added. These items could be collected from the P&L, but one should take care of to adjust it for taxes. In fact, in the case of financial revenues, there is a negative effect generated by the tax payment that turns into a decrease of the item, while in the case of financial expenses, the taxation results in a positive effect on flows (debt fiscal shield).

The variation of the *net debt* is calculated referring to the year in analysis versus the previous one. It positively affects cash flows in case it increases (e.g., new loans taken out as bank loans or bond emissions), as higher flows are available for shareholders, while it negatively affects flows in the case of a decrease (e.g., repayment of a previous debt).

Finally, the *increase in share capital* represents the increase of the company equity. It increases the FCFE, as the flows are available and are at the service of shareholders. A *decrease in share capital*, however, negatively weighs on the FCFE, as the amount is paid to the shareholders and is no longer available for them in the company. Typically, a company experiences a decrease in share capital in the moment it distributes dividends.

Table 2.2 FCFE Calculation
FCFF
+ Financial revenues, net of tax
− Financial expenses, net of tax
+/− ΔNet Debt
+ Increase in share capital
− Decrease in share capital
= FCFE

Both logics (invested capital and shareholders capital) are conceptually correct; nonetheless, the invested capital logic is more common in practice.[3]

2.1.1.2.3 Terminal Value and Real Options

As previously discussed, beyond the forecasting horizon $(0-T)$, the precise estimation of cash flows is substituted by a synthetic measure; in the past, this measure was usually the projection of the last NCF available (Year T) on an infinite horizon of time. Now, companies draw from a wider range of possibilities for defining the terminal value, such as

- Enlargement of the forecasting horizon for cash flow estimation
- Adopting perpetuity
- Adopting annuity
- Multiple estimation
- Real options.

The first alternative is the *enlargement of the forecasting horizon*, which means estimating NCFs for a higher number of years so that the remaining time can be neglected because it is considered marginal. This is actually only a deceptive solution; in turbulent and complex settings—such as those nowadays—extending the horizon period beyond T could generate unrealistic or even misleading results.

Perpetuity instead hypothesizes that the NCFs of the last year of the forecasting period (T) will stay unchanged for the subsequent years. Under this hypothesis, the terminal value can be calculated as follows:

$$TV(0) = \sum_{t=T+1}^{+\infty} \frac{NCF_T}{(1+k_T)^t} = NCF_T \sum_{t=T+1}^{+\infty} \frac{1}{(1+k_T)^t} = \frac{NCF_T}{k_T}$$

In the case of an asset-side analysis (invested capital logic), the terminal value could be computed as:

$$TV_{EV} = \frac{FCFF_T}{WACC_T}$$

while in the case of an equity-side approach (shareholders capital logic), it must be computed as:

$$TV_E = \frac{FCFE_T}{k_{e,T}}$$

A variation is obtained considering a constant growth rate of NCFs. With g equal to the growth rate, the terminal value becomes:

$$TV = \frac{NCF_T \times (1+g)}{k_T - g}$$

which is then, respectively,

---

[3] Usually in companies, the management of financing is centralized; consequently, it is not possible to identify the precise composition of the capital employed by each unit of the company, as required by the shareholders capital logic. Often this leads to the application of the invested capital logic using the WACC.

$$TV_{EV} = \frac{FCFF_T \times (1 + g)}{WACC_T - g}$$

$$TV_E = \frac{FCFE_T \times (1 + g)}{k_{e,T} - g}$$

in the case of an asset-side or equity-side approach.

The perpetuity approach is simple to apply, yet it is rather unrealistic in turbulent contexts, where there is no guarantee that the enterprise will be able to maintain activities and performances as they are in the last year of the NCF forecast. Several modifications can emerge:

- Present activities could be abandoned in the face of an unfavorable evolution of the market
- Enterprise resources could generate innovative projects, with characteristics that are significantly different from present performances.

Consequently, the future value will depend not only on the characteristics of the activities available at present but also from the company's capability to modify its portfolio to be in line with these changes.

The *annuity* approach is useful if the company is not likely to experience regularity or growth of its net cash flows on an infinite time horizon, but only in a certain number of years (*n* in the following formula).

In this case, the terminal value becomes, in the case of a constant or growing net cash flow, respectively:

$$TV = \frac{NCF_T}{k}\left[1 - \frac{1}{(1+k)^n}\right]$$

$$TV = \frac{NCF_T}{k - g}\left[1 - \frac{(1+g)^n}{(1+k)^n}\right]$$

where *n* indicates the number of years the company is supposed to generate those flows, exceeding the period *T*.

Table 2.3 shows how to apply these formulas according to the approach, the time horizon, and the growth rate chosen.

Table 2.3 Perpetuity and Annuity in Calculating Terminal Value

		Asset-Side Approach	Equity-Side Approach
Infinite time horizon besides T	$g = 0$	$TV_{EV} = \frac{FCFF_T}{WACC_T}$	$TV_E = \frac{FCFE_T}{k_{e,T}}$
	$g > 0$ (but $g <$ cost of capital)	$TV_{EV} = \frac{FCFF_T \times (1+g)}{WACC_T - g}$	$TV_E = \frac{FCFE_T \times (1+g)}{k_{e,T} - g}$
Finite time horizon besides T (equal to n)	$g = 0$	$TV_{EV} = \frac{FCFF_T}{WACC_T}\left[1 - \frac{1}{(1+WACC_T)^n}\right]$	$TV_E = \frac{FCFE_T}{k_{e,T}}\left[1 - \frac{1}{(1+k_{e,T})^n}\right]$
	$g > 0$ (but $g <$ cost of capital)	$TV_{EV} = \frac{FCFF_T \times (1+g)}{WACC_T - g}\left[1 - \frac{(1+g)^n}{(1+WACC_T)^n}\right]$	$TV_E = \frac{FCFE_T \times (1+g)}{k_{e,T} - g}\left[1 - \frac{(1+g)^n}{(1+k_{e,T})^n}\right]$

However, the choice of the constant growth rate g has a high impact on the company valuation, as small changes in this rate could bring larger ones in the company valuation. The sensitivity of the value to the g rate is very relevant and must be taken into consideration. Usually, a sensitivity analysis is performed to assess its trustworthiness.

Another way to compute terminal value is through *multiple estimation* (refer to Section 2.1.2.4 How to Adapt Relative Valuation to Estimate Terminal Value for further details). This means to deduce an appropriate multiple that is an indicator derived from the market comparison or transactions trend and apply it to the company.

Finally, terminal value can be calculated with *real options*. Companies value the possibility of using their resources in alternative projects, trying to create economic value in the face of emerging risks and opportunities. Accordingly, the terminal value of the company becomes the value of all the options available at year T (the end of the forecasting horizon). Real options are linked to several "sources." The most common of these are:

- Quantitative options, related to the possibility of growth or (conversely) of dismissing declining businesses
- Options based on the possibility of varying the mix of product and services
- Options to abandon new projects before they are achieved.

The term *real options* was initially proposed by Kester (1984); this term is now commonly used and provides an analogy between potential projects and financial options (Table 2.4). Financial options are the right—but not the obligation—to buy (or sell) an underlying instrument at a specified price (strike price) in the future; at the expiration date of the option, the transaction will be carried out only if the market price is higher (or lower) than the specified price. Similarly, in the case of real options, an enterprise has the right to implement a project in the future; the actual implementation, however, will be carried out only if market conditions favor this choice at the moment in which the decision must be made.[4]

Several approaches have been proposed to value real options; these have used similar methods with financial options and have been extensively researched. However, financial options methods are based on some hypotheses that are hardly applicable to real options. These are:

- *Portfolio division*: With financial options, investors can divide the invested money in portions as desired. On the contrary, real options are discrete. If a company only realizes 60% of a research and development investment, it will not attain 60% of the results.

Table 2.4 Real Options and Financial Options

Real Option	Financial Option
Present value of the project or investment cash flows	Value of the underlying asset
Additional investment for exercising the action (option)	Strike (or exercise) price
Time until the decision must be made	Time until the option expires

[4]The same logic is applied to abandonment decisions; a company can decide whether to maintain its activities. The decision will be made on the basis of the context evolution. In the rest of this section, we refer to investment options, yet the same analysis can be applied to disinvestment opportunities.

- *Market tradability*: Financial options are traded on the market, where there is comparable information; instead, real options are proprietary in nature, with no market-comparable alternatives.

However, real options have calculative advantages compared to financial options. In particular, they do not require continuous valuation models; a discrete time horizon is sufficient (simultaneously considering all events happening in a specific year), and the level of precision required is lower than the one required for financial options. To account for this, a specific method of valuation is preferable, which is the adaptation of the decision tree model.
Specifically

- The entity of the investment required to open the option is defined, as well as the investment to exercise it.
- A scenario analysis is carried out, identifying variables influencing the decision to exercise the option.
- Each scenario is then associated with its probability and the sum of its discounted cash flows.

The value of the option at year T (the "exercise" year) is calculated as:

$$\sum_{i=1}^{N} \max[(\mathrm{PV}_i(T) - I); 0] \times p_i \tag{2.3}$$

where

N, number of possible scenarios
p_i, probability associated with each scenario i
PV_i, present value (at year T) of the cash flows generated by exercising the option in relation to each scenario i
I, additional investment needed to exercise the option.

To clarify this approach, an example is provided. A company has a patent for a manufacturing process that leads to products based on graphene. One of the applications of the process under development is related to water treatment, which is expected to be one of the major challenges in the future. This prototype opens up the possibility for the company to build super-eco-adsorbent recyclable materials for oil spill clean-ups. The actual use of the technology needs engineering but depends on the governments' decision to adopt this technology in water treatment. The investment for the engineering activity is valued at 40 million €, and it can be delayed until the political scenario is more stable. At present, three scenarios can be defined:

- WORST scenario, with a probability of 0.3, which hypothesizes that the water treatment will not change due to established service providers; in this case, the graphene technology will generate low actualized cash flows equal to 1 million €.
- GOOD scenario, with a probability of 0.5, which assumes that a new favorable law will be approved but that other enterprises will be able to enter the market; in this case, actualized cash flows are equal to 80 million €.
- BEST scenario, with a probability of 0.2, which assumes that a new favorable law will be approved and that competitors will not be able to enter the market with a competitive product; in this case, expected actualized cash flows are equal to 100 million €.

The option value is calculated, taking into account that the water treatment engineering will be done only with favorable conditions (GOOD and BEST scenarios); applying Eq. (2.3), the option value is (in million €):

$$0.5 \times (80 - 40) + 0.2 \times (100 - 40) + 0.3 \times (0) = 32$$

If the graphene company had decided to invest in engineering since the beginning, the expected present value would have been (in million €):

$$0.5 \times (80 - 40) + 0.2 \times (100 - 40) + 0.3 \times (1 - 40) = 20.3$$

Hence, this value is lower compared to the previous calculation (real option value).

2.1.1.3 Present Value Computation: Enterprise and Equity Value

After computing the flows, discount rates, and terminal value, it is possible to evaluate the company, which means defining its enterprise value or equity value according to the approach chosen. In fact, in the case of opting for the asset-side approach, the value estimated is called the enterprise value and represents the value of the company for all its investors; using the equity-side approach, the equity value is immediately reached.

As shown in Eq. (2.2), the company value is the present value of the forecasted discounted cash flows. Thus, according to the asset-side approach, the company enterprise value (EV) is:

$$EV = \sum_{t=0}^{T} \frac{FCFF_t}{(1+WACC_t)^t} + \frac{TV_{EV}}{(1+WACC_T)^T}$$

while according to the equity-side approach, the company equity value (E) is:

$$E = \sum_{t=0}^{T} \frac{FCFE_t}{(1+k_{e,t})^t} + \frac{TV_E}{(1+k_{e,T})^T}$$

It is possible to estimate the EV through the equity-side approach or, vice versa, to deduce the E through the asset-side approach. To do so, the net financial position, which is equal to the difference between debt and cash, should first be computed.

$$NFP = Debt - Cash$$

In fact, the EV and the E of the same company differ for the net financial position.

$$EV = E + NFP$$

2.1.2 Relative Valuation

Relative valuation is a widely used approach to estimate the company value. It compares the (target) company with other similar listed ones with the idea that the value of the target company should be in line with that of comparable companies. Generally, it is used with the NCF direct measurement method, aiming to compare different methods looking for a convergence of the different results. The idea of this method is to estimate a multiple based on comparable company parameters and then apply it to estimate the target company value.

In general terms, it is necessary to identify some comparable companies (i) for which either EV or E could be easily defined. Starting with the EV or E, the multiple is the ratio between the value of each comparable company and a parameter that could

Figure 2.3 Steps for valuing a company through the relative valuation approach.

usually be extracted from each comparable company's balance sheet (e.g. EV/EBIT, EV/EBITDA, and so forth). In formulas, for each comparable company, the multiple could be estimated as:

$$\text{multiple}_i = \frac{\text{Value}_i}{\text{parameter}_i}$$

For example, a company whose EV is 12 billion € and whose expected EBITDA is 3 billion € has an EV/EBITDA multiple equal to 4 (EV/EBITDA = 4x). The year from which to use data must be determined to perform the analysis. Generally, analysts use the later year on which data are available or the average between the two previous years.

Figure 2.3 shows the steps required to value a target company through the relative valuation approach. The following subsections discuss these steps in detail.

2.1.2.1 Defining Comparable Companies

The identification of comparable companies is one of the most difficult tasks of this approach to valuation. Comparable companies are not just the same as the company's competitors: in fact, also non competitors can be considered. For example, comparable firms for a luxury watch firm could include a luxury fashion apparel firm.

In addition, it is quite difficult to find companies in the same business of the target company, especially if the target company is a multidivisional firm. In this case, it is possible to find comparable companies for each division, estimating the value of the different divisions and then deriving the one of the company.

One suggestion is to previously identify the target company value drivers (as shown in Section 2.2.1 with the performance tree) and then identify those companies with the same value drivers. In addition, it is important to pay attention to the specific properties of the companies—e.g., the market in which they operate, their dimensions (measured either by assets or sales), the presence of comparative advantages allowed by national laws (if applicable), and the presence of concessions and their expiration dates.

2.1.2.2 Defining Possible Multiples

Multiples are divided into two categories with reference to the two methods for calculating the company value: enterprise value (EV) and equity (E).

2.1.2.2.1 Enterprise Value Multiples

EV multiples are those that support the valuation of the target company enterprise value looking at the EV of comparable companies. The main assumption is that if a sample of comparable companies is valued by the market a certain number (n) of times a given balance sheet parameter, the target company, if really comparable, can be valued the same way—i.e., the same number n of times the same given balance sheet parameter:

$$\text{multiple}_i = \frac{EV_i}{\text{parameter}_i}$$

Among the EV multiples, there are those with a wider diffusion and application, such as the EV/EBITDA, the EV/EBIT, the EV/FCFF, the EV/sales, and the EV/CE.

The *EV/EBITDA* is the ratio between the EV of a company and its EBITDA. In economic terms, it represents the number of years the EBITDA should be multiplied by to obtain the company enterprise value. It is one of the most commonly used EV multiples when dealing with industrial companies. The EBITDA is the first approximation of the company cash flows but is not a good choice for companies for which outsourcing is relevant because of the overvaluation of the *EBITDA*. This multiple could be easily adjusted to have a more powerful application in some cases. Thus, the EV/EBITDAR (earnings before interest, taxes, depreciation, amortization, and rent) is often used for air companies and in the case of analyzing companies with an actual different level of rent that is supposed to change in future years. This indicator can be further adjusted by dividing EBITDA by the growth (g) and obtaining EBITDAG; in this case, the multiple is the EV/EBITDAG and allows for a better analysis of forthcoming growth perspectives.

A second option for calculating multiples is the *EV/EBIT*, which is the ratio between the EV of a company and its EBIT. It represents the number of years the EBIT should be multiplied by to obtain the enterprise value. The EBIT focuses on the operating management, but it does not consider the different choices made by companies regarding depreciation and amortization.

The *EV/FCFF* is the ratio between the EV of a company and its FCFF. It represents the number of years the FCFF should be multiplied by to obtain the enterprise value.

The *EV/sales* is the ratio between the EV of a company and its sales. It represents the number of years the sales should be multiplied by to obtain the enterprise value.

In companies with negative EBITDA, EBIT, or FCFF, the previously described multiples become senseless. Due to the positive sales at each company, this multiple becomes the first choice in such cases. However, it has the serious disadvantage of not taking the company's profitability into consideration.

The *EV/CE* is the ratio between the EV of a company and its capital employed. Because it compares the EV with its balance sheet asset value, it runs the risk that the balance sheet data may not be representative of the asset market value. It is often used for companies that operate in the luxury segment.

The list of EV multiples is quite long and can be longer. It takes a great deal of practice to determine the best alternative to calculate the EV of a company. It is not possible to say at the beginning which one is the best. It can depend on different industries, different business models, and different value drivers. The multiple that can express the value of the company in the most complete way must be determined on a case by case basis.

2.1.2.2.2 Equity Multiples

Equity multiples allow analysts to directly evaluate the company equity value. The equity multiples have as a numerator the market capitalization of the company or, equally, its stock price. The market capitalization of the company is given by the price of the stock on the official exchange multiplied by the number of outstanding shares.

Similar to the EV multiples, the process to estimate the target company equity value comes from the estimation of the comparable companies' (i) multiple values:

$$\text{multiple}_i = \frac{E_i}{\text{parameter}_i}$$

Among equity multiples, the P/E,[5] the P/FCFE, and the P/BV are the most commonly used.

The *P/E* is the ratio between the market capitalization of a company and its earnings or, equally, the ratio between the price of the stock and the EPS (the ratio between earnings and the number of outstanding shares). It represents the number of years the EPS should be multiplied by to obtain the company market capitalization (the stock price). It is one of the multiples that can always be computed (for listed companies), as it is easy to calculate and understand. However, the earnings of a company suffer from depreciation and amortization policies, its financial structure, and the profit or loss of discontinued operations. To avoid the latter, the *adjusted P/E* adjusts the earnings in order not to be affected by the profit or the loss of discontinued operations.

The *PEG* is the ratio between the P/E and the earnings growth. This allows for a better analysis of forthcoming growth perspectives of the company.

The *P/FCFE*, the ratio between the market capitalization of a company and its FCFE, represents the number of years the FCFE should be multiplied by to obtain the company market capitalization.

The *P/BV* is the ratio between the equity market value (i.e., the market capitalization) of a company and its equity book value. It represents the equity value of a company in relation to its book value. It is often used for banks and real estate companies and less so in the industrial sector. In fact, for a lot of companies, the equity book value (assets and debts) is not the best indicator of the company value.

2.1.2.3 From Multiples to Value

To choose the best multiple to be used in valuing a company, it is possible to identify a subset of multiples that are significant from a theoretical point of view, as described in the previous sections.

However, for each of these multiples, the second step is to identify one or more drivers that could explain the variance among the multiples of the different comparable companies. Suppose you have identified some comparable companies and you believe the EV/EBITDA to be a possible multiple to evaluate your target company. In general terms, comparable companies could have different EV/EBITDA values, sometimes with huge variability. In addition, you also consider P/E to be of some interest and note that its value variability among companies is lower. You might conclude that the

---

[5]P/E means price to earnings. In this case, "E" is earning and not equity. The practice is used to adopt the acronym "P/E," meaning the ratio between the stock price and the earnings per share. That's why it is possible to also use "P/Eps" to mean "price to earnings."

Table 2.5 Examples of EV/EBITDA and P/E in the Retail Dress Apparel Sector				
	Comparable Company A	Comparable Company B	Comparable Company C	Comparable Company D
EV/EBITDA	3.8×	6.6×	5.4×	4.1×
P/E	10.9×	10.1×	11.5×	11.8×

second multiple—i.e., the P/E—is better than the former just because the comparable companies' values are more similar.

Table 2.5 shows some data of comparable companies in the retail dress apparel sector.

To assess what the best multiple is, one should identify some drivers that could explain the variability of the multiple itself. For example, both EBITDA growth and the EBITDA margin could be drivers to explain the variance among the EV/EBITDA of the different comparable companies.

Thus, a regression analysis could be performed for each couple multiple—the explanation driver and the choice of the multiple to be used (the best multiple) is related to the highest R^2 fit reached by the analyses.

Going back to the example, suppose now that you separately regress EV/EBITDA versus EBITDA growth and the EV/EBITDA versus EBITDA margin and that the latter shows the highest R^2.[6] This is the multiple to be chosen.

After identifying the best multiple and knowing the value of the target company indicator (EBITDA or EBIT), it is possible to estimate its value.

In our case, knowing the target company EBITDA margin, it is possible to calculate its multiple (the target company EV/EBITDA) through a simple substitution in the corresponding estimated regression equation and then derive the target company value (the target company EV) by multiplying for its EBITDA.

2.1.2.4 How to Adapt Relative Valuation to Estimate Terminal Value

Relative valuation could be useful even to estimate the terminal value to be used in the discounted cash flow approach (refer Section 2.1.1.2.3 Terminal Value and Real Options).

The first steps require choosing either an enterprise value or an equity value multiple and computing its value for comparable companies i:

$$multiple_i = \frac{EV_i \text{ or } E_i}{parameter_i}$$

Then, either the average or the median of these comparable companies' multiple values must be calculated:

$$multiple_{comparables} = avg. \text{ or median of multiples}_i$$

Finally, the terminal value of the target company could be identified by multiplying the average multiple of the comparable companies and the target company parameter.

$$TV_{target} = multiple_{comparables} \times parameter_{target}$$

[6]R^2 is the correlation coefficient that explains how two different parameters are related.

For example, to estimate the terminal value for a real estate company, some comparable firms are identified, and the P/BV is computed for each of them. Then, an average P/BV is calculated as the average of the comparable companies' P/BV values.

Furthermore, by multiplying the average of the comparable companies' P/BV values and the target company's book value, one could estimate the target company's terminal value.

However, use caution: when using an equity multiple (like the one in the example), the terminal value could be used in an equity-side approach, while an enterprise value multiple will lead to a terminal value useful in an asset-side valuation approach.

2.1.3 VB Proxies

To further analyze the measurement of the present value with direct or relative methods, some proxies have been introduced that try to approximate the value in a simplified way. The number of indicators proposed is very high; here, we illustrate three metrics that are often used:

- Total business return (TBR)
- Market value added (MVA)
- Total shareholder return (TSR).

Referring to an accounting period, TBR is defined as:

$$V(1) + CF(1) - I(1) \tag{2.4}$$

This index measures two elements of the value in a period:

- $V(1)$, which is the present value at the end of the period
- The net cash flows generated during the period, specifically $CF(1) - I(1)$.

Hence, TBR is a different formulation of the present value, as shown in Eq. (2.1).

MVA and TSR are two indicators that use market value as a proxy for the present value. MVA is an absolute indicator defined as:

$$\text{Market value} - \text{invested capital} \tag{2.5}$$

TSR is a ratio indicator referring to a specific period, usually a year:

$$\text{TSR} = (\text{increase in market value} + \text{dividends})/\text{initial market value} \tag{2.6}$$

The key characteristic of these last two indicators is the use of the market value. Although they are quicker to calculate, the market value is equal to the company present value only if markets are perfect (e.g., perfect information, perfect factor mobility, zero entry and exit barriers, and zero transaction costs). Yet adopting market value rather than present value actually means to substitute the company's own estimations of its future, with the assessment of the market, which is less informed. As a result, the two indicators are less precise compared to the direct measurement of the present value, although they are less costly and more measurable.

Finally, MVA and TSR can be used only for listed companies and not for single business units or unlisted companies.

2.1.4 Risk Value Indicators

Risk value indicators aim to measure risk in financial terms, alternatively or simultaneously addressing two elements: expected results and capital employed.

In the last decade, due to the increasing turbulence of markets but also the increasing pressure of various stakeholders to manage risks and prevent failures, several indicators have been developed with the objective of capturing the probability and impact of loss in economic value. In this section, we illustrate the most diffuse indicators across sectors[7]:

- Value at risk (VAR)
- Economic capital (EC)
- Risk-adjusted return indicators.

VAR measures the maximum potential loss in the value of a risky asset or portfolio over a defined period for a given confidence interval. For example, if the VAR on the company's assets is 500 million € at a 1-year 95% confidence level, there is only a 5% chance that the value of the company's assets will drop more than 500 million € in 1 year.

VAR has two basic parameters:

- The *time period* considered—that is, the duration of the period in which an asset or a portfolio of assets is held (holding period). The holding period varies according to the type of asset/investment; usually it ranges from 1 day to 1 year.
- The *confidence interval* for performing the estimation. Most companies adopt confidence levels that range from 95% to 99%.

The traditional version of VAR is based and calculated on the hypothesis of a normal distribution of yield; accordingly, gains and losses have a Gaussian shape, where the average is the average yield, and the variance is the asset/investment volatility.

This hypothesis of normal distribution is considered one of the main limits of VAR in its original formulation and led to the development of alternative models that consider abnormal distributions in VAR. Another limit of VAR is its past orientation; VAR is based on statistical analysis of historical values where possible future changes are neglected.

Finally, another limit is the coherence of the measure when used to compare different portfolios; for example, considering two portfolios X and Y, $VAR(X + Y)$ can be the higher value of $VAR(X) + VAR(Y)$.

Even with these problems, VAR has received great attention and is commonly used, especially in sectors exposed to market and commodities risks. The main benefits associated with VAR are:

- Due to its diffusion, VAR is a risk measure that is widely accepted all over the world and is often used as a standard reference.
- VAR is synthetic, collecting several risks under a unique number and also the probability (translated through the confidence level).

EC is the amount of capital that a company requires to achieve a sufficient level of protection (target solvency standard) against adverse circumstances in the net asset value. Its calculation is not always univocal, and different formulations are available; in particular, EC is proposed as:

- The maximum amount of capital required for losses; in this case, EC is equal to VAR.
- The amount of capital needed for unexpected losses; in this case, there is a difference between EC and VAR, as shown in Figure 2.4.

---

[7]Financial risk and value risk indicators have developed more widely in the financial and insurance sectors due to their exposure and specific regulation; the treatment of these indicators is beyond the scope of this book. For further reference, see Jorion (2007).

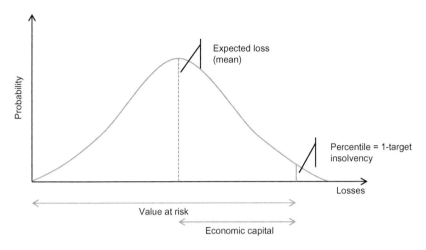

Figure 2.4 EC calculated as the amount of capital needed for unexpected losses.

The use of EC is two-folded. The first use of EC, which is commonly used in the energy and finance sectors, is its allocation to different business units and projects. This approach can be seen as an alternative to traditional assessment approaches, where the level of risk is reflected in different discount rates, as developed by Michelin (Thierny and Smithson, 2003).

The second use is the calculation of profitability risk-adjusted indicators, again particularly used throughout the finance sector: return on risk-adjusted capital (RORAC), risk-adjusted return on capital (RAROC), and risk-adjusted return on risk-adjusted capital (RARORAC). In the following sections, we provide reference definitions, but it is important to remember that there is great heterogeneity in the application of these indicators across sectors and companies.

RORAC is the profitability ratio where the denominator is adjusted depending on the risk associated with the asset or the project.

$$\text{RORAC} = \frac{\text{net profit}}{\text{economic capital}}$$

In RAROC, the risk is instead put at the numerator, which is reduced depending on the risk associated with the instrument or project.

$$\text{RAROC} = \frac{\text{net profit} - \text{expected loss}}{\text{invested capital}}$$

RARORAC assesses risk both at the numerator and denominator and can be considered a combination of RAROC and RORAC.

$$\text{RAROC} = \frac{\text{net profit} - \text{expected loss}}{\text{economic capital}}$$

All three indicators are used to calculate the percentage profitability considering risks.

2.1.5 Characteristics of VB Indicators

The main limit of VB indicators is their *timeliness*. They require, in fact, the translation of several data points in monetary terms (market share, product characteristics, and competitive position). Furthermore, VB indicators encompass the estimation of future results. This process further lengthens the analysis, reducing the possibility to make a frequent collection of information and, consequently, a timely identification of possible problems.

Regarding advantages, along with their precision given their alignment with present value, *long-term orientation* is indeed a strength; these indicators force companies to evaluate both short-term results and long-term implications and strategies.

Tracing *specific responsibilities* instead is not straightforward because it is difficult to identify the specific contribution of each organizational unit to the value creation. For this reason, Value-Based Management indicators are mainly adopted to control company performances overall.

Completeness is generally high, although it varies according to the thoroughness of the analysis performed to build the indicators. In particular, moving across the pentagon of value (from Steps 1 to 5) and including the evaluation of real options, the completeness of the analysis (and derived indicators) increases. The increase in completeness implies a decrease of *measurability*. This is a critical problem when VB indicators are adopted for motivational purposes. To use VB indicators as key indicators for motivation, target values of NCFs should be defined for each year of the time horizon $(0-T)$, further to a target value for TV.

Yet after 1 year, only the actual NCF of the first year is measureable; if the assessment of organizational units is based on this variance, the resulting measure will be short-term oriented, losing the main advantage of these indicators: long-term orientation. To be employed, the assessment should be complemented by an analysis of how actions and decisions were made during the year and how they impacted the present value, revising the estimation of NCFs and terminal value. These estimations, however, are based on information provided by organizational units that are under assessment. This situation potentially leads to opportunistic behaviors—for example, to underestimate near-future cash flows and overestimate growth in distant years. In this case, the measure also stimulates short termism, going against the logic of VB indicators.

CHAPTER 3

Accounting-Based Measures

This chapter presents accounting-based measures, which consist of indicators defined starting from financial statements, namely Profit and Loss statement (P&L), Balance Sheet statement (BS) and Cash Flow statement (CF). Through these indicators, it is possible to provide an overview of the enterprise's main results in terms of profitability, liquidity and financial structure. These measures are therefore particularly relevant for external accountability purposes to support the evaluation of the overall organizational performances.

In order to compute accounting-based measures two intermediate steps are required:

- Reclassification and adjustments of annual reports. Through this activity, items included in annual reports are aggregated and reorganized to highlight some intermediate results that can easily support the understanding of organizational performance and the subsequent computation of accounting-based measures.
- Time series and common size. This analysis highlights trends and the relative importance of items in annual reports over time.

Following this view, this chapter is organized into three main sections: reclassification and adjustments of annual reports; time series and common size analysis; accounting-based indicators.

3.1 RECLASSIFICATION AND ADJUSTMENTS

The activities of reclassification and adjustments of annual reports are required preliminary operations to highlight some key financial elements that will support the subsequent computation of accounting-based measures. The annual report is indeed prepared in accordance with civil law, such as IAS/IFRS or the specific local GAAP of each country (e.g. in Italy IV Directive CE). This implies that annual reports cannot be comparable with each other, not lastly because of the different regulation they endorsed in presenting each item. For this reason, when the purpose is to analyse organizational activities and compare measures of different organizations, often through accounting-based measures, annual reports are reclassified. For example, through reclassification and adjustments it is possible to highlight intermediated results that are not visible looking at a general annual report, such as net working capital or net financial debts.

Both the Balance Sheet and Profit and Loss account can be reclassified.

3.1.1 Reclassification of the Balance Sheet

The reclassification of the balance sheet highlights some key items that are not visible by looking at document prepared following a civil law approach, such as Net Working Capital (NWC) and Net Financial Debt (NFD). The balance sheet is usually reclassified distinguishing between Net Invested Capital and Coverage (see Table 3.1).

Table 3.1 Net Invested Capital versus Coverage

Balance Sheet (Ias/Ifrs)		Reclassified Balance Sheet	
Total Assets	Total Liabilities and Equity	Net Invested Capital	Coverage
1. NON-CURRENT ASSETS	**4. SHAREHOLDERS' EQUITY**	**1. FIXED CAPITAL**	**4. SHAREHOLDERS' EQUITY**
1.1 Property, plant and equipment	4.1 Issued capital	1.1 Property, plant and equipment	4.1 Issued capital
1.2 Investment property	4.2 Reserves	1.2 Investment property	4.2 Reserves
1.3 Goodwill	4.3 Net profit/loss for the financial year	1.3 Goodwill	4.3 Net profit/loss for the financial year
1.4 Other intangible assets	**5. NON-CURRENT LIABILITIES**	1.4 Other intangible assets	**9. NET FINANCIAL DEBT**
1.5 Equity investment	5.1 Bonds	1.5 Equity investment	5.1 Bonds (non current + current)
1.6 Other non-current financial assets	5.2 Bank debts	1.6 Other non-current financial assets	5.2 Bank debts (non-current + current)
1.7 Deferred tax	5.3 Other financial non-current liabilities	1.7 Deferred tax	5.3 Other financial current and non-current liabilities
2. CURRENT ASSETS	5.4 Provisions for liabilities and charges	**8. NET WORKING CAPITAL**	2.4 Cash and cash equivalents
2.1 Trade and other receivables	5.5 Pensions and similar obligations	2.1 Trade and other receivables	
2.2 Inventories	5.6 Deferred tax liabilities	2.2 Inventories	
2.3 Ordered work in progress	**6. CURRENT LIABILITIES**	2.3 Ordered work in progress	
2.4 Cash and cash equivalents	6.1 Bonds	5.4 Provisions for liabilities and charges	
3. ASSETS CLASSIFIED AS HELD FOR SALE AND DISPOSAL GROUPS	6.2 Bank debts	5.6 Deferred tax liabilities	
	6.3 Trade and other payables	6.3 Trade and other payables	
	6.4 Other financial current liabilities	6.5 Current tax liabilities	
	6.5 Current tax liabilities	**5.5 Pensions and similar obligations**	
	7. LIABILITIES DIRECTLY ASSOCIATED WITH ASSETS CLASSIFIED AS HELD FOR SALE AND DISPOSAL GROUPS	**3–7) ASSETS CLASSIFIED AS HELD FOR SALE AND DISPOSAL GROUPS AND RELATED LIABILITIES**	

The Balance Sheet prepared following IAS/IFRS shows assets and liabilities according to the time horizon, distinguishing between current and non-current assets/liabilities. The reclassified balance sheet instead distinguished between Net Invested Capital and Coverage. The logic behind this classification is to distinguish between the total available capital (i.e. shareholders' equity + net financial debt) and net investments.

More specifically, the Net Invested Capital comprises the sum of Fixed Capital (i.e. investments in tangible, intangible and financial assets), Net Working Capital and Pensions and similar obligations. Coverage instead comprises Shareholders Equity and Net Financial Debt. The items "Assets held for sales" and "Liabilities associated with assets classified as held for sales" are included in the "net invested capital section".

The key item showed by this reclassification comprise:

- Fixed Capital (FC);
- Net Working Capital (NWC);
- Net Financial Debt[1] (NFD).

Several approaches can be adopted to compute each of these items. We are now presenting the most common ones.

Fixed Capital

It highlights investments in tangible, intangible and financial assets. This item usually corresponds to the Non-Current Asset item of the IAS/IFRS Balance Sheet

The distinctive elements of fixed capital are twofold: first, the listed resources are available for a time horizon higher than one year; second, the listed resources consist of long-term investments for the enterprise. Table 3.2 shows an example of fixed capital for the Company Snam Rete Gas.

Net Working Capital

The Net Working Capital (NWC), in some cases simply called working capital, is a first measure that highlights the ability of an enterprise in managing the operating cycle (i.e.: receivables, payables, inventories). More precisely, it represents the capital available to finance short-term activities with the available short term resources (without including cash and cash equivalents).

Table 3.2 An example of fixed capital for the Company Snam Rete Gas

BALANCE SHEET (IAS/IFRS)	RECLASSIFIED BALANCE SHEET
1. NON-CURRENT ASSETS	**1. FIXED CAPITAL**
1.1 Property, plant and equipment	1.1 Property, plant and equipment
1.2 Investment property	1.2 Investment property
1.3 Goodwill	1.3 Goodwill
1.4 Other intangible assets	1.4 Other intangible assets
1.5 Equity investment	1.5 Equity investment
1.6 Other non-current financial assets	1.6 Other non-current financial assets
1.7 Deferred tax	1.7 Deferred tax

[1]Shareholders equity does not vary from the BS prepared according to IAS to the reclassified schema. Assets classified as held for sales and related liabilities also do not vary: they are included in a unique item (asset held for sales-liabilities associated with assets held for sales) in the net invested capital section.

In some cases, it is roughly calculated as the difference between Current Assets and Current Liabilities. However, this is a non-precise approach since in this formula comprises cash items as well as non-cash and operative items such as inventories or receivables.

A more precise approach is usually adopted, which accounts for current assets and liabilities that have the following characteristics: they are non-explicitly related to cash (i.e. cash and cash equivalent) and they concern a short term time horizon. The most common approach to compute the NWC consist in the following formula (some other computations can also be found):

As you can see from the table (Table 3.3), it is calculated by summing receivables, inventories and orders in progress (from the current assets) adjusted by provisions for liabilities and charges, deferred tax liabilities, payables and current tax liabilities (from non-current liabilities). It does not correspond to the mere difference between Current Assets and Current Liabilities since "cash" as well as financial short term debts are not included. The value of the NWC, as it can be detected from its constitutive items, strongly depends on the operating cycle of the enterprise, in terms of time for collecting payables and receivables, which, in turn, impact on short term cash.

The next table (Table 3.4) further details the correspondence between the IAS/IFRS Balance Sheet and the reclassified NWC value.

This is a relevant item that supports the computation of some liquidity indicators (see Section 3.3).

Table 3.3 An example of computing the NWC

Snam – Half Year Report 2014

(€ million)	31.12.2013	30.06.2014	Change
Fixed capital	20.583	20.746	163
Property, plant and equipment	14.851	14.969	118
Compulsory inventories	363	363	
Intangible assets	4.710	4.735	25
Equity investments	1.024	1.008	(16)
Financial receivables held for operating activities	2		(2)
Net payables for investments	(367)	(329)	38

Table 3.4 The correspondence between the IAS/IFRS Balance Sheet and the reclassified NWC value

8. NET WORKING CAPITAL
2.1 Trade and other receivables +
2.2 Inventories +
2.3 Ordered work in progress −
5.4 Provisions for liabilities and charges −
5.6 Deferred tax liabilities −
6.3 Trade and other payables −
6.5 Current tax liabilities

Net Financial Debts

Net Financial Debts (NFD) consist of the total debts of the company less available cash (i.e. cash and cash equivalent). This item can be considered as a driver of the ability of the enterprise to reimburse its debts if they were all due today: a high net financial debt can underline a critical financial condition for the enterprise since it might find difficulties to repay debtors.

Following its definition, NFD can be computed by summing all financial debts (both current and non-current) and deducting cash and cash equivalent (see Table 3.5).

Table 3.5 Computing the NFD		
BALANCE SHEET (IAS/IFRS)		**RECLASSIFIED BALANCE SHEET**
1. NON-CURRENT ASSETS	**4. SHAREHOLDERS' EQUITY**	**8. NET WORKING CAPITAL**
1.1 Property, plant and equipment	4.1 Issued capital	2.1 Trade and other receivables
1.2 Investment property	4.2 Reserves	2.2 Inventories
1.3 Goodwill	4.3 Net profit/loss for the financial year	2.3 Ordered work in progress
1.4 Other intangible assets	**5. NON-CURRENT LIABILITIES**	*5.4 Provisions for liabilities and charges*
1.5 Equity investment	5.1 Bonds	*5.6 Deferred tax liabilities*
1.6 Other non-current financial assets	5.2 Bank debts	*6.3 Trade and other payables*
1.7 Deferred tax	5.3 Other financial non-current liabilities	*6.5 Current tax liabilities*
2. CURRENT ASSETS	5.4 Provisions for liabilities and charges	
2.1 Trade and other receivables	5.5 Pensions and similar obligations	
2.2 Inventories	5.6 Deferred tax liabilities	
2.3 Ordered work in progress	**6. CURRENT LIABILITIES**	
2.4 Cash and cash equivalents	6.1 Bonds	
3. ASSETS CLASSIFIED AS HELD FOR SALE AND DISPOSAL GROUPS	6.2 Bank debts	
	6.3 Trade and other payables	
	6.4 Other financial current liabilities	
	6.5 Current tax liabilities	
	7. LIABILITIES DIRECTLY ASSOCIATED WITH ASSETS CLASSIFIED AS HELD FOR SALE AND DISPOSAL GROUPS	

3.1.2 Reclassification of the Profit and Loss Statement

The reclassification of the P&L statement is aimed at highlighting the key performance of an organization in terms of Added Value, EBITDA and EBIT. These intermediate data support some preliminary considerations about the economic and profitability position of the enterprise, while at the same time they identify intermediate results that will support the computation of some accounting based measures.

The reclassified P&L statement usually follows the schema presented in Table 3.6, which allows to highlight the following intermediated results:

- **Added Value**. It is computed as the difference between revenues and production costs without considering personnel costs. It is the value firms add to external resources used (i.e. materials and services purchased from third parties) and that is then distributed to employees (through wages and salaries), government (through taxes), lenders (through debt repayments) and shareholders (through shares).
- **EBITDA (Earnings Before Interests Taxed Depreciation and Amortization)**. It is the margin calculated before costs that are not cash outflows (i.e. depreciation and amortization), hence computed by deducting personnel costs from the Added Value measure. This measure can be considered as a proxy of cash generated: it provides a first insight about the ability of the organization to produce cash through its operations given that it does not account for financial activities (i.e. interest expenses), governmental activities (i.e. taxes) and accounting decisions (i.e. depreciation and amortization). A low EBITDA value highlights a critical situation for the enterprise from a profitability perspective as well as from a cash perspective. On the contrary, a high EBITDA means that the company is profitable at the operating level and it also has the capability to generate cash. This measure is used in several accounting-based indicators (e.g. EBITDA margin).
- **EBIT (Earning Before Interests and Taxes).** It is the margin calculated before Interests and Taxes, therefore deducting depreciation and amortization from the EBITDA measure. It is also called Operating Income Before Taxes. It evaluates the operating profitability of the organization without accounting for taxes and financial activities. EBIT can be useful to compare results of similar companies in the same industries when they have different capital structure and, like EBITDA, it supports the computation of some accounting-based measures such as ROI (Return on Investments). EBIT and EBITDA are similar, but they present some significant differences: they both provide insights about the operating activities of the enterprise. Yet, EBIT does not include taxes and interests, while EBITDA excludes also depreciation and amortization. This difference can have a significant impact in organizations with huge investments in fixed capital, which will have a high value of depreciation and amortization.

Table 3.6 Schema for reclassifying a P&L statement
9. NET FINANCIAL DEBT
5.1 + 6.1 Bonds (non current + current) +
5.2 + 6.2 Bank debts (non-current + current) +
5.3 + 6.3 Other financial current and non-current liabilities −
2.4 Cash and cash equivalents

3.2 TIME SERIES AND COMMON SIZE ANALYSIS

Time series and common size analysis provide some early insights about how an organization is performing. In particular, time series analysis compares a single enterprise over time: this means that some organizational results, such as EBIT, EBITDA, revenues or total assets, are compared over the years. This year-to-year comparison facilitates the identification of causes of changes, which can be helpful in supporting the definition of future actions for an organization.

Table 3.7 provides an example of time series analysis for the company ENI: each item in the annual report is provided over a time horizon of three years to highlight some significant trends. For example, by looking at the value of the item "Profit before taxes" it is possible to observe a significant decreasing from 2013 to 2015. This can be an early signal of some (potential) profitability problems or existence of particular situations that could be investigated further.

A major limitation of time series analysis is represented by the adoption of absolute values in the year-to-year comparison. This might create problems when there are size differences over time.

This limitation is overcome by common size analysis that expresses annual report data in percentage terms to highlight the differences over time. As for time series analysis, also common size analysis aims at comparing annual report data over time. However, unlike time series, common size analysis provides this comparison in percentages. More specifically, in horizontal analysis each line of the annual report is expressed as a percentage of the base year, which is usually the first year shown. This is particularly useful to highlight trends over the years. Table 3.8 provides an example of horizontal analysis with reference to the previous financial results of BP: each item is expressed as a percentage of the same item of the base year, represented by 2012.

Table 3.7 An example of time series analysis for the company ENI
RECLASSIFIED INCOME STATEMENT
Total Revenues
Raw Material
General and administrative expenses
VALUE ADDED
Personnel costs
EBITDA
Depreciation and Amortization
EBIT
Net financial Expenses (income)
Earnings before tax and extraordinary items
Extraordinary gain (losses)
Pretax Income
Tax
NET INCOME

Table 3.8 An example of horizontal analysis with reference to the previous financial results of BP

	2013	2014	2015
Total revenues	**99,664**	**94,226**	**68,945**
Purchasing and other operating costs	78,108	74,067	53,983
Personnel costs	2,657	2,572	2,778
Other operating income (costs)	(71)	145	(485)
Depreciation and amortization	10,961	10,147	14,480
Operating profit	**7,867**	**7,585**	**(2,781)**
Financial Income (Expenses)	(999)	(1,181)	(1,323)
Net Income (Expense) from investments	6,083	469	124
Profit before taxes	**12,951**	**6,873**	**(3,980)**
Taxes	(9,055)	(6,681)	(3,147)
Net profit (Loss)	**4,959**	**850**	**(9,378)**

Table 3.9 An example of vertical analysis with reference to a balance sheet

	2014	2013	2012
Profit before taxation	6412	31769	19769
finance costs and net finance	1462	1548	1638
taxation	947	6463	6880
non-controlling interests	223	307	234
profit for the year	3780	23451	11017
	2014	**2013**	**2012**
Profit before taxation	32%	161%	100%
finance costs and net finance	89%	95%	100%
taxation	14%	94%	100%
non-controlling interests	95%	131%	100%
profit for the year	34%	213%	100%

Vertical analysis instead expresses each financial statement line item as a percentage of the largest amount of the statement. More specifically, on the Profit and Loss account, the largest amount is represented by net sales, while on the Balance Sheet, this is represented by total assets. Table 3.9 provides an example of vertical analysis with reference to a balance sheet, where each item is compared to the value of total assets.

3.3 ACCOUNTING BASED INDICATORS

This section presents the accounting-based indicators (see Table 3.10), which are grouped into four clusters according to two dimensions:

- *Type of indicator*: ratio or absolute. This dimension takes into account the structure of the indicator, which can be a ratio, if it compares two different values, or an absolute indicator, if it is constituted by a unique standalone value.

Table 3.10 Accounting-based indicators					
	2010	2011	2012	2013	2014
Total assets	*100%*	*100%*	*100%*	*100%*	*100%*
Total non-current assets	65%	66%	63%	68%	69%
Non-current assets held for sale	2%	3%	6%	0%	0%
Total current assets and receivables	33%	31%	31%	32%	31%

Table 3.11 Measurement principle: accrual or cash logic			
		Accrual	Cash
Ratio	*Profit*	***Shareholders' perspective***: ROE; Net profit Margin; Payout Ratio ***Overall company perspective***: ROA; ROI; ROCE; ROACE; EBIT Margin; EBITDA Margin; Quality of Operating Earning; Asset Turnover ratio ***Stakeholders' perspective***: Debt-to-Equity ratio; Interest Coverage Ratio; Cost of Debt; Effective Tax rate	EM; CFRoi; CF-to-Debt Ratio; Short-term Debt Coverage; Capital Expenditure Coverage
	Liquidity	Current Ratio; Quick Ratio; Inventory Turnover Ratio; Average Collection Time of Trade Receivables	
Absolute		RI; EVA	Cash EVA; CVA

- *Measurement principle*: accrual or cash logic, see Table 3.11. This dimension takes into account the nature of the indicator, either if it is computed from accrual data or from cash data. Usually, indicators computed starting from Balance Sheet and Profit and Loss accounts are actual indicators, while measures computed starting from cash flow statement are cash indicators.

The next sections will detail indicators in each dimension.

3.3.1 Ratio/Accrual Indicators

These indicators can be distinguished between indicators that evaluate profitability and liquidity, depending on the specific aspect of the enterprise they investigate.

Profitability indicators can be further differentiated on the basis of the perspective through which they analyse the profitability of the company:

- Shareholders' perspective;
- Overall company perspective;
- Stakeholders perspective.

Profitability Indicators: Shareholders perspective
These indicators comprise:

- ROE
- Net Profit Margin
- Payout Ratio

ROE (Return on Equity) is a synthetic indicator of the overall profitability of an enterprise and it is defined as:[2]

$$ROE(\%) = \text{Net Profit}/\text{Equity}$$

ROE shows the percentage return against shareholders' capital (Equity). ROE traces the overall profitability of then enterprise, encompassing operating activities (the capability to transform input in output), financial activities (the use of capital for financial activities and debt management), fiscal and discontinued operations.

Net Profit Margin, also known as bottom line margin, measures the percentage of profit that shareholders can gain from revenues. It is defined as follows:

$$\text{Net Profit Margin } (\%) = \text{Net Profit}/\text{Revenues}$$

In other words, Net Profit Margin measures the portion of revenue that is net profit. The higher the value, the higher the profitability from selling activities.

Payout Ratio, also called dividend payout ratio, measures the percentage of net profit that is returned by cash to shareholders. It corresponds to the monetary reward of shareholders. It is computed as follows:

$$\text{Payout ratio } (\%) = \text{Dividends per share}/\text{Earning per shares}$$

The data about the dividend per share is usually provided in the statement of changes in equity, and in some cases it is also showed at the bottom of the profit and loss account. This value can be different from one organization to another since dividend policies can vary widely from companies to companies. For example, in companies that pursue a "continuous investment" strategy, the non-distributed profit is not translated into dividends but invested in other activities; hence, the company is self-financing rather than borrowing capital.

For this reason, together with the payout ratio, it is often also calculated the **Sustainable Growth Rate**:

$$\text{Sustainable Growth Rate: ROE} * (1\text{-Payout ratio})$$

It provides an indication about how quickly a company can grow without borrowing money from external actors. In other words, it measures the enterprise's maximum growth rate using internal financial resources without increasing the level of debt or increasing the value of equity. Assuming that this value for a given company is 8%, this means that the company, by using only internal financial resources, can grow at slightly 8% without asking external financial. Above this value, external resources are needed to allow the company to grow.

Profitability Indicators: Overall company perspective

These indicators evaluate profitability of the company as a whole. The most common indicators under this perspective comprise the following:

- ROA;
- ROI;
- ROCE;
- ROACE;
- EBIT Margin;

[2]In (2.1) Equity can refer to both the initial or the final value of the balance sheet. The first option usually underestimates the value, the second to overestimate it. An intermediate solution is the average between the two.

- EBITDA Margin;
- Quality of Operating Earning;
- Asset Turnover Ratio.

ROA (Return on Assets) measures the profit (EBIT) generated by the enterprise through the use of all the available assets. It is computed as:

$$ROA\ (\%) = EBIT/Total\ Assets$$

This measures evaluates the ability of managers to use assets to generate operating profit.

With the same intent of ROA, **ROI (Return On Investments)** still measures the profit generated by the enterprise thorough the use of the net invested capital. Unlike, ROA, ROI considers the ability of managers in using the invested capital.

$$ROI\ (\%) = EBIT/Net\ Invested\ Capital$$

Where

Net Invested Capital = Total assets − Liabilities without an explicit interest rate
Or
Net Invested Capital = Fixed Capital + Net Working Capital (from reclassified Balance Sheet)

There are different computational formulas for the invested capital. It can be derived from the IAS/IFRS statement by computing the difference between total assets and liabilities without an explicit interest rate. Some other companies, instead, consider the NIC (Net Invested Capital) calculated in the reclassified Balance Sheet as the sum of Fixed Capital and Net Working Capital. Both of the approaches are correct, but it is important to ensure coherence during an eventual time series analysis or benchmarking with competitors.

This indicator is quite common and it can be used to evaluate the overall profitability of the enterprise as well as to evaluate individual organizational projects: in this last case, the EBIT of the specific project is compared against the Invested Capital of the same under evaluation project.

With the same logic to evaluate the overall profitability of the enterprise, other two indicators can be also adopted: ROCE and ROACE.

ROCE (Return on Capital Employed) measures the profit (i.e. EBIT) generated by the enterprise through the use of the employed capital, intended as the sum of equity and long term debt (hence short term liabilities are not included)

$$ROCE\ (\%) = EBIT/Capital\ Employed$$

Where

Capital Employed = Equity + Long Term Debts
Which corresponds to Capital Employed = Total assets − Current Liabilities

The higher this value, the higher the ability of managers using resources to generate profit.

ROACE (Return On Average Capital Employed) instead corresponds to the same ROCE computation, but instead that using the Capital Employed at a given point of time, it considers the average value of the Capital Employed:

$$ROACE\ (\%) = EBIT/Average\ Capital\ Employed$$

Where

$$\text{Average Capital Employed} = \text{Average Equity} + \text{Average Long Term Debt}$$

By accounting for the average value of the employed capital, ROACE provides a more precise estimation of the company profitability since it is not affected by the fluctuation of equity and Long Term Debts during the year.

EBIT margin measures the company overall profitability in terms of EBIT as a percentage of total revenues.

$$\text{EBIT margin (\%)} = \text{EBIT}/\text{Revenues}$$

It can be considered as a proxy of the overall profitability of an organization. Higher EBIT margins signal higher profitability over revenues. This indicator, when compared against competitors of an enterprise provides some insights about the reasons behind high or low margins, which can be due to the contingencies of a particular industry or specifically related to the profitability of the company.

EBITDA margin measures the company overall profitability in terms of EBITDA as a percentage of total revenues.

$$\text{EBITDA margin (\%)} = \text{EBITDA}/\text{Revenues}$$

As for the EBIT margin, it provides an indication about the overall profitability of the enterprise. However, it is often preferred than EBIT margin since it seeks to minimize the accounting decisions that are specific to each organization (i.e. depreciation and amortization), which are instead included in the EBIT margin. By excluding the value of depreciation and amortization, which is strictly dependent upon internal decisions, EBITDA margin is frequently used to compare the operating profitability between different organizations.

Quality of operating earnings measures the quality of earnings, posing particular emphasis on effects of accrual games on operating profit (i.e. EBIT).

$$\text{Quality of operating earnings (\%)} = \text{Operating Cash Flow}/\text{EBIT}$$

A value of this ratio higher that 1 usually highlights high quality earnings since it compares a cash value (operating cash flow) with its analogous accrual value (EBIT). Hence it allows to highlight internal accrual decisions that might increase EBIT while not affecting cash results. The reference logic is that a high quality operating earnings should be reflected into operating cash flow.

Asset Turnover Ratio measures the efficiency of operations of an enterprise. It is computed by comparing revenues against total assets. Some organizations might use the average value of total assets rather than the value at a given point of time.

$$\text{Asset Turnover Ratio (\%)} = \text{Revenues}/\text{Total Asset}$$

This indicator evaluates the ability of the organization to translate assets into sales revenues. The higher this value, the higher the efficiency of the organization to produce revenues from assets. For example, a value equal to 1 means that the organization is generating 1 euro of sales per each euro of invested assets.

Profitability Indicators: Stakeholders' perspective

These indicators evaluate profitability of the company from the perspective of all stakeholders. The most common indicators under this perspective comprise the following:

− Debt-to-Equity ratio;
− Interest coverage ratio;

- Cost of debt;
- Effective tax rate.

Debt-to equity ratio, also called gearing or leverage and often abbreviated as D/E, compares total liabilities with shareholders' equity highlighting the proportion between shareholders' capital and debts.

$$\text{Debt-to-equity ratio} = \text{Total Liabilities}/\text{Shareholders' Equity}$$

Where

- Total Liabilities = Current Liabilities + Non-Current Liabilities
  Or
- Total Liabilities = Net Financial Debts

Total liabilities can be computed either as summing Current and Non-Current Liabilities or by looking at the solely debts and considering the Net Financial Debt item from the reclassified Balance Sheets.

It provides an indication about the dependency of the organization from third parties and, more specifically, the relationship between third parties capital and shareholders capital. This indicator is of particular importance for third parties, especially creditors, given that it underlines situations of high dependency from third parties by the organization. A value higher than 1 means that debts are higher than shareholders' equity, signalling potential problems of financial sustainability. A value lower than 0 underlines the absence of dependency from third parties; however, this can also be a negative hint since it indicates that the organization is not investing.

Interest Coverage Ratio, sometimes also called as times interest earned ratio, is quantified as the ratio between EBIT and Interest Expenses. It provides an indication about the excess of operating profit over interests. The logic is that the higher this value, the higher the probability that a company will be able to meet interest expenses.

$$\text{Interest Coverage Ratio (\%)} = \text{EBIT}/\text{Interest Expenses}$$

This indicator provides an estimation about the ability of the organization to meet payment schedules since cash to cover interest expenses is expected to come from operating profit.

Cost of debt highlights the impact of interest expenses over debts (with an explicit interest rate). It measures the interest rate paid by a company because of its debt.

$$\text{Cost of debt} = \text{Interest Expenses}/\text{Debt with an explicit interest rate}$$

This indicator is often used, together with the Debt-to-Equity ratio to better understand the level of dependency of an organization from third parties. A higher value underlines a high cost of debt and therefore a high dependence from third parties.

Effective Tax Rate quantifies the average incidence, in percentage terms, of taxes. It is computed by dividing the amount of taxes with the profit before taxes.

$$\text{Effective Tax Rate (\%)} = \text{Taxes}/\text{Pre-tax profit}$$

Liquidity Indicators

These indicators measure the financial health of an enterprise with reference to the availability of liquidity/assets to obligations when they become due. The most common indicators include the following:

- Current Ratio;
- Quick Ratio;
- Inventory Turnover Ratio;
- Average Collection Time of Trade Receivables.

Current Ratio is the most common indicator to measures liquidity of an organization in the short term. It is calculated comparing current assets against current liabilities.

$$\text{Current Ratio} = \text{Current Assets}/\text{Current Liabilities}$$

Through this indicator, it is possible to evaluate if an organization has enough resources in the short term to cover liabilities that will become due during the next twelve months. A value near 1 or lower than 1 can underline a critical situation from a liquidity perspective since resources might not be able to cover current liabilities.

It is important to underline that current assets comprise, among the other items, inventories, which are not an immediate cash, but they are products in the warehouse that might not be translated into cash within the short term. For this reason, an optimal situation is usually considered with a current ratio equal or higher than 2.

To take into account the uncertainty of inventories to be translated into cash, a more cautious indicator is used, **Quick Ratio**, also known as Acid-Test Ratio. It has the same purpose of current ratio, but exclude inventories from Current Assets.

$$\text{Quick Ratio} = (\text{Cash} + \text{Short Term Investments} + \text{Receivables})/\text{Current Liabilities}$$

Therefore, the denominator remains the same as for Current Ratio, while the numerator excludes inventories from Current Assets. In this way, the numerator corresponds to the sum of all those items that will certainly become cash over the next year: cash, short term investments and receivables.

The **Inventory Turnover Ratio** measures the efficiency in managing inventories. It is computed by comparing revenues with inventories.

$$\text{Inventory Turnover Ratio} = \text{Revenues}/\text{Inventories}$$

This indicator quantifies how fast inventories are translated into sales, giving rise to revenues. A higher value is usually preferred since it highlights that more revenues is generated starting from a certain amount of inventories; or the other way round, given a certain revenue, less inventories are required to increase sales.

Average Collection Time of Trade Receivables, often simply called average collection period, quantifies the average number of days to receive payments from customers. It is computed by dividing the number of working days in the analysed period (usually the year) by receivables turnover ratio, intended as revenues divided by receivables. The denominators account for the portion of revenues that is represented by trade receivables.

$$\text{Average Collection Time of Trade Receivables} = 365/(\text{Revenues}/\text{Trade Receivables})$$

It highlights the average time customers take to pay the company, hence impacting on its liquidity with reference to cash availability. The lower the value, the lower the number of days needed before receiving cash from customers and therefore the higher the liquidity of the company.

3.3.2 Ratio/Cash Indicators

These indicators measure profitability and liquidity of an enterprise by relying on cash measures, rather than on accrual data. The most common cash indicators include:

- Economic Margin;
- CFRoi;
- Cash Flow to Debt Ratio;
- Short-term Debt Coverage;
- Capital Expenditure Coverage.

The first two indicators are often considered as a "cash version" of ROI. **Economic Margin**[3] (EM) was proposed by Obrycki and Resendes; it measures the operating Cash Flow generated by the invested capital and compares this value with the cost of capital (k)

$$EM = \text{Cash Flow from Operating Activities/Invested Capital} - k$$

Where:

- CF from Operating activities considers the cash from operating activities from Cash Flow Statement
- k is the cost of capital
- I is the invested capital, considered as the "Coverage" of the reclassified Balance Sheet. This value is therefore the sum of equity and net financial debts. In some other cases, it can also be computed as Total Assets - Equity

There are two major advantages connected with the adoption of EM rather than ROI. First, accounting decisions and distortion are not included since a cash value is adopted; second, it makes explicit that the company profitability should be put in relation to the cost of capital.

CFROI[4], developed jointly by Boston Consulting Group and HOLT Planning Associates is similar to EM, but it compares the Cash Flow from Operating activities with the Market Value of the Invested Capital

$$CFROI = \text{Cash Flow from Operating Activities/market Value of the invested capital}$$

The difference with the EM lies in the adoption of the market value of the invested capital and not making explicit the cost of capital. The reason behind the inclusion of a market value is the recognition that it is expected that the market defines the prices on the basis of cash flows.

The remaining three cash/ratio indicators are more traditional and they quantify, at a general level, the ability of the enterprise to use its operating cash flow to cover respectively debts, current liabilities and capital expenditures. More specifically, **Cash Flow-to-Debt Ratio** measures the ability of the organization to cover debts (short term debts and long term debts with an explicit interest rate) through its operating cash flow; **Short-term Debt Coverage** quantifies the ability of the company's operating cash flow to cover short term debts, while **Capital Expenditure Coverage** measures the ability of operating cash flow to cover capital expenditures (CAPEX). For all these three indicators, a high

---

[3]Economic Margin™ and Economic Margin Framework™ are trademarks of The Applied Finance Group, LTD.
[4]CFROI® is a registered trademark of Credit Suisse.

value indicates that a company will be more likely to cover its obligations, in terms of debts and capital investments, through its cash flow from operations.

$$\text{Cash Flow-to-Debt Ratio} = \text{Operating Cash Flow}/\text{Debts}$$
$$\text{Short-term Debt Coverage} = \text{Operating Cash Flow}/\text{Current Debts}$$
$$\text{Capital Expenditure Coverage} = \text{Operating Cash Flow}/\text{Capital Expenditure}$$

3.3.3 Characteristics of Ratio Indicators

The characteristics of ratio indicators can be analysed with reference to two measures used in assessing the enterprise profitability, ROE, which aims at capturing the overall profitability of the company for shareholders, and ROI, which refers to the operating activity.

A first weakness of these indicators is the low timeliness. Calculating ROE and ROI (and similar indicators) requires in fact:

- Measuring physical transaction (for example an operation on a product)
- The economic translation of physical transaction (referring to the previous example the cost of the operation);
- The aggregation of all the information to construct the financial statements;
- The indicators calculation based on the financial statements.

Two of these phases, the economic translation of physical transactions and the aggregation of information, can require a lot of time, particularly for enterprises characterized by large product ranges and articulated organizational structures. The length of this procedure limits the *timeliness* of the indicators system, both directly and indirectly for the cost of the procedure which induces companies to reduce the frequency of data collection and analysis (usually monthly or quarterly).

A second disadvantage is their scarce long term orientation: they focus on past financial results rather than on forecast or signal indicating future results. Consider for example a company for which two alternative solutions are under evaluation. Solution A plans to eliminate any form of quality control, selling outside a considerable quantity of defected products; solution B instead plans to control each product and re-work defected products. In the medium term Solution B will likely result better than A because it will avoid problems on the market and the reduction of revenues. Nonetheless, in the short term Solution A allows to have lower operating costs (quality control) and ROI will go up. So, the use of ROI could lead to favor solution A over B in contrast with the objective to create economic value.

Another example is training; the reduction of training provides an immediate increase of EBIT, hence of ROI, without significant impacts, in the short term, on the company results. The training reduction will have a negative impact[5] in the long run on human resource performances, consequently on the creation of economic value.[6]

To summarise, ROI, and similarly ROE, favour the maximisation of short term results, overlooking long term results.

These indicators are instead better performance in term of *completeness*. Given that ROE and ROI report yearly performance, the analysis of their completeness means verifying their capability to synthetize the diverse factors which can contribute to the

---

[5]This analysis is obviously valid when training interventions are economically significant.
[6]Similar considerations can be made for other categories, such as research and development.

creation of economic value in a single accounting year. These factors are expressed, analytically, by this formula:

$$\text{Cash Flows}/(1 + k)$$

In this perspective, the disadvantage of ROE and ROI are limited to:

- Misalignment between cash flows and accrual flows; specifically, while NPV refers to cash flow, ROE and ROI refers to accrual flows.
- The lack of risk consideration, hence of the cost of capital. Focusing on comparing ROE and ROI across two accounting years, or actuals with budgeted figures, the contribution to the value creation cannot be assessed[7]. This problem is more evident when ROI is adopted to evaluated heads of business units (BU) or divisions of an enterprise; generally, these divisions are not characterized by the same level of risk, consequently a simple comparison of actual ROI for the BU is an incomplete measure of their performances.[8]

Regarding *precision*, the most critical issue in the use of ROI and ROE is their relative nature (ratio indicators), while the economic value is an absolute measure.

Consequently, ROI and ROE tend to favour smaller actions and project compared to what happens with the economic value. This situation can be clarified referring to the relation between economic value and profitability. Making the hypothesis of stability of profitability and growth of equity, we have:[9]

$$V/E = \left(\text{ROE}/k - g/k\right)/\left(1 - g/k\right)$$

Where V is the economic value of the enterprise, E the shareholders' capital, g the growth rate and k the cost of equity capital.

The creation of economic value depends hence not only on the profitability in the use of resources (ROE), but also on the size of the company, both at present (E) and across time (g). ROE neglecting these two elements tend to favour smaller project and actions.

Also for this reason, ROE and ROI can be used opportunistically leading what is called "denominator management": reducing the denominator an improvement of indicators can be obtained in an easier way than acting on the "numerator".

Finally, financial accounting ratios trace well *specific responsibilities* only at top levels. Specifically, ROI is appropriate for measuring performance of BU which gave the opposability to influence revenues, costs, and invested capital; ROE for organizational units that can manage also financing sources. On the contrary ROE and ROI are too aggregate to trace specific responsibilities for operational units, which usually do not control simultaneously costs, revenues and investments.

Accounting ratios are instead characterised by a good *measurability*, because their calculation is based on precise rules. The discretion in some items (e.g. depreciation or inventories value calculation) are not particularly relevant for their managerial use if

- Homogenous rules are adopted for different units across the company;
- When there are changes in financial accounting policies, data belonging to different years must be homogenised.

---

[7]This problem is reduced by adopting indicators of liquidity and financial structure, which are signals of the company risk.

[8]This problem can be solved using the extra-profitability instead of ROE and ROI, where the extra-profitability is calculated as difference between ROE and the cost of equity capital; and ROI taking away the interest coverage rate.

[9]See Hax e Majluf [1991].

The discussion above highlights that the most important characteristics of ratio indicators are completeness, with the exception of risk consideration, and, moreover, *measurability*.

On the contrary the major limitations are the low *timeliness* and the scarce *long term orientation*. This short summary allows to conclude that ratio indicators have to be used carefully with enterprise operating in stable contexts, where short term profitability can be seen as an indicator of the competitive capability of the company. In turbulent contexts, instead, the correlation between past results and future performances is indeed weaker; furthermore, the greater the turbulence the higher is the need to have quick information (timeliness).

3.3.4 Absolute/Accrual Indicators

These indicators comprise RI (Residual Income) and EVA (Economic Value Added). **Residual Income** (RI), which was defined for the first time by Preinreich (1938),[10] measures the economic result of an enterprise net of the invested capital cost; it is defined as:

$$RI = EBIT - k * I$$

Where:

- OP is the Operating Profit
- k is the cost of capital
- I is the invested capital, considered as the "Coverage" of the reclassified Balance Sheet. This value is therefore the sum of equity and net financial debts. In some other cases, it can also be computed as Total Assets − Equity.

At the conceptual, level RI is similar to ROI; a decision has a positive impact on the RI of an enterprise if its ROI is higher than its cost of capital. On the contrary, yet, RI is an absolute indicator, consequently is more precise and limit the "denominator management".

An example can clarify this; consider a BU (Business Unit) characterised by:

- EBIT = 100,000,000€
- Invested capital = 400,000,000€
- K = 10%

The BU has to decide to make or not an investment of 100,000,000€, which will increase EBIT of 20,000,000€/year. The investment should be done because it remunerates the cost of capital; however, as highlighted in Table 3.12, if the BU receive incentives based on ROI, they will tend to refuse the investment; RI instead lead to a more correct decision (Table 3.12).

This phenomenon is more general: given that RI is an absolute indicator, it value rises when an investment return is higher than the cost of capital. However, RI is built upon the same measures of ROI (EBIT and Invested Capital), hence all the other characteristics are similar. Specifically, RI does not solve the major problem of ROI (and ROE): the scarce long term orientation and the limited timeliness.

An additional problem of RI, and similar absolute indicators, is related to their capability to trace specific responsibilities of BUs. The cost of capital (k) is usually a leverage of the corporate level, which stems from the integrated management and

[10]Preinreich, G., 1938, Annual study of economic theory: the theory of depreciation, *Econometrica*, July, 219,241.

Table 3.12 Difference in calculation between using ROI and RI		
	BU with investments	**BU without investments**
EBIT	120	100
I	500	400
ROI	24%	25%
RI	70	60

assessment of the financial position and risk of the enterprise. Because RI include explicitly the cost of capital its use at BU level could violate the specific responsibility "principle". Actually the difference between ROI and RI is more formal and real; although ROI does not include "k" in the formula to fully assess BU performance against ROI achievements the comparison with cost of capital is needed.

Economic Value Added (EVA) is a similar indicator which has received significant attention across years. EVA was introduced by Stern Stewart[11] with this formula[12]:

$$EVA = EBIT - k * I$$

This formula is similar to RI; nonetheless Stern Steward suggested that the calculation needs a preliminary step to adjust financial statements data to better show the capability of the company to generate incomes. Dozens of adjustments are suggested; following some examples:

- Capitalization of research and development costs, which influence both EBIT and invested capital;
- The actualisation of non-capitalized loans;
- The inclusion of not goodwill not yet recorded
- The inclusion of extraordinary loss after tax

Stern Steward suggests that these adjustment makes EVA a better proxy of the economic value of an enterprise (Stewart, 1991). This statement has been contested at both the theoretical and empirical level. At the theoretical level Bromwich (1998) highlighted that EVA, being based on actual results, is not able to measure future implications and trends. Accounting adjustments can reduce the short-termism but cannot eliminate the problem. For eliminating misalignments companies should introduce an adjustment equal to the different between NPV at the beginning of the period and at the end (Bromwich, 1998); yet this value is unknown.[13]

As a consequence, also EVA lead manager to short term behavior, against long term results as we saw for RI and ROI.[14] Several empirical analysis[15] confirmed that the correlation between EVA and economic value is not higher than the relation between RI and the economic value.

---

[11]EVA® is a registered trademark of Stern Stewart.
[12]Some firms refer to this indicator as *Shareholder Value Added*.
[13]This adjustment is actually the replacement of EVA with a direct measure of economic value.
[14]Bromwich (1998) pointed out that incentives based on EVA aimed at aligning managerial choice to companies' goals are based on too strict unrealistic hypotheses.
[15]See for example, Biddle *et al* (1997).

3.3.5 Absolute/Cash Indicators

This last set of indicators still are based on absolute values, but they differ from the previous ones for their use of cash flows rather than accrual measures. The most common indicators comprise Cash EVA and Cash Value Added (CVA).

Cash EVA is another version of the previous EVA, but in this case, operating profit is replaced by the Cash Flow from operating activities.

$$\text{Cash EVA} = \text{Cash Flow from Operating activities} - K * I$$

This indicator provides an estimation of the cash generated by the invested capital. The logic behind this approach is that value is created when operating cash flow generated by investments exceeds the cost of that invested capital.

Less used in practice is instead the **Cash Value Added** (CVA), defined as:

$$\text{CVA} = \text{Cash Flow from operating activities} - \text{Cash Flow Required for operating activities}$$

CVA is more a measure of the liquidity of an enterprise rather than of its profitability, hence with a low correlation with the creation of economic value.

CHAPTER 4

Value Drivers

Coauthored by Marika Arena

Politecnico di Milano, Department of Management, Economics & Industrial Engineering

This section illustrates a third set of indicators: value driver measures. This term is used to denote indicators that provide *earlier signals* (drivers) of the value creation. Three types of drivers are presented:

- Nonfinancial indicators of the present *performance* of the enterprise
- Nonfinancial indicators of the *resource state* (which measure the potential of the present enterprise resources to generate future value-added projects)
- Drivers of *risks* which provide early signals and allow monitoring of probability and impact of risks (events that influence the capability of an enterprise to achieve its objectives).

The rationale behind these indicators can be understood by referring to the value tree presented in Chapter 2. The tree shows that the value creation is driven by the capability of the company to improve performance related to critical success factors; by monitoring critical factors through nonfinancial performance measures, companies can predict value creation. The characteristics of these indicators also enable companies to more quickly collect data and perform analysis compared to financial indicators.

4.1 NONFINANCIAL PERFORMANCE INDICATORS

Nonfinancial performance indicators measure the current output of projects and activities. Referring to the value tree components, indicators can be both revenue drivers and cost drivers and be measured by different competitive factors: time, quality, flexibility, productivity, environment, and social responsibility. The following sections discuss the indicators according to these factors.

4.1.1 Time Indicators

The first category of indicators refers to time as a competitive factor. Time is a driver for both costs and revenues, potentially covering all the phases of the supply chain and product/service development. Time indicators can be further divided into two broad types of indicators in relation to their expected impact on financials:

- Internal-oriented indicators, driving efficiency, and thus a reduction of costs
- External-oriented indicators, driving customer value, and monitoring how companies respond to actual and potential customers.

Internal-oriented indicators aim to follow time efficiency across the supply chain by measuring—more or less indirectly—value-added activities. A widespread indicator is *cycle time*, which monitors possible internal inefficiencies across the manufacturing or

Table 4.1 Example of Delivery Time			
	Due Date	Number of Days Delayed	Working Days Needed to Deliver to the Final Client
Machine A	Today	0	1
Machine B	Yesterday	1	1
Machine C	Last week	5	1

service delivery cycle, anticipating the impact on diverse cost items such as costs of supervision, production planning and control, and operating working capital.

An interesting indicator is the *cycle time efficiency*, which is defined as:

$$\frac{\text{Time for value-added activities}}{\text{Total cycle time}}$$

This indicator explicitly states the amount of nonvalue-added activities; a value near 0 would indicate a very high level of inefficiency, while values near 1 indicate a cycle without waste.

A final example of an indicator for internal-oriented measures is *setup time*, which measures one of the activities most often considered nonvalue-added.

External-oriented time indicators can be divided into two types:

- Metric of delivery time for catalogue products aimed at evaluating the competitiveness of the logistical system of the enterprise; examples are the *average delivery time* and *on-time deliveries*.
- Measures of the time needed for developing new products aimed at assessing the competitiveness of the process for developing new products and services. A widespread indicator in this cluster is *time to market*, which is defined as the time period between the start of product design and the sale of the first unit of the product on the market.

Each indicator measures only one component of the impact of time performances against enterprise value; as a result, to have a complete overview, several indicators must be used. The selection of indicators is crucial and may be done consistently with strategy. Yet there are problems that appear to be "technical" but influence motivation and decision making.

To clarify this issue, we use an example. Suppose a company is producing machines and has a critical success factor of delivery time; at the moment, they have three consignments in the cycle: A, B, and C (refer to Table 4.1). Machine C already has a 5-day delay, B is due today (end of the day), and A is due tomorrow. All three consignments need one working day to be delivered, and they cannot be processed in parallel.

The delivery time performances can be measured with different indicators, for example:

- Average delay
- Maximum delay
- Percentage of delayed orders.

The adoption of a specific metric has implications on the decision to prioritize one machine or the other (Tables 4.2 and 4.3).

Table 4.2 shows the impact of this decision on the number of days a product is delayed; this decision can be influenced by the type of metric adopted (Table 4.3).

Table 4.2 Impact of Prioritization on Delays					
		Present Situation (Start of the Day)	Situation Prioritizing Machine A	Situation Prioritizing Machine B	Situation Prioritizing Machine C
	Due Date	Number of Days Delayed	Number of Days Delayed	Number of Days Delayed	Number of Days Delayed
Machine A	Today	0	0	1	1
Machine B	Yesterday	1	2	1	2
Machine C	Last week	5	6	6	5

Table 4.3 Impact of Metric Choice on Decisions				
Type of Metric	Present Situation (Start of the Day)	Situation Prioritizing Machine A	Situation Prioritizing Machine B	Situation Prioritizing Machine C
Average delay (days)	2	2.7	2.7	2.7
Maximum delay (days)	5	6	6	5
Percentage of delayed order	66.7%	66.7%	100%	100%

If the company adopts the average delay, the decision maker can choose indifferently (A, B, or C) because the impact on performance will be the same.

When the maximum delay is adopted, the decision maker is led to prioritize the order with the highest delay to avoid a further worsening of performance.

Finally, if the percentage of delayed deliveries is used as an indicator, the decision maker is led to process Machine A first to avoid the indicator increasing from 66.7 to 100% of delayed deliveries.

4.1.2 Quality Indicators

The second category of nonfinancial performance indicators addresses *quality*, tackling the characteristics of products/services/processes. Indicators can also be articulated in this case according to their internal or external orientation.

External-oriented measures assess the quality of products/services in relation to customer needs. There are several classifications of quality dimensions that can be classified in three categories, however, design quality, conformance, and customer responsiveness. All three of these performance dimensions can be measured by objective metrics and subjective metrics; the former is based on the direct measurement of performance features (e.g., battery duration in mobile phones); the latter is based on customer perception (qualitative judgment of battery duration).

Design quality indicates operational, esthetic, and technical features of products/services, which determines its positioning and differentiation. For example, laptops can be characterized by processor speed, battery duration, weight, screen size, and resolution. Design quality has been a fertile topic for many commercial or consumer websites, which offer comparisons of product/service characteristics in different sectors, such as computers, mobile phones, insurance services, and bank services.

Customer responsiveness moves the attention away from design features to their focus on clients; it refers to the capability of a product/service to respond to the needs and wants of present and potential customers. For an example, we refer to the characteristics of student support services. The overall satisfaction of students for these services is judged by several features, such as personnel courtesy and front-office opening hours. To understand the importance of these features, customer satisfaction surveys can be employed, correlating each feature performance against the overall satisfaction with the service. In particular, importance-performance analysis (IPA) can be used (Figure 4.1) as a visual tool. The x-axis indicates the attribute importance as measured by standardized coefficients and the y-axis shows its performance (satisfaction with service quality). The means are used to split the axes. The performance and importance values divide the matrix into four quadrants, giving university managers a visual indication of where they should focus their efforts to improve overall student satisfaction.

Finally, conformance indicators assess the conformity to design of products and services delivered to customers. These indicators include the number of returned products and the number of claims.

Internal-oriented indicators focus on internal processes, evaluating waste, scrap, and reworked products. Most often, internal quality measures refer to manufacturing and logistical processes, but similar measures can be used in administrative processes; for example, in order management, the quality can be assessed by the number of incomplete order forms.

Internal and external quality partially overlap—in particular, improvements in process quality increase the conformity of delivered products/services, maintaining the same control activities.

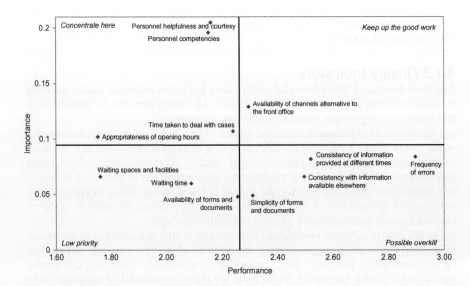

Figure 4.1 IPA analysis. Source: Arena et al., 2010.

4.1.3 Productivity Indicators

Productivity indicators are one of the most traditional nonfinancial measures in enterprises; they are the ratio between output and input of a specific process/activity. Improving productivity implies an improvement of the capability to have a higher volume of output with the same input. These indicators are very often used in mass physical transformation where output is standardized, but they can also be adopted in routine support activities, such as invoicing. Indicators can be classified according to the measurement of inputs and outputs.

Starting from outputs, physical measurement is simple for "single-product" companies. In this case, the output can be expressed with the quantity produced. In multiproduct companies, to have a unique measure, a weighted average must be calculated to account for diversity. Two alternative solutions can be theoretically adopted: (i) physical weights, referring, for example, to size elements (length, weight, area) and (ii) monetary weight, using the price of each product/service as the weight. This latter method translates output in monetary terms. To avoid the disadvantages of financial indicators, standard prices, rather than actual prices, can be adopted; this speeds up the measurement process, allowing output to be measured without waiting for an account of actual sales.

The first alternative—physical weights—is adopted by companies with homogeneous products; monetary weights are favored when products are more diversified.

An issue to be considered in both cases is the influence of vertical integration on the measurements. When companies produce the same amount of output with different levels of vertical integration, the ratio between input and output changes. The company with the higher level of integration will be less productive due to the lower level of input. To avoid incomparability, products have to be weighted using a value-added method; this solution is usually more expensive and is suggested only for specific information needs.

Regarding input measurement, it is first useful to distinguish between partial productivity, where input encompasses a single production factor, and global productivity indicators, where a combination of different inputs is considered in the ratio.

Labor productivity (using the number of employees as input) and raw material use are widespread indicators of partial productivity. In the case of raw material, the input refers often only to the most valuable or scarce material (e.g., rare earth across several industries or water in some countries).

Productivity indicators are usually not calculated with reference to technological inputs; more frequently, enterprises measure the productivity of single machines using the ratio between output and production time.

The main disadvantage of productivity indicators is their sensitivity to variations of inputs. If enterprises invest in automation, their productivity per employee increases significantly, but it does not trace the exchange of input mix.

Global productivity indicators have been introduced to solve this problem—having a measure of productivity that is not dependent on input mix. Here, the input includes more than one factor and is calculated as their weighted average. Usually, weights are unit costs of resources; with this methodology, the input actually becomes the cost of production. Although standard values can be used, in this way, the indicators become financial. In particular, when economic weights are used for both output and input, the obtained measure is the ratio between sales and the cost of production, quite similar to return on sales.

4.1.4 Flexibility Indicators

Flexibility is the capability to respond to changes within limited cost and time ranges. The link with change highlights the importance of flexibility indicators to environmental changes. Contrary to the other types of nonfinancial performance analyzed, flexibility becomes a driver of cost or revenue according to the strategy of the company. With a reactive strategy to change, flexibility is more a cost driver, tracing the capability of the company to respond with limited costs. Companies can also use the proactive approach of *stimulating changes* by introducing a higher number of innovations compared to their competitors. In this case, flexibility is a revenue driver.

Because there are different types of changes, flexibility is a multidimensional concept—dimensions are more or less relevant for different companies or even for the same company over time. As seen for quality, there are several classifications of flexibility measures (e.g., Vokurka, O'Leary-Kelly, 2000), which sometimes express the concept in dozens of categories. A review of the literature goes beyond the scope of this book; here, we suggest a categorization useful to cover all the dimensions with reference to products and services delivered using a manageable number of categories.

These flexibility categories are described referring to two characterizations of change:

- Type of change, distinguishing between *quantitative* changes linked to positive or negative variations of demand of products/services of enterprises and *qualitative* variations related to changes in the type of product/service produced.
- Entity of change, which can be divided into three categories:
  - *Small changes*, which do not require structural variations of enterprise resources.
  - *Large changes*, which require structural changes in enterprise resources.
  - *Range* of allowed changes, referring to the set of environmental changes that the company is capable of sustaining without structural modification; this capability usually increases when modular reconfigurable resources are employed.

Combining the two categorizations of change, six types of flexibility are obtained.

Table 4.4 gives the six categories, showing examples of indicators. Starting from flexibility with small changes, *product flexibility* is the ability to modify resources for

Table 4.4 Flexibility Dimensions			
Entity of Change	Type of Change	Flexibility Dimension	Examples
Small	Qualitative	Product	Time for engineering a new product
	Quantitative	Volume	Operating leverage
Large	Qualitative	Operation	Time for introducing a new handling system that can transport materials of different shapes
	Quantitative	Expansion	Maximum increase in warehouse space, loading capacity, and other distribution facilities
Range	Qualitative	Production	Range of products and services manufactured and delivered
	Quantitative	Mix	Average number of products in a period Spare capacity Setup time

introducing new products or services—a common measure is the time required for small modifications in activities such as engineering and logistics. *Volume flexibility*, which measures the impact on enterprises of small quantitative variations, can be measured by the operating leverage (ratio between fixed costs and variable costs). *Operation flexibility* is the ability to adapt to large qualitative changes; it can be measured by the time required for adapting enterprise resources to new requirements. *Expansion flexibility*, indicating the ability to respond to large changes in existing product demand, depends on the resource modularity; referring to logistics, an example is the maximum increase in warehouse space, loading capacity, and other distribution facilities. The qualitative range dimension is referred to as *production flexibility*, measured, for example, by the range of products and services manufactured and delivered by companies. *Mix flexibility*, which is defined as the ability of companies to withstand changes in the level of demand without additional investments, can be tracked by the average number of products in a period, spare capacity, and setup time.

4.1.5 Environmental and Social Responsibility Driver

The capability of companies to improve their behavior with regard to environment and society has become a crucial component of many companies' strategies. Attention to these issues is not only an ethical matter but also affects the creation of enterprise value.

Environmental and societal performance is particularly relevant for external accountability, positively influencing the company's image and sometimes affecting purchasing behaviors. Many companies are now devoting increasing attention to green consumers, developing innovations in line with ecologically conscious consumers and analyzing the determinants of their behavior.[1] Furthermore, some performances linked to human mistreatment or environmental neglect or harm can determine cash outflows. An extreme case of this is the BP oil spill in the Gulf of Mexico between April 20 and July 15, 2010.[2]

The more traditional use of this type of indicator is for *external accountability*, which is often included in sustainability reports. The indicators in these reports must be stable and standard in order to be externally credible and positively influence the company's external stakeholders. Furthermore, reports must be disseminated through official channels and linked to more traditional reports (e.g., financial reporting).

To improve the credibility of sustainability reporting, several reference frameworks have been developed. These frameworks vary in the terms of dimensions considered, as given in Table 4.5. The rows show the different items that frameworks might consider; the columns provide the main frameworks available (ordered from left to right) according to the coverage of items. Some frameworks focus only on environmental issues, such as the Sigma Project, while others concentrate only on social elements, such as the International Council on Human Rights Policy (ICHRP) and Ethical Trading Initiative.

The most complete framework is the Global Reporting Initiative (GRI), which is also the most used standard in enterprises worldwide.[3]

---

[1]Akehurst et al., 2012.
[2]http://en.wikipedia.org/wiki/Deepwater_Horizon_oil_spill
[3]http://www.pwc.com/id/en/publications/assets/Sustainability_Reporting-2012.pdf

Table 4.5 Sustainability Frameworks

Item	GRI (2013)	Facility Reporting Project (2005)	SIGMA Project (2003c)	BLIHR (2003)	BLIHR (2006)	ICCR (2003)	FEEM (1995)	ICHRP, (2002)	Ethical Trading Initiative	Environment (2000)	GEMI (1998)	CEFIC (2006)	DEFRA (2006)	SIGMA Project (2003a)	UNCTAD (1999)	WBCSD (2000)	UNCTAD (2004)	Investors in People (2004)	SIGMA Project (2003b)
Materials	X	X	X			X	X			X	X		X		X	X			
Energy	X	X	X				X			X	X	X	X	X	X	X	X		
Water	X	X	X				X			X	X	X	X	X	X	X	X		
Biodiversity	X	X	X							X									
Emissions	X	X	X			X	X			X	X	X	X	X	X	X	X		
Waste	X	X	X				X			X	X	X	X	X	X	X	X		
Products and services	X	X	X				X			X									X
Compliance	X	X	X				X			X	X		X						
Transportation	X		X							X	X	X		X					
Work practices and conditions	X	X	X	X	X	X	X	X	X		X	X		X					
Employment	X	X	X	X	X	X	X	X	X									X	
Industrial relations	X	X	X	X	X	X		X											
Workplace health and safety	X	X	X	X	X	X	X	X	X		X	X							
Training and education	X	X	X	X	X	X	X	X	X									X	
Diversity and equal opportun ties	X	X	X	X	X	X		X	X										
Human rights	X	X	X	X	X	X	X	X	X										
Investment and supply practices	X	X	X	X	X	X		X											
Nondiscr mination	X	X	X	X	X	X		X	X										

(Continued)

Table 4.5 (Continued)

Item		Framework																		
	GRI (2013)	Facility Reporting Project (2005)	SIGMA Project (2003c)	BLIHR (2003)	BLIHR (2006)	ICCR (2003)	FEEM (1995)	ICHRP, (2002)	Ethical Trading Initiative	Environment (2000)	GEMI (1998)	CEFIC (2006)	DEFRA (2006)	SIGMA Project (2003a)	UNCTAD (1999)	WBCSD (2000)	UNCTAD (2004)	Investors in People (2004)	SIGMA Project (2003b)
Freedom of association and collective bargaining	X	X	X	X	X	X		X												
Child labor	X	X	X		X	X		X	X											
Forced labor	X	X		X	X	X		X	X											
Security practices	X	X		X	X	X		X												
Rights of indigenous peoples	X	X		X	X	X		X												
Society	X	X	X	X	X	X	X													
Community	X	X	X	X	X	X	X													
Corruption	X		X	X	X															
Political contributions	X	X		X	X															
Anticollusion policy	X																			
Product responsibility	X	X	X	X	X	X														
Consumer health and safety	X	X	X	X	X	X	X													
Product and services labelling	X		X			X	X													
Marketing communication	X			X	X	X														
Privacy	X			X	X															
Compliance	X	X	X	X	X	X	X				X									

Table 4.6 Example of Indicators from GRI—Energy (Adapted from GRI Implementation Manual G4)[4]

Area	Indicator
Energy consumption within the organization	Total fuel consumption from nonrenewable sources in joules or multiples, including fuel types used Total fuel consumption from renewable fuel sources in joules or multiples, including fuel types used Consumption in joules, watt-hours, or multiples, including: • Electricity consumption • Heating consumption • Cooling consumption • Steam consumption In joules, watt-hours, or multiples, including: • Electricity sold • Heating sold • Cooling sold • Steam sold Total energy consumption in joules or multiples
Energy consumption outside of the organization	Energy consumed outside of the organization in joules or multiples Source of the conversion factors used
Energy intensity	Energy intensity ratio Types of energy included in the intensity ratio: fuel, electricity, heating, cooling, steam, or all of these
Reduction of energy consumption	Amount of reductions in energy consumption achieved as a direct result of conservation and efficiency initiatives in joules or multiples
Reductions in energy requirements of products and services	Reductions in the energy requirements of sold products and services achieved during the reporting period in joules or multiples

GRI standards[5] are divided into two main areas:

- General standard disclosures, addressing high level elements of sustainability, including strategy and analysis, organizational profile, identified material aspects and boundaries, stakeholder engagement, report profile, governance, and ethics and integrity. This part is more textual and qualitative, although several indicators are incorporated. For example, the organizational profile encompasses:
  - The total number of permanent employees by employment type and gender
  - The total workforce by employees and supervised workers and by gender
  - The total workforce by region and gender.
- A specific standard disclosure, which is divided into three categories: economic, environmental, and social. This is further divided into four subcategories: labor practices and decent work, human rights, society, and product responsibility.

The specific standard disclosure illustrates a broad and complete set of indicators for each area (Table 4.6).

The following table presents the detailed guidance for energy consumption within the organization (Table 4.7).

---

[4]https://www.globalreporting.org/resourcelibrary/GRIG4-Part2-Implementation-Manual.pdf
[5]Reference to G4 reporting standards: https://www.globalreporting.org/resourcelibrary/GRIG4-Part1-Reporting-Principles-and-Standard-Disclosures.pdf

Table 4.7 Example of Indicator Guidance for Energy Consumption Within the Organization (adapted from GRI Implementation Manual G4)[6]

Indicator	Guidance
Total fuel consumption from renewable fuel sources in joules or multiples, including fuel types used	Nonrenewable fuel sources include fuel for combustion in boilers, furnaces, heaters, turbines, flares, incinerators, generators, and vehicles that are owned or controlled by the organization. Nonrenewable fuel sources cover fuels purchased and fuels generated by the organization's activities, such as mined coal and gas from oil and gas extraction
Electricity consumption Heating consumption Cooling consumption Steam consumption	Using the identified types of energy (purchased for consumption and self-generated), calculate the total energy consumption within the organization in joules or multiples using the following formula: Total energy consumption within the organization = Nonrenewable fuel consumed + renewable fuel consumed + electricity, heating, cooling, and steam purchased for consumption + self-generated electricity, heating, cooling, and steam − Electricity, heating, cooling, and steam sold
Electricity sold Heating sold Cooling sold Steam sold	

In addition to external accountability, societal and environmental performances are relevant for internal accountability. Environmental performances in particular have a significant impact on the costs that enterprises sustain. Each of the GRI categories (energy, materials, water, and biodiversity) generates costs for organizations. Yet when indicators are used for internal purposes, a higher focus is required, with specific measures that can change over time according to decision-making needs.

As for the other value drivers analyzed so far, environmental and societal indicators provide information on specific issues, giving a partial view of enterprise behavior. To overcome this fragmentation, some companies have developed synthetic indicators in order to assess their sustainability more holistically. These indicators are developed with the weighted average sum of difference elements, and they are not usually available to the public, although there are exceptions, such as in the case of Apple. Apple provides the calculation of its environmental footprint on its website, which includes emissions generated from manufacturing and transportation, recycling of products, and the emissions generated by its facilities.

4.2 NONFINANCIAL RESOURCE STATE INDICATORS

Indicators of *resource state* aim to capture the potential for enterprises to innovate and grow. Indicators cover both tangible and intangible assets, such as intellectual capital. The latter are more difficult to analyze, and several classifications and metrics have been proposed.[7] In spite of the different labels and clusters, all classifications are

---

[6]https://www.globalreporting.org/resourcelibrary/GRIG4-Part2-Implementation-Manual.pdf
[7]For a summary, see Cuganesan and Dumay, 2009.

essentially four types of resources: financial, technological, human and organizational, and image and reputation.

Operationally, to use this indicator, each enterprise should define in detail the specific resources that they interested in monitoring. To support this process, King and Zeithaml (2003) developed a methodology that was tested in several companies in different sectors. Their approach is as follows:

- *Defining scope: Industry and organization selection*: In this phase, enterprises perform analysis of secondary sources on the industry and interviews with experts in order to identify a large set of resources that are potentially relevant for sector development and organization growth.
- *Protocol design*: This stage is a preliminary step to prepare for discussions and interviews with senior managers. The goal is to prepare a protocol of semistructured questions for Stage 3.
- *Top management discussion to identify organizational knowledge resources*: This list of resources is discussed internally during open interviews in order to arrive at a more focused list of resources that are relevant for the company specifically.
- *Operational management survey to measure resources*: The list from the top management discussion is then submitted to operational management through closed interviews in order to assess the relevance of each identified resource from their perspective.

The cycle is closed with the choice of the specific indicator to associate with each resource.

The choice of indicators is a delicate process, as we have also illustrated for performance indicators. To provide a guideline, the choice can be related to the four types of resources highlighted at the beginning of this chapter (financial, technological, human and organizational, and image and reputation), which are measured according to three dimensions: quality, quantity, and accessibility. The capability to innovate and grow in the long run is in fact related to the quantity of resources available; their quality (e.g., patents awarded and pending); and their accessibility, intended as the possibility to "increase" the specific resource (e.g., for human resources, the education level in the area). Metrics can either be objective—such as the number of employees by role—or subjective—for example, customer perception compared with competitors to evaluate ways to improve the company's image or reputation. Sometimes, financial indicators are adapted to value resources. A typical indicator for innovation and marketing is the cost associated with these activities; another example is the percentage of sales coming from new products (Figure 4.2).

To measure and visualize assets, several approaches have been proposed, and three areas have been developed: intellectual capital, human resources, and brand equity.

Intellectual capital joins different types of assets and is a model that includes three dimensions:

- Human capital, which refers to the skill, training, education, experience, quantity, and quality of an organization's employees.
- Relational capital, which encompasses relationships with customers and suppliers, brand names, trademarks, and reputation.
- Internal structural capital, which refers to intangible assets and knowledge embedded in organizational structures and processes; this dimension comprises patents, research and development, and technology.

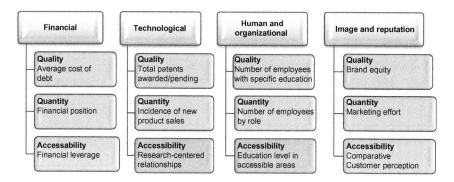

Figure 4.2 Resource state indicators: an example.

Among the various approaches proposed, Sveiby's (1997) Intangible Assets Monitor has become increasingly popular. According to this approach, each element is then measured according to three types of metrics: indicators of *growth/renewal*, such as the growth of the number of customers; indicators of *efficiency*—for instance, the proportion of professionals in the company; and indicators of *stability*, such as the frequency of repeated orders.

A limited number of indicators should be assigned to each of the three areas, providing a synthetic view of intangible assets.

Regarding *human resources*, several approaches have been tested that can be classified into three categories:

- Approaches focused on the *process* dimension, covering human resource management (HRM) practices; these methods measure the effectiveness and efficiency of recruitment, selection, training, and development of human resources without evaluating the actual impact on company value.
- Methodology providing one synthetic indicator, starting from the assessment of HRM, such as the Human Capital Index (HCI) proposed by Watson Wyatt, or the Human Capital Capability Scorecard proposed by Imperial Consulting.
- Approaches mainly devoted to external accountability, which provides ratings of human resources functions across the public sector. An exemplary country is the United Kingdom and particularly the National Health Service (NHS). Initially, the rating system focused on simple indicators about staff (total staff numbers; proportion of staff in each major staff group [ancillaries, nurses, doctors, etc.]); total staff cost; overtime cost; and use of part-time staff. More recently, the indicator system was changed, attempting to capture "softer" elements of human resources; for example, commitment to improving the working lives of staff (key target); health, safety, and incidents; and staff opinion surveys on HRM.

Finally, *image and reputation* has recently gained increasing attention, and several methods have been proposed. In particular for marketing functions, an important indicator is *brand equity*, which is the value added to products and services uniquely attributable to the brand (Keller, 1993).

Although there is not a universal metric, three approaches have been widely adopted:

- Young & Rubicam (Y&R) BrandAsset™ Valuator (BAV)
- Aaker Brand Equity Ten
- Moran Brand Equity Methodology.

The Y&R BAV was developed by the advertising agency Young & Rubicam and is based on a large survey of customers all over the world, who assessed brands in terms of four dimensions:

- Differentiation, measuring the uniqueness of a brand against others
- Relevance, gauging the perceived importance of a brand to a large sample of customers
- Esteem, assessing customer perception of the growing or declining popularity of a brand
- Knowledge, evaluating consumers' understanding and awareness of the brand's meaning.

BAV relates the first two elements (differentiation and relevance) to the potential of the brand, while the latter two (esteem and knowledge) are associated with the brand's present status.

The second model was developed by Aaker (1996) and measures brand equity across 10 dimensions: price premium, satisfaction/loyalty, perceived quality, leadership measures, perceived value, brand personality, organizational associations, brand awareness, market share, and price and distribution indices.

In terms of measurement, it is suggested that the majority of these factors be measured through a survey consistent with other brands, and specific questions are suggested; for the price premium, an alternative measure is the difference in price between comparable products.

The third approach is the Moran Brand Equity Index, which is based on three dimensions:

- Effective market share (EMS), which calculates the market share, dividing the market into segments with the following formula:

$$EMS = \sum_{i}^{N} \sigma_i \times S_i$$

where

i, index for segments
N, total number of segments
σ_i, market share in segment i
S_i, proportion of brand sales in segment i.

Table 4.8 shows an example of the calculation comparing three different brands (A, B, and C).

- Relative price (RP), which is the ratio between the price of the brand's product/service over the average price of a competing product/service:

$$RP = \frac{brand\ price}{average\ price}$$

- Durability (D), which is the measure of customer retention or loyalty, expressed by the forecast of the percentage of a brand's customers who will continue to buy the brand's goods next year:

$$D = \%Customer\ who\ will\ repurchase\ next\ year$$

Table 4.8 Example of Calculation for EMS (Moran Methodology)										
		Brands Assessed			Segment Proportion Over Brand's Total Sales			Share of the Market Segment		
Market Segment	Total Market	A	B	C	A	B	C	A	B	C
Asia	2000	400	800	600	25.0%	50.0%	37.5%	20%	40%	30%
Europe	2000	400	800	200	25.0%	50.0%	12.5%	20%	40%	10%
North America	2000	400	0	600	25.0%	0.0%	37.5%	20%	0%	30%
South America	2000	400	0	200	25.0%	0.0%	12.5%	20%	0%	10%
	8000	1600	1600	1600	20%	100%	100%	20%	20%	20%
Market share		20.0%	20.0%	20.0%						
EMS		20.0%	40.0%	25.0%						

The final equity index is the multiplication of the three factors:

$$\text{Moran BE Index} = \text{EMS} \times \text{RP} \times \text{D}$$

Comparing the three methodologies, the first method—Y&R (BAV)—is the simplest. It is based on consumer perception, which gives an immediate response but has the disadvantages of subjective methodology based on a survey. Furthermore, this indicator relies on relative evaluation against competitors, which implies a significant effort in data collection or the outsourcing of measurement. Similar characteristics can be outlined for the second indicator (Aaker model); however, this model is more complete and includes more dimensions. This comprehensiveness, on the other hand, renders the measurement procedure more complex and onerous.

Finally, the third indicator has the advantage of being an objective measure and, hence, does not require a consumer survey. The main disadvantage is the applicability to sectors where segmentation is not straightforward.

4.3 CHARACTERISTICS OF NONFINANCIAL PERFORMANCE AND RESOURCE INDICATORS

The main advantage of nonfinancial indicators compared to financial indicators is their timeliness. Financial indicators, regardless of their type, need several steps to translate physical events into financial transactions. For example, it is possible to monitor requests for maintenance on products daily, while the financial impact on costs would be visible periodically and only once costs are committed or sustained.

Another important benefit of nonfinancial indicators is long-term orientation. This is particularly true in comparison with accounting indicators. If chosen logically with the enterprise's critical success factors, nonfinancial indicators are a driver for competitive advantage and value creation. For instance, in the automotive industry, delivery time is a critical success factor; suppliers constantly monitor this factor, which can affect business relationships. If they realize that they are behind schedule, they can implement solutions to speed up delivery, sometimes even choosing costly solutions for transportation (e.g., air transportation).

Regarding *measurability*, nonfinancial indicators are comparable to accounting indicators, although each indicator must be carefully outlined in terms of metrics to avoid possible ambiguity. To clarify this problem, an example of productivity can be useful. Labor productivity is a common indicator in the manufacturing industry, but in order to be measured, output and input must be defined. These include the unit of analysis (company, plant, machinery, and batch) and how single products are then aggregated (weight choice). This problem is solved by implementing a protocol for each indicator, where the following information is included:

- Measure: Title of the measure
- Purpose: Why do companies want to measure this?
- Formula: How to calculate this measure
- Unit of analysis: What is the object of measurement?
- Frequency: How often do companies measure this?
- Source of data: Where does the necessary data come from?

Completeness is more critical for nonfinancial indicators. Financial indicators can aggregate several critical success factors into one value by translating their effect in accrual or cash flows; for example, product cost includes several categories (personnel, material, and depreciation) and several key factors (e.g., flexibility, productivity, and efficiency). Nonfinancial indicators measure specific performances (e.g., delivery time) without providing information on other performances (e.g., product quality). If the number of indicators adopted is very limited, the completeness of the systems is inappropriate, and employees motivate to improve few performances overlooking other factors critical for the long-term competitiveness. When this selective approach is adopted dynamically, frequently changing indicators to guarantee a fit with the strategy, very often this approach encounters problems due to the rigidity of management control and information systems.

On the contrary, when the indicator set is large, the information is more complete. The problem in this situation is the synthetic assessment of employees and organizational units, given that it is very unlikely that all indicators have the same trend (positive or negative). In order to have a unique overall evaluation, weights can be defined explicitly or implicitly. Both of these solutions have behavioral implications. If weights are transparently defined, the "controlled" unit will be led to favor the performance with a higher weight—risks similar to very selective systems. If companies decide to assign weights implicitly, without transparently involving the assessed unit/employees in their definition, this creates uncertainty around the assessment process, negatively affecting motivation and potentially causing conflicts among peers.

In all cases, nonfinancial indicators do not have a linear relationship with revenues/cost, but often there are saturation effects: Once a critical threshold is achieved, further improvement in single performance (e.g., service quality) has a small impact on revenues and cost.

Finally, concerning *precision*, nonfinancial indicators are good drivers of value creation. Internal-oriented indicators measure the enterprise's capability to efficiently manage its resources; an improvement of these metrics is potentially translated in the increase of economic value by reducing cash outflows for manufacturing and supporting activities. Improvements in nonfinancial indicators often indicate only potential savings; for example, a reduction of nonvalue-added activities is an actual cost savings only if personnel can be employed in other activities or removed.

Regarding external-oriented measures, the impact on value creation is linked more to competitors' comparative performance rather than to an absolute increase in nonfinancial performances. If indicators improve but are worse compared to competitors, this is unlikely to have a positive impact on value creation. Even in this case, nonfinancial metrics provide partial indication of the capability to create enterprise value. To reduce this risk, absolute indicators can be substituted by relative indicators using benchmarking techniques.

4.4 RISK DRIVERS: KEY RISK INDICATORS

Chapter 2 introduced some risk indicators that are calculated and based on financial figures and provide a synthetic overview of the probability and impact of variations in value creation. In line with the rest of the chapter, in this section, we focus on risk indicators, which attempt to provide early signals. These indicators are called[8] KRIs and are defined as metrics that monitor and provide early signals on the probability and impact of one or more events (risks) that influence the capability of enterprises to reach their goals.

To clarify the meaning and role of KRI, think of the telecommunication companies that lose customers due to the availability of prepaid phone programs. The chain of events is set in motion starting with this risk:

- *Risk event* (to object of control): Customer loss
- *Intermediate event* (a metric anticipating the risk event but not explaining the original cause): Lack of credit recharging
- *Root cause*: Better offers provided by competitors.

KRIs can examine all three events, but it is evident that monitoring root causes and intermediate events increases the time available to make decisions.

The definition of KRIs should be carried out in synergy with risk management processes (see Chapter 6) given the importance of carefully identifying the risks affecting the company; then, the most appropriate KRI should be selected.

Regardless of the type of risk addressed (e.g., regulatory, market, or operational), KRIs can also vary in terms of the metrics adopted—specifically, these can be:

- Objective or subjective: The former refers to metrics derived from the measurement of objective phenomenon; subjective KRIs refer to metrics derived from stakeholders' perceptions (managers, clients, employees, etc.).
- Single or composite, referring to the number of events the indicators monitor: Single KRIs monitor a single event (e.g., oil price); composite KRIs assess more than one factor (e.g., synthetic country risk indicators take different factors into account).

Table 4.9 provides examples of each category.

4.4.1 Characteristics of KRI Indicators
KRIs can be analyzed in terms of their contributions/characteristics for managerial control.

---

[8]The label *key risk indicator* is used by several academics and practitioners but lacks a unique definition.

Table 4.9 Key Risk Indicators		
	Single	**Composite**
Objective	• Brent price • Exchange rates	• Cost of capital • Inflation rate
Subjective	• Supplier failure risk	• SACE country risk

The most important advantage of KRIs is their *timeliness*; observing events that can undermine the achievement of company goals, they provide prompt signals to managers, allowing the company to supervise performance even earlier than performance drivers.

Completeness is very similar to what was outlined previously for nonfinancial performance and resource indicators; as they track specific dimensions of risk, the completeness of the control system is determined by the coverage of the risk drivers. From this perspective, it is possible to check the extent to which different potential risks are covered in connection with a company's perimeter distinguishing between:

• Microenvironment, which refers to the internal environment of the company, including issues such as human resources, technological resources, assets, processes, and the portfolio of assets.
• Mesoenvironment, which specifically tackles the elements that infringe on the company's perimeter, including, for instance, the extended supply chain (suppliers, distributors, and customers); competitors and regulators; and key stakeholders.
• Macroenvironment, which refers to the macroeconomic context and the global market.

Precision is controversial; KRIs track the potential variation in probability and impact of risks, which then affect performances. The precision of KRIs is hence related to the relation between KRIs, risk, and performance trends. When risks have a "history," meaning that it is possible to analyze past correlations (e.g., financial and commodity risks), the precision tends to be quite high; when companies cannot rely on significant past occurrences to determine a relationship, precision is lower.

Similar to what was illustrated previously for performance and resource drivers, *measurability* is high only when metrics are carefully outlined to avoid possible ambiguity.

Regarding *specific responsibility*, indicators vary in terms of the types of events monitored and the possibility to isolate the impact of different factors. For instance, one common metric to assess reputational risk is based on the analysis of the shared market reaction to reputational events, such as an accident or a violation of regulations (Arena et al., 2014). However, this approach does not assess the influence of different events that happen in the same time frame on the market share value—i.e., distinguishing which quota of decrease in the market share can be directly attributed to the reputational event and which quota is related to other market dynamics.

CHAPTER 5

Scorecards

The previous chapters introduced different types of indicators that can be adopted for measuring performances: value-based indicators, accounting indicators, and value drivers. All three types have advantages and disadvantages, emphasizing that it is impossible to build a good performance measurement system (PMS) without a mix of indicators. This situation has led several enterprises to build indicator scorecards, which are groups of different types of indicators that together can fulfill all managerial needs. Obviously, indicators included in the scorecard must be consistent with the company's competitive position and its organizational configuration.

The correlation between the adoption of scorecards and value creation is not easy to trace, yet some studies (Evans, 2004; Davis and Albright, 2004) have shown a positive effect, in particular when the scorecard includes an integrated set of indicators consistent with the strategy (Davis and Albright, 2004). Actually, the adoption of scorecards is often linked to strategic needs (Speckbacher et al., 2003; Arena and Azzone, 2005).

More generally, the adoption of indicator scorecards includes:

- Defining the scorecard's format—that is, how indicators are organized.
- Defining the process by which different measures are selected.

In the remaining sections of this chapter, some solutions are proposed, starting with the current most widely used application—the balanced scorecard (BSC).

5.1 BALANCED SCORECARD

Among the various methodologies proposed to build an indicator scorecard, the most widely used is the BSC (Kaplan and Norton, 1992); it is so common that often the label *balanced scorecard* is considered a general term to specify an indicator scorecard.

According to the initial proposal by Kaplan and Norton (1992), the BSC is designed as constituted by four groups of indicators related to four perspectives:

1. Financial
2. Customer
3. Internal processes
4. Innovation (subsequently renamed "learning and growth").

Figure 5.1 shows the graphical format of the BSC (adapted from Kaplan and Norton, 1992), where the four areas related to the strategy are in the center.

The *financial perspective* reports indicators that are useful to analyze companies' trends against shareholders' expectations in terms of size (e.g., market share, revenues); profitability (e.g., ROE, ROI, EVA, EBIT); and cash generation (cash flow).

The *customer perspective* highlights performances related to the relationship between the enterprise and its market in terms of:

- Range of products/services and frequency of new product introductions
- Customer response time
- Partnership with key clients
- Customers' perception of the company.

These factors can be measured with both financial and nonfinancial metrics.

Metrics included in the *internal processes perspective* are aimed at analyzing efficiency and performances of internal activities of companies; here, also, both financial and nonfinancial indicators can be included, such as:

- Frequency of introduction of new products, tackling research and development processes.
- Average production costs and time efficiency, addressing production performances. Time efficiency allows companies to indirectly monitor setup time and the existence of bottlenecks.

Finally, metrics related to the *learning and growth perspective* can include indicators such as time to market or time in between the launches of two totally different products. In the first case, design and development are emphasized; in the second case, basic and applied research is stressed. Even operating activities can be addressed in this area, measuring learning phenomena, for example, with the incremental reduction of production time due to experience curves.

The BSC, as shown in Figure 5.1, is very complete, including a wide range of indicators that follow the creation of enterprise value, specifically:

- Metrics within the financial perspective include synthetic economic and financial indicators of the results at the enterprise or business-unit level.
- The customer perspective addresses performances linked to customer relations and perception, monitoring who buys products and services.

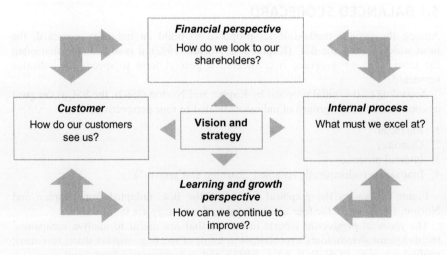

Figure 5.1 BSC structure. Adapted by Kaplan and Norton (1992).

- Indicators in the internal processes perspective include measures monitoring the company's processes, potentially covering all the critical success factors (CSF) (flexibility, time, productivity, etc.).
- Finally, the learning and growth perspective focuses on the enterprise's resources, encompassing indicators such as innovation, human resources, technology, and intangible assets.

5.1.1 Choosing Indicators: Second-Generation BSC

As previously discussed, the quality of the BSC depends on the indicators selected and included in each of the four quadrants, which should be linked by causal relationships and updated according to changes in the company's strategy.

To achieve this result, a tailored design is required for each company; in the second-generation BSC, Kaplan and Norton illustrate the process to follow for doing so.

The first phase is the *construction of a strategic map* of enterprise goals. At the start, general goals are identified and then usually expressed by synthetic and financial indicators; these are positioned in the financial perspective area. Each general goal is afterward divided into subobjectives through a cascade process (refer to Figure 5.2), positioning each objective in the corresponding areas referring to the original areas of the BSC (first-generation). Usually, relations are from the top to the bottom or within the same level. The cascading process can, however, skip one or more areas.

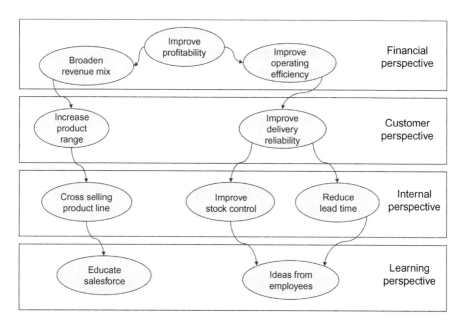

Figure 5.2 The cascading process.

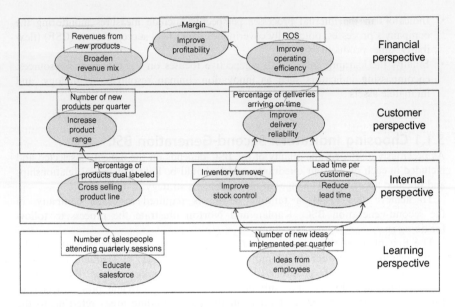

Figure 5.3 An example of a strategy map.

Once objectives are selected, an indicator is then assigned to each of them; the four sets of indicators defined become the indicators to be included in the BSC. Figure 5.3 shows an example of a strategy map with actions and indicators designed for a car dealership.

5.1.2 Other Types of Scorecards
In addition to the approaches illustrated in the previous section, several other types of scorecards have been proposed, including:

- Tableau de bord (TdB)
- Third-generation BSC
- Risk scorecard.

TdB (Epstein and Manzoni, 1998; Bourguignon et al., 2004) was first introduced during the 1950s in France, where it had considerable success. This scorecard is designed starting with the company objectives, which are then translated into CSF. Each CSF is then associated with one or more performance indicators. The TdB structure also dictates that the company goals be disaggregated at the business-unit level and then across organizational units within business units. Both levels are hence assigned a TdB with a process similar to what was adopted for the company overall.

TdB is a less structured method compared to the BSC because both the visualization format and the process for selecting indicators are less stringent. However, the differences between the two methods are minor and more often are linked to the way in which the approaches are implemented rather than their original characteristics, as defined by proponents.

The label *third-generation BSC* was introduced by Lawrie et al. (2004) to distinguish their proposal from the original BSC (Figure 5.1) and the strategy map (Figure 5.3). The third-generation BSC attempts to overcome two problems:

1. The difficulty in linking each indicator to a specific target; in particular, a weakness may be defined in abstract terms and then only after trying to define the target for a specific period.
2. The difficulty in defining objectives starting with the company's BSC to create a detailed BSC for organizational units; to do this, enterprise goals must be translated to be specific to certain departments. For example, it is not easy to understand what a single organizational unit must do to increase EVA overall.

To avoid these problems, two devices are introduced. First, the selection process starts with what are called destination statements, which are statements in which enterprises directly define the target values to be achieved. According to Lawrie and Cobbold (2004), this approach allows companies to more easily achieve consensus within the organization. Second, the BSC is divided into only two levels, which emphasize: (i) expected results, derived directly from the objectives in the destination statements; and (ii) the activities that will be carried out to achieve these objectives.

Given that activities are easily associated with specific organizational units, this conceptualization favors the identification of goals to be assigned to each organizational unit. The set of indicators identified and their target values is the scorecard available to management. Table 5.1 gives an example of destination statements.

Although this method is called a BSC, similarities with the original BSC are negligible. Instead, the freedom in structuring indicators and the emphasis on the integration among objectives of different organizational levels show that this method has more in common with TdB. Compared with TdB, the third-generation BSC is more structured and more easily implemented.

Finally, there is a recent evolution of the BSC: the risk scorecard. Calandro and Lane (2006) introduced a separate scorecard based on the four areas of the traditional BSC, where different types of risks are identified and categorized. Figure 5.4 illustrates the risk scorecard.

Table 5.1 An Example of Destination Statements	
Financial results	• Achieve an EVA of 100 million € • Reduce time for collecting trade receivable to 20 days
Internal processes	• Improve manufacturing productivity by 15% • Reduce defective products by 10%
Innovation	• Reduce time to market to 1 month
Clients	• Reduce delivery time to 5 days • Increase customer satisfaction

Financial Risk Perspective	
Risk	Measure
Financial Market	Weighted Average Cost of Capital Capital Asset Pricing Model
Solvency	Debt-to-Equity Cost of Debt Value-at-Risk
Tax	Expected-to-actual affective tex rate

Customer Risk Perspective	
Risk	Measure
Portfolio	% customers satisfied # of customer complaints Purchase frequency variance Receivables' quality Bad debt reserve fluctuations
Competition	# of new entrants % share lost
Marketing	Actual-to-Expected Revenue

Internal Risk Perspective	
Risk	Measure
Technological	# of help tickets issued # of security breaches
Human Resource	Employee turnover Employee morale/satisfaction # (or %) of top performers who leave
Process	# of unsatisfactory internal audit findings # of positive controls rationalizations % of manual-to-automated processes
Organizational	# of regulatory complaints Price of insurance

Learning & Growth Risk Perspective	
Risk	Measure
Learning	Productivity or trained employees % of employees sent for training that are promoted % of suggestions implemented
Growth	Expected-to-actual growth M&A synergy variance Trend of the expected-to-actual process improvement benefits

Figure 5.4 Risk scorecard. Calandro and Lane (2006, p. 35).

CHAPTER 6

Target Setting: Budgeting and Risk Management

Coauthored by Marika Arena

Politecnico di Milano, Department of Management, Economics & Industrial Engineering

The first part of this book explained how companies can measure enterprise value through different type of indicators and visual tools (e.g., scorecards). This chapter begins the second part on performance management, addressing a major problem: setting performance targets.

Traditionally, target setting is carried out with budgeting, aimed at defining a reference value, particularly financial indicators; however, in recent years, market turbulence and the financial crises have increased companies' awareness of the importance of not only setting performance targets but also predicting variability and events causing potential variances. This attention has culminated in the popularity of ERM systems.

This chapter illustrates both budgeting and ERM in terms of relevance, process, output, and roles, concluding with an analysis of their possible relationships at the organizational level.

6.1 BUDGETING

Budgeting is a set of procedures and activities aimed at assigning targets to organizational units—i.e., reference values for their performances—and the resources needed to achieve these results. Budgeting has a long history in enterprises; however, its boundaries and components are not always clearly defined. The model and phases of the budgeting process are strictly intertwined. Traditional textbooks tend to identify distinct stages in the budgeting process, including communicating strategy, considering options, preparing the sales budget, initially preparing various budgets, negotiating with superiors, coordinating and reviewing the budget, obtaining final acceptance of the budget, and performing ongoing reviews. However, this traditional perspective has been highly criticized, favoring the adoption of reduced approaches to the budget (Hansen et al., 2003) which presents a simplified sequence of stages.

The second relevant feature in budgeting is the role of people involved in the process. Budgeting is a broad process in which different roles are involved, including:

- Managers responsible for organizational units
- Managers and employees working within organizational units affected by target setting (e.g., in terms of individual incentives)
- Accounting and finance functions supporting the process.

Due to its broad organizational and behavioral impact, budgeting design is important, and two main elements may be considered: (i) the choice between explicit or implicit systems for defining targets (see Section 6.1.1) and (ii) the way through which targets of different organizational units are integrated (see Section 6.1.2).

6.1.1 Defining Targets: Explicit and Implicit Systems

Budgeting systems can be divided into two categories:

- Systems in which targets are explicitly tied to a value (*explicit targets*)—e.g., a logistics department may want to decrease delivery time by 5%.
- Systems in which targets are not defined with reference to a specific value (*implicit targets*); instead, only the desired direction of the performance trend is defined. For example, an implicit target for a logistics department would be to decrease delivery time.

Explicit targets assigned to organizational units are supposed to be the result of negotiation processes between the head of each organizational unit and management. Negotiation should:

- Identify challenging—but achievable—targets adhering to the goal-setting theory illustrated in Chapter 1.
- Focus not only on targets but also on action plans needed to achieve those targets. In this way, without limiting the autonomy of managers, both parties involved potentially increase their understanding of the actual attainability of targets.

There are two main obstacles to this process. First, information asymmetry between managers and their superiors; managers who propose targets have more information regarding the attainability of the targets. Second, there is the possibility of opportunistic behaviors; managers proposing targets for their units and people are inclined to underestimate the objectives that can be achieved, creating reserves (slack) to guarantee easier achievement of results.

A PMS can diminish the impact of these problems, providing common information to both superiors and workers and favoring the identification of a shared solution. Without agreement, the system based on explicit targets loses its effectiveness. If objectives are defined autonomously by superiors with a top-down process, there is a risk that targets will be too ambitious and, hence, demotivating; furthermore, workers tend to become less proactive. If objectives are defined autonomously by workers (responsible for organizational units), usually, the targets are not challenging.

At any rate, even when the negotiation process is balanced, the definition of explicit targets can be critical. This system has some issues:

- Targets tend to provide a limit for organizational units. Once targets are achieved, managers have fewer incentives to bolster improvements; this problem is particularly relevant in turbulent contexts, where targets are difficult to identify in advance.
- Targets are likely to set organizational priorities in a fixed way; again, this situation is more problematic in turbulent contexts, where external conditions and goals vary frequently.

Adopting implicit target systems, during the budgeting phase, managers and their superiors define the performances that are important for the department to contribute to the achievement of overall company goals, without defining a reference value for these performances. This choice has an impact on all the phases of the planning and control process. In particular, a formal variance analysis cannot be done after the measurement of actual results, given that there are no targets for comparison; here actual results provide a potential basis of discussion between managers and their superiors for analyzing the unit trend and then possible corrective actions.

Systems based on implicit targets use performance indicators with different purposes compared to explicit target systems. According to Simons' (1995) terminology, the latter can be associated with diagnostic systems (formal systems that managers use to monitor actual results against expected results to guarantee the achievement of objectives), while systems based on implicit targets are more interactive, calling for regular and frequent interactions between managers and their superiors, including discussions about performances and related decisions.

Although they are more flexible, implicit target systems have two main problems. First, managers responsible for organizational units may be uncertain about year-end results, which are subjectively evaluated by upper management. Second, the higher autonomy given to managers can lead to inconsistencies in decision making among different organizational units, negatively affecting the company's overall results.

The first problem cannot be solved but can be diminished if superiors adopt highly participative and transparent processes to assess workers' results. The second problem requires the development of two further levels of control (Simons, 1995): *belief* and *boundary*.

Belief systems entail sharing values and behavioral rules across the organization; in so doing, top management needs to communicate the common priorities and goals to all organizational units and ensure that lower managers comprehend and buy into these beliefs.

Boundary systems require constraints to action and behaviors. These systems are not a novelty in planning systems. For example, public administration and some non-profit organizations operate with this system, defining a threshold for expenses during the budget that has to be respected during the year. In both cases, financial constraints aim to limit broader consequences due to the erroneous behavior of organizational units. In the past, this approach has been used as an alternative to performance measurement, when assigning performance indicators to some organizational units was considered impossible; nowadays, companies more frequently use both methods in an integrated way.

6.1.2 Integrating Targets Among Organizational Units

Targets of individual organizational units cannot be seen as independent from the rest of the organization; for example, the objectives of production units depend on marketing and selling and procurement functions. A revealing element of the budgeting process is the way in which objective integration is handled. There is a wide range of solutions that can vacillate between two extremes: an *integrated* process and an *adaptive* process. The following two sections illustrate these approaches.

6.1.2.1 The Integrated Approach: Master Budget

The master budget is both a document and a process that attempts to define forecasted financial statements. There is great variation among companies in this process in terms of:

- Planning horizon, which is the longest period of time for which formal plans are prepared.

- Content of plans, in which both quantitative and qualitative areas are included.
- Length and timing of the process defining the final document.

In this chapter, we illustrate an example of the master budget for manufacturing companies, which can be one of three types of plans:

- Operating budgets, which originate from the typical (characteristic) management of a business; they define the economic flows of raw materials, components, finished products, and services.
- Capital expenditure budgets, which define the use of financial and human resources for the medium and long term.
- Financial budgets, which evaluate the impact of operating and investment plans on cash inflows and outflows.

Manufacturing organizations' operating budgets typically include the sales budget, production and inventory budget, cost of sales budget, and period costs budget. These schemes can be modified in service organizations or utilities companies to take their specific features into account.

6.1.2.1.1 Sales Budget

The *sales budget* is a central phase in the budgeting process: sales are the basis for forecasting all other operational budgets and even cash flow budgets, which are influenced by the cash inflows coming from sales. To be drafted, the sales budget needs the marketing and sales functions as primary actors in generating sales; the budget must also consider the accounting and finance staff, which triangulates their information with the broader organization's forecasts in the medium to long term. Assembling these data, sales information is forecasted in terms of quantity and price, usually with a monthly projection. Often, information is disaggregated or reorganized according to multiple dimensions such as clients, geographical areas, and product lines (Table 6.1).

6.1.2.1.2 Production Budget and Budgeted Inventory Level

Once sales have been forecasted, it is possible to define the quantity of output for product i (P_i) that the enterprise has to produce to meet the selling plan (V_i), taking into account the presence of initial (opening) inventories (SI_i) and the target final (closing) inventories (SF_i). This budget is expressed in terms of quantity following the analytical formula:

$$P_i = [V_i + (SF_i - SI_i)] = P_i$$

This calculation has to be carried out for each product that is planned to be sold for the next year.

Table 6.1 Example of a Revenue Budget

Product	January			[Each month of the year]			December			Total		
	Price	Volume	Sales	Price	Volume	Sales	Price	Volume	Sales	Price	Volume	Sales
A	100€/u	200u	20,000€									
B												
C												

The construction of the production plan requires the verification of the availability of resources and their congruence with what is needed according to sales plans; for each resource j (e.g., machinery, labor), the following verification is needed:

$$\sum_{i=1}^{N} P_i \times t_{ij} \leq T_j$$

where t_{ij} is the unit quantity of the resource j required for product i and T_j is the available capability for the resource j.

When planned sales are higher than available production capacity, a revision of the production and sales plan is required. In particular, there are four types of actions—not necessarily alternatives—to search for feasibility:

- Changing the sales policy; for example, if there is elasticity in prices, an increase in the price of goods will reduce the quantity to be produced but will achieve the same level of sales.
- Revising the inventory policy; for instance, reducing the closing inventory of finished goods and work in progress.
- Modifying the production capacity or investing in manufacturing processes; this solution requires longer decision making time compared to the other options and is more suitable when changes in sales are permanent and not contingent.
- Outsourcing the production of goods (or part of the production); this solution can be risky in terms of know-how and quality control. Outsourced work may be given to those who may not have the same level of expertise, and quality control may suffer as a result.

6.1.2.1.3 Cost of Sales Budget

When the production plan that is compatible with resource constraints is defined, the next stage is to verify economic implications.

Process engineering—defined as the standard quantity of material, components, and direct labor needed for meeting production requirements—includes:

- The total quantity of direct material and components to purchase to meet planned production levels; on the basis of this information and the forecasted prices, this is estimated by the procurement staff. The direct material usage and purchase budget are defined (Tables 6.2 and 6.3).
- The outsourcing entity.

Table 6.2 Direct Material Usage Budget

Component/ Material	Quantity Necessary to Meet Production Requirements	Component/ Material Price	Total Cost	
X (Product A)	10,000 kg	3€/kg	30,000€/kg	
Y (Product A)	...	...	...	Total usage of Product A
X (Product B)	...	...	...	
Y (Product B)	...	...	...	Total usage of Product B

Table 6.3 Direct Material Purchase Budget

	Material X (Quantity)	Material Y (Quantity)
Quantity needed to meet the usage need	100,000 kg	2000 units
Planned final inventory	15,000 kg	150 units
Less planned initial inventory	20,000 kg	100 units
Total units to be purchased	95,000 kg	2050 units
Planned unit purchase price	3€/kg	60€/unit
Total purchases	**285,000€**	**123,000€**

Table 6.4 Direct Labor Budget

	Product A	Product B	Total
Budgeted production (unit)	1000	1500	
Hours per unit	20	10	
Total budgeted hours	20,000	15,000	35,000
Budgeted hourly rate (€/h)	15	15	
Total wages	**300,000**	**225,000**	**525,000**

- Conversion costs related to the transformation of input into the finished product; here, there are three budgets: the direct labor budget (Table 6.4) and manufacturing overhead. Manufacturing overhead is divided into variable overhead (which varies in proportion to the quantity produced) and fixed overhead (which remains constant over a relevant range of output).

After these calculations, it is possible to also define the value of closing inventory and the cost of sales:

Total purchase + conversion costs − inventory variation (WIP and finished products)

6.1.2.1.4 Period Cost Budget

Period costs include selling and administrative expenses; their definition is often problematic in the budgeting cycle. As previously discussed, it is difficult to observe a standard relation between the level of output and the amount of period costs. Among the approaches proposed in the literature and adopted in practice, three methods are noteworthy:

- Incremental approach
- Zero-based budget (ZBB)
- Activity-based budgeting (ABB).

The incremental approach defines budgeted period costs on the basis of expenses incurred in the last accounting year; more specifically, budgeted costs are obtained by multiplying historical values by a coefficient that takes into account inflation and, if any, the expansion of the company's activities. The advantage of the incremental model is the simplicity of its application; however, there are problems at the conceptual level:

- A linear relation is assumed between the activity level and the amount of period costs; this relation can be considered correct for structural costs, but it is inappropriate for discretionary expenses, which occur occasionally. These expenses are sustained for specific reasons and are not repeated every year.
- Future expenses are based on historical data, implying amplification over time of possible inefficiencies.

With a ZBB approach, the budget of period costs is entirely redefined every year. More precisely, heads of organizational units are required to identify:

- A set minimum of resources needed to efficiently run the department
- A set of alternative packages of activities and their costs.

The level of expenses more appropriate for each unit is hence redefined every year on the basis of enterprise priorities.

With ZBB, the company history does not affect future allocation, and managers are forced to render explicit the use of requested resources, reducing the problems related to the incremental approach. Although this is an advantage, ZBB is more time-consuming: it needs high involvement from upper management and accounting and finance staff.

In some cases, a hybrid approach is adopted, wherein ZBB is used every 3–4 years, whereas the incremental approach is employed annually.

Finally, ABB is based on the following steps:

- The identification of activities that consume period costs (e.g., for procurement units, an activity is order fulfillment)
- The definition of activity drivers that justify the level of activity (regarding order fulfillment, the driver is the number of orders)
- The unit consumption, which is the relation between the activity cost and the driver quantity (in our example, the cost for order fulfillment).

The planning phase of period costs is carried out by defining the expected level for each driver, multiplying these values for the activity unit cost, and summing all activity costs to obtain the total period costs.

ABB is the most precise solution, but it is cumbersome; usually, this method is adopted if activity-based costing is also used as an accounting system for sales and administrative expenses.

6.1.2.1.5 Capital Budget

A capital budget highlights the portion of investments that enterprises are expected to sustain next year in order to:

- Face medium- to long-term goals defined during strategic planning
- Solve capacity problems that emerged during the budgeting process (as seen above in the production budget).

At the operational level, a distinction between investments in fixed assets and human resources is made to take into account the diverse characteristics of resources and the different organizational units that govern their planning.

Table 6.5 Example of a Capital Budget				
Investment Projects	**2014**	**2015**	**2016**	**2017**
Approved in previous accounting years				
Investment A				
...				
Investment F				
Total investments approved in previous years				
Approved during the current year				
Investment G				
...				
Investment L				
Total investments approved during the current year				
Under approval				
Investment M				
...				
Investment R				
Total investments under approval				

In particular, a capital budget for fixed assets shows investments that have already been approved or that are under approval, detailing cash outflows needed to implement specific projects (Table 6.5).

The budget for human resource investments encompasses forecasts of costs related to the search, selection, hiring, and training of enterprise personnel.

6.1.2.1.6 Cash Budget

A cash budget attempts to verify the financial sustainability of the budget for the year—on one hand, the development of cash budget analyses of the capability to self-finance, collect credit, and risk capital; on the other hand, the cash trend over the year according to the forecasted operational plan.

Here, two budgets are considered:

- A budgeted cash flow statement for the overall analysis of the financial sustainability of operational budgets
- A detailed cash budget, wherein subperiods are analyzed to avoid the risk of insolvency.

6.1.2.1.7 Budgeted Cash Flow Statement

As mentioned previously, the budgeted cash flow statement analyzes the overall financial sustainability of the operational and investment plan. There are two methods for calculating the cash budget:

- Directly, by registering future cash inflows and outflows
- Indirectly, wherein economic results based on the accrual logic are adjusted in order to define cash flows for the year.

Table 6.6 Budgeted Cash Flow Statement
EBIT
+ *Depreciation and amortization*

+ Δ *Net working capital* =
   (Opening account receivable − closing account receivable)
   + (Closing account payable − opening account payable)
   + (Opening inventories − closing inventories)

Δ *Capital expenditures (CapEx)* =
   Investments in fixed assets
     − disinvestments in fixed assets

− *Taxes*
= **Free cash flow to firm (FFCF)**
+ Cash flows from financial revenues, net of tax
− Cash flows for financial expenses, net of tax
+ Cash for increase in share capital
− Cash due to decrease in equity (including dividends)
+ Δ Net debt
= **Free cash flow to equity (FCFE)**

In this section, we analyze the indirect method, as it is the most widely used practice. The direct method is illustrated in presenting the detailed cash budget.

Table 6.6 illustrates the budgeted cash flow statement carried out with the indirect method. The starting point is EBIT, which is first adjusted by taking into account non-monetary operational costs: depreciation and amortization. Depreciation and amortization come directly from the operating budgets that were previously defined.

The second adjustment is to add the variation of net working capital, which encompasses accounts receivable, inventory, and accounts payable.

The following adjustment is to add the variation of capital expenditures: it comprehends planned acquisitions the fixed capital investments (capital budget) decrease by disinvestments and disposals of fixed assets.

Subtracting expected taxes,[1] the first important cash figure is determined: FFCF. As illustrated in Chapter 2, FFCF is the cash flow available for both debt and equity holders. A further step is to move from FFCF to FCFE) considering cash flows related to the financing activity, specifically:

- Inflows from financial incomes are added.
- Outflows for financial expenses are subtracted.
- Inflows from share capital increase are added.
- Outflows linked to the decrease in share capital; the main item is usually dividends paid to shareholders.
- Variation in the net debt calculated referring to the difference between the budgeted year and the current one. This positively affects cash flows if they increase (e.g., new loans taken out as bank loans or bond emissions) and negatively affects cash flows if they decrease (e.g., repayment of a previous debt).

---

[1]The tax rate applied here is usually based on historical data, adjusted with possible changes in taxation known at the time of budget definition.

Table 6.7 Cash Budget: Inflows Scheme

	Month				
Inflows from:	*January*	*February*	*March*	*...*	*December*
Revenues	1500				
Accounts receivable	250				
Other items	100				
Total operating inflows	**1850**				
New loans	250				
Bonds	0				
Equity increase	0				
Disinvestments	0				
Other financing items	100				
Total financing and investment inflows	**350**				
Total inflows	**2200**				

It is clear that if the FCFE is positive (financial surplus), enterprises are not required to take action; if the budget highlights a cash problem (financial need), then companies are obliged to find solutions such as:

- Finding more financing sources—for example, increasing debt or issuing bonds (refer to Chapter 11 for an analysis of financing strategy)
- Reducing investments or canceling or delaying projects
- Revising initial operational plans and targets.

6.1.2.1.8 Detailed Cash Budget

The detailed cash budget more deeply analyzes cash coming in and out over the planning horizon; the plan shows subperiods (usually months) to provide continuous monitoring of the liquidity situation. Starting from expected opening available cash, companies forecast total expected inflows, outflows, and a synthesis (refer to Table 6.7). The monthly cash figure is then compared to the target cash in order to take action to increase or reduce availability of needs.

Drafting the detailed cash budget is the final stage of the budgeting process before preparing the overall financial statements. The cash budget requires several input data from other documents, including revenues, purchases, investments, inventory, and financing lines of credit. As for all the other budgets, even here budgets can go through several cycles before the final definition is decided; when, for instance, cash is too low compared to company targets, further cash needs to be found by increasing debt or searching for alternative sources of income (Tables 6.8 and 6.9).

6.1.2.1.9 Budgeted Financial Statements

The final step in the budgeting process is preparing financial statements, including the P&L and balance sheet. The previous budgets provide all the elements needed, with the exception of one element: discontinued operations.

Table 6.8 Cash Budget: Outflows Scheme

	Month				
Outflows from:	*January*	*February*	*March*	...	*December*
Material purchases	1000				
Accounts payable	200				
Wages and cost of labor	500				
Services	100				
Selling expenses	200				
Other operating items	0				
Total operating outflows	**2000**				
Taxes	0				
Financial interest	150				
Loans	0				
Other debts	0				
Fixed assets	0				
Total financing and investment inflows	**150**				
Total inflows	**2150**				

Table 6.9 Cash Budget: Synthesis Scheme

	Month				
	January	*February*	*March*	...	*December*
Opening level of cash	25				
Total inflows	*2200*				
Total available cash in the period	2225				
Total outflows	*2150*				
First cash balance	75				
Minimum level of cash required	(20)				
Cash balance	*55*				
Opening debt position	(4860)				
Financial interest on current accounts	30				
Closing debt position	*(4835)*				

The budget for discontinued operations includes all revenues and costs due to disposal and disinvestment; these items have been already included in the cash flow budget as cash, but an accrual perspective is needed.

After this final analysis, both the P&L and balance sheet can be prepared. The following tables illustrate these documents (Tables 6.10 and 6.11).

Table 6.10 Budgeted Profit and Loss Account

Budget Profit and Loss Account

Revenues

− Operating costs

= **Operating income** *(or net operating income) (or operating profit) (or earnings before interest and taxes [EBIT])*

+ Financial incomes

− Financial expenses and adjustments

Profit before taxes from continuing operation

− Taxes

Profit after taxes from continuing operation

Profit or loss from discontinued operations

Net profit

Table 6.11 Budget Balance Sheet

Budget Balance Sheet

Noncurrent assets	Shareholders' equity
Property, plant, and equipment	Subscribed (issued) capital
Investment property	Share premium account
Goodwill	Revaluation reserve
Other intangible assets	Other reserves
Equity investments	Profit or loss brought forward
Other noncurrent financial assets	Profit or loss for the financial year
Accounts receivable and others	
Deferred tax	
Current assets	**Noncurrent liabilities**
Trade and other receivables	Bonds
Inventory	Bank debt
Other assets for sale	Other financial noncurrent liabilities
Ordered work in progress	Provisions for liabilities and charges
Short-term financial assets	Pensions and similar obligations
Cash and cash equivalents	Deferred tax liabilities
	Current liabilities
	Bonds
	Bank debt
	Trade and other payables
	Advanced payment for ordered work in progress
	Financial current liabilities
	Income taxes
	Other current liabilities

6.1.2.2 The Adaptive Approach

The process of developing the master budget is long, especially in large organizations, and can take as long as 4–9 months. Also, when there are variances, companies have to redefine targets for organizational units and then the overall company through renegotiation. In turbulent contexts, such a process conflicts with the need to make quick decisions.

The adaptive approach is an alternative that favors better capability to adapt to environmental changes. In this process, top levels do not define an overall complete plan but instead:

- The set of enterprise objectives to be achieved
- The leverage that an organizational unit has.

The targets for each manager are actually independent; this explains why the overall behavior of the enterprise can sometimes appear paradoxical, with conflicting decisions. The process for defining a balanced scorecard described in Chapter 5 is an example of this approach: Starting with the company objectives, there is a series of specific objectives (e.g., the goal to increase residual income can be associated with the increase of market share and reduction in production costs), but the approach does not ensure the completeness of the breakdown process in terms of activities and organizational units.

From this perspective, adaptive processes call for using different performance management tools in order to enable the devolution of performance responsibility.

When companies use the adaptive approach, some procedures are suggested to avoid a complete disintegration among goals; in particular, companies use *top-down* guidelines and *bottom-up* information flows.

With the adaptive approach, upper management is required to emphasize the importance of the company's objectives through their actions and decisions to increase knowledge and awareness throughout the organization. Top-down guidelines should ensure that managers' actions are within limits.

It is appropriate to disseminate information exchanged during the budgeting process. In the integrated approach, only information to be formalized in documents is exchanged; qualitative information and weak signals are usually overlooked. For example, the procurement unit can communicate that the expected price for material is 5€/unit, but they may neglect to communicate the information that supplier delivery time is expected to increase. In the adaptive process, the dissemination of this information can prevent future problems in the production process, the logistical chain and, finally, the final product delivery. It is hence suggested to prepare quantitative plans but also integrate qualitative elements or simple comments (Figure 6.1).

6.2 ENTERPRISE-WIDE RISK MANAGEMENT

Several times in this book, we have stated that nowadays companies operate in a turbulent, uncertain, and complex environment. In such contexts, any type of planning, regardless of the approach undertaken, has a certain level of risk, which means a high probability that the actual results and plan will diverge from the expected ones. This situation poses significant risk factors for budgeting and planning.

In addition, in recent years there has been increasing emphasis on risk management systems, particularly on adopting ERM. In this section, the origin, framework, and components of ERM are discussed.

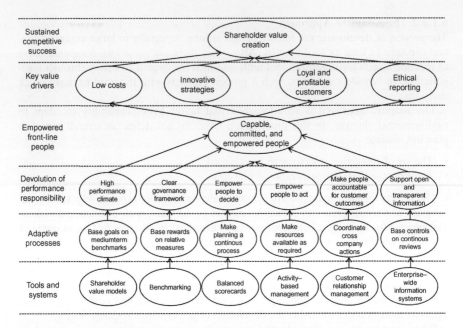

Figure 6.1 Adaptive approach and devolved organization. Source: Player, 2003.

6.2.1 Origin of ERM

Recent years have seen an explosion of interest in risk management (Power, 2007; Arena et al., 2010), which has moved from peripheral functional areas of the organization to the corporate level. Publications, corporate websites, and official reports often contain specific sections devoted to how organizations manage their risk. A wide array of risks are considered, including financial exposure, information system interruptions, fraud, raw material price rises, client bankruptcies, regulatory changes, and failure to understand customers' needs. The rise of risk management, which started in the mid-1990s, can be attributed to a number of factors. One, from a rational-economic perspective, is the change in the external and internal competitive environment, with a tendency toward greater turbulence and complexity. This is indeed borne out by the types of risks that organizations themselves take into account: the ongoing trend toward business process outsourcing; more complex forms of public sector contracts with private–public partnerships; the emergence of organized stakeholder groups who may put the spotlight on environmental or social issues; undermining the company's reputation; globalization; and the challenges of offshoring.

A second cause of the upsurge of risk management that did coincide with that time was a series of major financial and business scandals, in particular those that occurred during the 1980s and the beginning of the 1990s, such as Mirror Group Newspapers, Barings Bank, Polly Peck, Maxwell, and Guinness. These events starkly demonstrated not only that companies can fail but that the consequences of such failures can affect a huge number of actors: banks, consulting firms, managers, shareholders, bond holders, citizens, and government authorities. Governments and financial control bodies responded to the situation by issuing new codes of practice and regulations. The first was the Cadbury Committee Report, published in 1992 in the United Kingdom (the

Cadbury Code). The report set forth recommendations on the control and functions of boards and on the role of auditors, with the aim of "contributing positively to the promotion of good corporate governance as a whole" (Cadbury Code, 1992). Though recognizing that governance had been sound in the United Kingdom, the committee cited some recent cases of bankruptcy and fraud that suggested a need to intervene to diminish risks for companies and for the UK economy as a whole. This code proved to be highly influential internationally, ushering in a spate of self-regulatory approaches (Jones and Pollit, 2004; Power, 2007). On a more practical level, the Cadbury Report recommended certain specific matters to be put on the agendas of company boards, among which were risk management policies (Cadbury Code, 1992, p. 4.24). The publication of the Hampel Report (Committee on Corporate Governance, 1998) and the Turnbull Report (ICAEW, 1999) in the following years was a further significant step toward establishing an "enforced self-regulatory" framework (Power, 2007). Although risk management was also cited in the Cadbury Code, the Turnbull Report is generally considered to mark the start of the development of risk-based approaches to internal control (Spira and Page, 2003). From its very first pages, the Turnbull Report underlines the importance of risk assessment, treating risk management and internal control as effectively synonymous. In 2001, public interest in these issues was again significantly raised by the highly publicized financial scandals of Enron, WorldCom, and Tyco. These failures were attributed to poor corporate governance, leading to the promulgation of the Sarbanes-Oxley Act (SOX). SOX further reinforced the need for risk-based internal controls, creating a sense of urgency among firms to legitimize themselves through risk-based approaches, which became "an all-pervasive organizational, legal and regulatory principle" (Power, 2004).

All the aforementioned regulations framed risk management as a corporate governance requirement, implying a relation with internal control (see, for instance, Fraser and Henry, 2007; Spira and Page, 2003) and a broadening of the scope for detecting risk. Although risk management had existed since the 1950s (Bickley, 1959), it was initially associated with the insurance-purchasing function and, later, with specific processes such as workplace safety or information systems security. With its incorporation into internal control, the concept of risk became broader and more systemic, covering a wide array of events that might affect the attainment of corporate objectives. This emergent, all-encompassing approach was formalized in 2004 by the Committee of Sponsoring Organizations of the Treadway Commission (COSO) and was further revised in 2013. This framework has become the most widely used framework for ERM systems and is discussed in the next section.

6.2.2 ERM Framework and Components

The new enterprise-wide approach to risk management was formalized in 2004 (COSO), which issued a "definitive guidance" for building effective ERM (COSO, 2004). COSO (2004) defines ERM as follows: "Enterprise Risk Management is a process, effected by an entity's board of directors, management and other personnel, applied in strategy setting and across the enterprise, designed to identify potential events that may affect the entity, and manage risks to be within its risk appetite, to provide reasonable assurance regarding the achievement of the entity's objectives" (COSO, 2004).

ERM is represented as a three-dimensional matrix where organizational layers (entity, division, organizational unit, and functions) and risk typologies (strategic, operational, and reporting and compliance goals) are crossed and connected by ERM components. The first version of ERM entailed eight components: (i) internal environment, (ii) objective setting, (iii) event identification, (iv) risk assessment, (v) risk response, (vi) control activities, (vii) information and communication, and (viii) monitoring (COSO, 2004). A revised version for internal control (COSO, 2013) listed five elements of ERM: (i) control environment, (ii) risk assessment, (iii) control activities, (iv) information and communication, and (v) monitoring activities.

Beginning more broadly and referring to standards such as AIRMIC (2002), ERM approaches can be divided into four main phases: risk identification, risk assessment, risk treatment, and risk monitoring.

Risk identification is the recognition of internal and external events that could affect the achievement of the organization's objectives. Events can be differentiated by:

- Events that may have a negative impact, which are risks
- Events that may have a positive impact, which are referred to as opportunities.

Risk identification is an important phase of ERM that is usually guided by a "risk catalogue"—a reference classification of the events for the company. Table 6.12 shows an example of a risk catalogue where 10 categories of risks are reported and classified into five areas: market, management operations, finance and purchasing, human resources, and legal.

Risk assessment is the analysis and evaluation of potential risks that considers two elements:

- Impact
- Frequency of occurrence.

Risk assessment can be based on either qualitative or quantitative techniques. Qualitative techniques include tools such as qualitative scales, factor ratings, and risk priority numbers. Quantitative techniques refer to financial measures (e.g., Value at Risk, economic capital, and Risk-adjusted return on capital), which are becoming more common among profit companies for internal and external risk reporting purposes and key risk indicators (KRIs).

Often, companies adopt a combination of approaches, arriving at characterizing events (risk events) in terms of:

- *Inherent risk*: The risk to a company in the absence of any security controls or actions that can be taken to mitigate or reduce the likelihood or impact of an event.
- *Residual risk*: The probability of loss that remains to a company after security measures or controls have been undertaken.

Regardless of the assessment methodology adopted, there is a widespread tool that is used in companies to represent the overall picture of risk: the risk map (Figure 6.2).

The risk map is a visualization matrix wherein the two axes show the impact and the probability of occurrence. Mapping events onto the two axes provides a holistic visualization of all the selected risks that can be accordingly prioritized: upper right events (high impact and probability) are the priority for enterprises and are usually red; at the opposite end, there are risks with low impact and probability (usually green); the remaining areas represent risk with intermediate priority according to the two axes.

Table 6.12 An Example of a Risk Catalogue

1	Market/Industry	3–6	Operations Management	7	Finance
1.1	Technology/Innovation	3	Technology/Product Development	7.1	Currency
1.2	Substitution	3.1	Development-Time to Market	7.2	Interest
1.3	Product Life Cycle	3.2	Development Processes/Design to Cost	7.3	Credit
1.4	Business Cycle/Market Prices	3.3	Others	7.4	Country
1.5	Customer	4	Production/Logistics	7.5	Pension liabilities
1.6	Competitor Behavior	4.1	Manufacturing and Value Creating Processes incl. Outsourcing/Make or Buy	7.5	Others
1.7	Industry-specific conditions	4 2	Quality	8	Purchasing
1.8	Others	4.3	Delivery Time in Construction/Projects	8.1	Supplier Engagement/Behavior/Structure
		4.4	Internal Logistics Process	8.2	Purchase Prices/Supplier Market Place
		4.5	Others	8.3	Infrastructure Services
		5	Strategy/Marketing/Sales	8.4	Others
		5.1	Strategy Processes	9	Human Resources
		5.2	Marketing, Order Processing, and Customer Service	9.1	Availability of qualified Personel (R&D, Marketing, etc.)
		5.3	Distribution channels	9.2	Key Personnel
2	Management	5.4	Others	9.3	Reward Systems/Development
2.1	Market/Product/Service Definition	6	Organization/IT/Corporate Governance/External Communication	9 4	Read Court Reduction
2.2	Capacity/Locations/Regional Structure	6.1	Organization Structure/Decision Making Processes	9.5	Others
2.3	Definition of Business Segments/Internal Competition	6.2	Knowledge Management	10	Legal
2.4	Market Position	6.3	IT	10.1	Reaction to Changes in Legal/Accounting/Taxation Environment
2.5	Cost Management/Cost Position	6 4	Corp. Govemance/External Communication/Investor Relations	10.2	Environmental Affairs
2.6	Project Management	6.5	Others	10.3	Patents/Intellectual Property
2.7	M&A Activities/Management of Alliances/Joint Ventures			10.4	Competition law
2.8	Others			10.5	Others

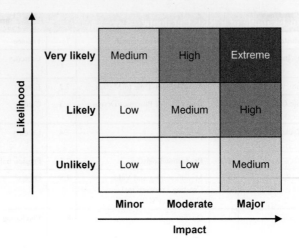

Figure 6.2 The risk map.

The third phase is *risk treatment*, in which organizations identify proper actions for responding to risks, such as:

- Avoiding risks and undertaking appropriate interventions (e.g., the risk associated with a supplier failure can be avoided by insourcing operations).
- Reducing risks in terms of probability and impact (e.g., accidents can be reduced by adopting security measures for workers).
- Transferring risks (for instance, through insurance or by hedging operations).

Theoretically, if none of these interventions allow a company to reach an acceptable risk threshold, targeted objectives could be redefined, with reiteration for the budgeting process.

In the end, *monitoring* consists of ongoing management activities for verifying and improving the effectiveness of the process.

6.3 BUDGETING AND ERM: ORGANIZATIONAL CONFIGURATIONS

Budgeting and ERM can be seen as two facets of the same problem: supporting companies in setting targets and variability, highlighting possible causes of change.

At the organizational level, budgeting and ERM are related in different ways. There are four types of configurations: *integration*, *combination*, *alignment*, and *coexistence*.

In *integration*, the constitutive parts are not distinguishable. The key element that characterizes integration is the development of shared ideas, practices, and knowledge. Integration entails the development of a common set of principles and ideas related to the organization of activities and tasks based on a shared system of values and conceptions of the object to be managed. For instance, shared corporate strategic ambitions, risk appetite, or core values of the organization (e.g., off-limit actions and behaviors) may constitute the basis for performance planning, risk assessment and, ultimately, decision making. A common language is developed to describe the originally constitutive areas and the impact of significant arising events (e.g., control failures, new regulations). Shared technologies are deployed to provide voice and representation (e.g., risk workshops, strategy meetings) but also to hold managers accountable for performances (e.g., risk measures linked to incentives). Finally, integration is supported by a common knowledge basis in terms of both abstract knowledge and practice (data collection, skills, and coordinating roles).

The category of *combination* is based on the notion of complementary rather than overlapping features: the idea of one area joining another, with the first providing support to the second. If one removes the elements of one area, the second area will be affected. Combination entails the presence of a shared set of principles and ideas and the development of a common language throughout the two areas. It also entails a converging knowledge basis, eventually fostered by data collection that serves a common purpose (e.g., risk identification for risk assessment and performance planning). Yet contrary to integration, it is possible to notice a dominant element—i.e., risk is supporting budgeting or vice versa. This means that one "championship" is prevalent in a given moment of time. However, the turbulent regulatory environment adds to the potential instability of the combination category, in the end opening up possible competition between functional experts when the direction of the relationship is challenged.

The category of *alignment* highlights the possibility to observe distinct features of the two areas. Yet the processes underlying the two (or more) areas are aligned—arranged in a line—by creating formal links and joint deadlines and by using common inputs and outputs. Contrary to combination, if one removes one area, the second would not be affected and could still continue to work properly. In the case of alignment, we have separate principles, ideals, and idioms to describe the two areas and enhance the performance of related techniques, although a shared understanding of these elements is not precluded. The important element of alignment is the creation of formal links—i.e., organizational roles, moments of discussion, and deadlines that jointly consider the outputs of the two processes. These links can stem from an aspiration for a common understanding of the outputs of the two processes by individuals and groups of individuals. Yet in terms of expertise, the two areas have distinct spheres of influence. In theory, this separateness could limit competition, although the dynamic nature of struggles for jurisdictional claims (Abbott, 1988) does not preclude the contrary.

Finally, the category of *coexistence* emphasizes the absence of elements of contact between the two areas. Contrary to alignment, there is a lack of formal links and moments of discussion on inputs and outputs of the two processes.

CHAPTER 7

Long- and Short-Term Decision Making

Decision making is a central factor of internal accountability and is crucial for managing company performances. Managers are required to continuously make decisions, but different criteria need to be used, taking time and the impact of decisions into account. In this chapter, we illustrate:

- Long-term decision making based on value-based measures and investment appraisal techniques
- Short-term decision making, where three uses are analyzed: breakeven analysis, contribution margin decisions, and full cost analysis.

7.1 INVESTMENT APPRAISAL: LONG-TERM DECISIONS

Nowadays, enterprises are more and more often required to make decisions that have a long-term impact, such as new product development or production capability investments. These decisions are particularly important for project-based companies because this process must be activated every time a new order is considered. Think, for example, of the production of aircrafts or ships: the commitment of resources has long-term economic impacts that must be carefully assessed.

The process of analyzing these impacts is called investment appraisal and refers to our objective function (present value):

$$PV = \sum_{t=1}^{T} \frac{NCF_t}{(1+k)^t} + \frac{TV_T}{(1+k)^T}$$

Referring to this function, we illustrate four methods that can be practically applied in appraising investment:

- Net present value (NPV)
- Profitability index (PI)
- Internal rate of return (IRR)
- Discounted payback function.

These methods are also called *discounted cash flow* (*DCF*) methods, given that they consider the time value of money. Some companies might use other methods known as *not discounted cash flow* (*not DCF*) methods, such as return on investment (ROI). These methods are not appropriate for analyzing investments because they neglect the actualization of cash flows.

7.1.1 Net Present Value

Net present value (NPV) is simply the sum of the discounted cash flows associated with a specific investment. The analytical formula for NPV for investments with a useful life of T is:

$$NPV = \sum_{t=0}^{T} \frac{NCF_t}{(1 + k)^t}$$

NPV is an absolute appraisal criterion that measures the increase of enterprise value due to a specific investment; this is the most obvious criterion for assessing investments. Hence, the other methods are analyzed against this.

The economic meaning of NPV can be directly derived from its definition: It is the value of the enterprise realizable from the investment. The acceptance condition for the investment can be derived from its formulation:

- Single investments are accepted when they increase economic value (when $NPV \geq 0$).
- When alternative investments are considered, the most convenient investment is the one generating more value—hence, the investment with the highest NPV.

7.1.2 Profitability Index

The profitability index (PI) is a relative appraisal criterion defined as the ratio between the discounted cash flows and the discounted investment:

$$PI = \frac{\sum_{t=0}^{T}(CF_t)/((1 + k)^t)}{\sum_{t=0}^{T}(I_t)/((1 + k)^t)}$$

There is a strict relation between NPV and PI; NPV is, in fact, the difference between two terms constituting the ratio in PI. This relation allows for the formulation of acceptance criteria for PI, starting with NPV.

$$PI = \frac{\sum_{t=0}^{T}(NCF_t + I(t))/((1+k)^t)}{\sum_{t=0}^{T}(I_t)/((1+k)^t)} = \frac{\sum_{t=0}^{T}(NCF_t)/((1+k)^t)}{\sum_{t=0}^{T}(I_t)/((1+k)^t)}$$

$$+ \frac{\sum_{t=0}^{T}(I(t))/((1+k)^t)}{\sum_{t=0}^{T}(I_t)/((1+k)^t)} = \frac{NPV}{\sum_{t=0}^{T}(I_t)/((1+k)^t)} + 1$$

As a result, the condition $NPV \geq 0$ is equivalent to the condition $PI \geq 1$, which represents the threshold to accept investments according to PI. In the case of alternative investments, PI suggests selecting the investment with the highest PI.

While PI and NPV never diverge with the appraisal of single investments, they may diverge with investment portfolios. In particular, differences arise in the case of alternative investments with different sizes; in these cases, NPV—being an absolute criterion—favors large investments, whereas PI—being a relative indicator—tends to favor smaller investments.

7.1.3 Internal Rate of Return

The internal rate of return (IRR) is a discount rate at which NPV is equal to 0; analytically:

$$\sum_{t=0}^{T} \frac{\text{NCF}_t}{(1 + \text{IRR})^t} = 0$$

Theoretically, this equation may have T solutions, yet in economic terms, IRR is meaningful only when it is universally defined—hence, when the equation has a unique positive solution. In a sufficient mathematical condition to employ IRR, coefficients of the IRR formula change signs (negative to positive or vice versa) only once. In economic terms, this is a common condition: Usually, net cash flows (NCFs) are negative the first year(s) of the investment and when they turn positive, they remain so until the termination of the investment.

The decision criteria for adopting IRR are:

- In the case of single-project analysis, investments are accepted if IRR is at least equal to the cost of capital: $\text{IRR} \geq k$.
- When alternative investments are considered, the investment to be selected is the one with the highest IRR.

In the case of mandatory investments, IRR can be applied without knowing the cost of capital (k).

Contrary to NPV, IRR is a relative indicator and is the percentage yield of capital still employed in the investment. In other words, if we assume that every year, the difference between k and IRR is a sort of reimbursement that reduces the capital invested, NCFs generated by the investments allow remuneration equal to IRR on the capital still "stored." IRR is hence an intrinsic yield of the investment and is easily understandable by potential investors, who can compare this rate with those that characterize alternative investments (e.g., bonds).

Similar to NPV, IRR, being a relative indicator, does not account for the investment size.

7.1.3.1 Possible Contrast Between NPV and IRR

When enterprises assess a single—not mandatory—investment project, NPV and IRR do not conflict in the case of a unique value of IRR (real and positive). In this case, the NPV curve as a function of the discounting rate is similar to what is shown in Figure 7.1. NPV suggests accepting investments only if NPV is positive—that is, when the cost of capital of the enterprise is on the left of the intersection between NPV(k) and the x-axis. This condition can be expressed as $k \leq \text{IRR}$, which is the condition for accepting investments with the IRR criteria.

With mutually exclusive investments, there could be contrasts between NPV and IRR; this contrast is shown in Figure 7.2. If the discounting rate (k) of the enterprise is lower than the x value of the intersection between the two curves NPV$_1$ and NPV$_2$ (Fisher intersection), NPV favors Investment 1, while IRR favors Investment 2.

The economic reasons for the contrast between NPV and IRR are related to differences between assessed projects in terms of:

- Magnitude of the investment
- Time distribution of capital invested
- Useful life.

Different solutions can be adopted to solve this divergence according to the cause.

When the cause is the diverse time distribution of returns, the divergence is linked to different underlining hypotheses for reinvesting flows generated during the investment; the solution is to render explicit the causes of contrast, highlighting the actual reinvestment rate (j). On the basis of this rate, it is possible to introduce two alternative criteria—NPV* and IRR*—that do not diverge; both indicators are defined starting from the terminal value (TV)—that is, the quantity of money available at the end of the useful life. Given that NCFs are reinvested at the rate j, this quantity is:

$$TV = \sum_{t=1}^{T} NCF_t \times (1 + j)^{T-t}$$

NPV* is defined as the present value of TV, net of the initial investment:

$$NPV^* = \frac{TV}{(1 + k)^T} - I_0$$

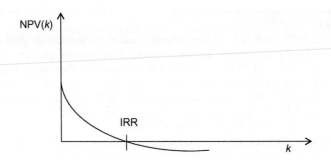

Figure 7.1 The relation between NPV and IRR for single investments.

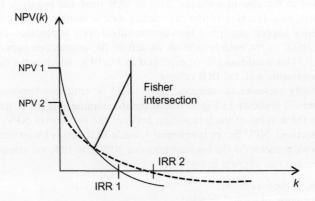

Figure 7.2 NPV and IRR: graphical representation of possible contrast.

IRR* may then be defined as the value of the discount rate, which renders NPV* = 0:

$$IRR* = \left[\frac{TV}{I_0}\right]^{1/T} - 1$$

In both cases, the criteria favor solutions with the higher TV.

If investments have different useful lives, the problem is similar to what was illustrated in the case of diverse time distribution. The presence of the different parameter T does not guarantee the absence of contrast between NPV* and IRR*. Before applying these modified criteria, it is first necessary to put the two assessed projects on the same time horizon by:

- Stopping all the investments at the shortest useful life (T_{min}); in this case, all the flow generated in the following year will be summarized in the terminal value of T_{min}.
- Lengthening all the projects to the maximum useful life T_{max}; in this case, reinvestment activities have to be determined.

Both solutions are formally correct and conceptually equivalent, yet they hide some problems at the managerial level. When the longest time horizon is taken as a reference, enterprises are forced to think of possible reinvestment activities for the shortest project between T_{min} and T_{max}—this process is often not easy. In the second situation (shortest as reference), again analyzing the problem from a managerial point of view, this may imply not considering specific technological solutions that need a longer time frame to be implemented.

7.1.4 Discounted Payback Time

The discounted payback time is a time function that measures the discounted cumulated value of NCF generated over time by the investment. Analytically, it is expressed as follows:

$$Payback(t) = \sum_{\tau=0}^{t} \frac{NCF_\tau}{(1 + k)^\tau}$$

Figure 7.3 shows the typical shape of the payback function where some features are visible: the y-axis value at $t = 0$ is usually <0 due to the initial investment;

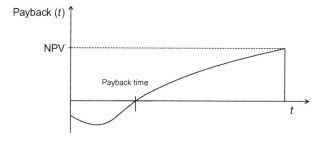

Figure 7.3 Graphical representation of payback function.

when the curve trend turns positive, it remains this way until the end of the investment period.

The payback function monitors the liquidity of the project at each moment of the investment horizon; from this curve, two indicators can be obtained:

- *Net present value*, measured by the value assumed by the function at the end of the period considered (investment horizon).
- *Discounted payback period*, which is the time needed to compensate cash outflows with cash inflows. Graphically, it is the intersection between the curve and the x-axis. Analytically, it is:

$$\sum_{\tau=0}^{PB} \frac{NCF_\tau}{(1 + k)^\tau} = 0$$

Adopting the payback period, the acceptance criterion is the comparison with a predefined time threshold. In the case of alternative investments, the projects with a lower payback time are favored. This criterion is actually highly prudential and aims to achieve quick returns. Yet the payback period might contrast with NPV when two alternative investments are assessed; this situation is represented in Figure 7.4. Two investments are represented here: Project 1, with higher initial investments (dotted curve), and Project 2, with lower initial investments.

Graphically analyzing the two projects, it is possible to see the misalignment between the two criteria: NPV and payback period.

The payback period favors a quicker return—hence, Investment 2—although Investment 1 provides a higher return in terms of the discounted cumulated cash generated. NPV maximizes the generation of discounted cash flows; consequently, it favors Investment 1.

NPV is a preferable criterion given its alignment with the enterprise value; however, when forecasting capability is very low, companies might adopt the payback period as the criterion in order to be more prudent.

When NPV is adopted, the payback period can be used as complementary indicator of the investment liquidity.

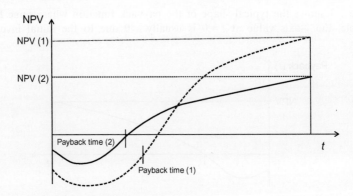

Figure 7.4 Misalignment between NPV and payback time.

7.2 SHORT-TERM DECISION MAKING

Decisions in enterprises must always be analyzed regarding PV; there are, however, decisions that have a limited impact on time and scope and do not modify enterprise assets. These decisions are called short-term decisions and include:

- The variation of activity volume when an increase in manufacturing capability is not required.
- The choice whether to accept an additional order for a nonstrategic client (without implications for the company's competitive position).
- Make or buy decisions that have no implications in the long run.

There are two main decision criteria for short-term decisions and their use:

1. Contribution margin
2. Cost−volume−profit (CVP) analysis and breakeven analysis.

7.2.1 Contribution Margin Analysis

Short-term decision making allows for some simplifications in the decision criteria, although the reference function is still PV—in particular:

- The impact of short-term decisions on enterprise value is equal to the impact of NCF on the first accounting year not discounted.
- Given that there are no investments in assets, NCF is equal to CF.
- Finally, due to the equivalence between cash and accrual flows, revenues are taken as a reference for cash inflows and avoidable costs of cash outflow:

$$CF \rightarrow Revenue - avoidable\ costs$$

When avoidable costs are equal to variable costs, the previous expression is equal to the total contribution margin (M):

$$M = p \times V - c_v \times V = (p - c_v) \times V$$

where

p = selling price
V = quantity to be sold and produced
c_v = variable costs.

If alternatives are characterized by the same selling quantity, the maximization of the total contribution margin is the same as the maximization of the *unit* contribution margin (m), equal to the difference between price and variable unit cost.

Setting the contribution margin as the criterion for short-term decision making questions the usefulness of full cost systems in enterprises. Full cost systems are, in fact, not appropriate, given that they include fixed costs, which are usually unavoidable.

The adoption of full cost systems for decision making is justified only in a complex context. Consider, for example, the choice of production mix. In the case of N products using M different production resources, this choice can be formulated as follows:

$$\max \sum_{i=1}^{N} x_i \times (p_i - ca_i)$$

with these constraints

$$x_i \leq x_i^* \qquad \text{with } i[1 - N]$$
$$\sum_{i=1}^{N} x_i \times t_{ij} \leq T_i \quad \text{with } j[1 - M]$$

where x_i is the quantity produced, p_i is the unit price, and ca_i is the unit avoidable cost of the i product. The two constraints impose that the quantity produced must be lower than demand (x_i^*) and that for each resource j, the overall quantity required (obtained by the unit consumption of the resource $[t_{ij}]$) must be lower than the available capacity T_j.

Also, this theoretical formulation includes only avoidable costs, thus usually not neglecting fixed costs. Although it has a high number of products and resources with a limited manufacturing capacity, the solution of the previous equation is cost-consuming and sometimes not compatible with the time needed to make decisions.

A simplified empirical model can be adopted in these situations: Products are selected on the basis of their profitability calculated with reference to product costs in absolute and percentage terms. To explain the results, assume that products are ordered differently if their profitability is calculated against avoidable cots (O_{ac}) or full costs (O_{fc}). Selecting products from the two ordered lists until the manufacturing capacity is saturated, two different mixes are obtained: M_{ac} and M_{fc}. Simulations on significant statistical samples have highlighted that with this empirical approach, M_{fc} provides a better mix than M_{ac} in terms of profitability. The advantage increases with the number of products considered. This result is due to the inclusion of fixed/indirect cost in full cost configurations, which reflects the use of manufacturing assets.

7.2.2 CVP and Breakeven Analysis

CVP analysis studies the relationship between changes that occur in the output (typically volume, but this may refer to activity levels) and changes in revenues, expenses, and profit. It attempts to define what happens to the financial results if a specified level of activity or volume changes. It is important to keep in mind that the relationship between output, costs, revenues, and profit is studied within a short period of time.

Managers use CVP analysis to help answer questions such as:

- How will total revenues and total costs be affected if the output level changes—for example, if we sell and produce 2,000 more units?
- If we raise or lower our sales price, how will that affect the output level?

Analytically, the relation between costs, volume, and profit is referred to as the operating margin (EBIT):

$$\text{EBIT} = \text{revenues} - \text{costs} = (p \times V) - [(c_v \times V) + C_F]$$

where

V = volume or activity level
P = selling price
c_v = variable costs
C_F = fixed costs

Table 7.1 shows the analysis in a simple case wherein price and costs are kept as fixed while simulating units to be sold (from 0 to 50).

Table 7.1 shows an important value of volume: V at which EBIT is 0—this point is called the breakeven point (BEP). Using analytical formulas, it is possible to calculate the value of single variables (volume, cost, and revenue) by which enterprises reach the BEP.

The following equation provides an example using the volume as reference. To find the BEP volume, EBIT is equal to 0:

$$\text{EBIT} = 0 \rightarrow (p \times V) - [(c_v \times V) + C_F] \rightarrow V(p - c_v) = C_F$$

which allows the calculation of the BEP volume:

$$V_{\text{BEP}} = \frac{C_F}{(p - c_v)}$$

We can also use the equation for introducing a profit element (target EBIT); in this case, the equation becomes:

$$\text{Target EBIT} = (p \times V) - [(c_v \times V) + C_F] \rightarrow V(p - c_v) = C_F + \text{target EBIT}$$

$$V = \frac{C_F + \text{target EBIT}}{(p - c_v)}$$

Figure 7.5 shows the graphical representation of CVP analysis and BEP. BEP is calculated in terms of quantity (the same can be done in terms of revenues).

Table 7.1 A Simulation of CVP Analysis						
Number of Units to Be Sold	0	5	10	20	30	50
Price (€/u)	100	100	100	100	100	100
Unit variable cost (€/u)	70	70	70	70	70	70
Fixed cost (€)	300	300	300	300	300	300
Revenue (€)	0	500	1,000	2,000	3,000	5,000
Total variable cost (€)	0	350	700	1,400	2,100	3,500
Contribution margin (€)	0	150	300	600	900	1,500
Fixed cost (€)	300	300	300	300	300	300
EBIT	−300	−150	0	300	600	1,200

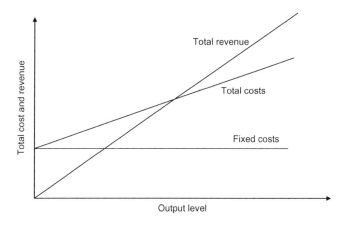

Figure 7.5 Graphical representation of CVP analysis and BEP.

CHAPTER 8

Performance Control for Organizational Units

Coauthored by Deborah Agostino

Politecnico di Milano, Department of Management, Economics & Industrial Engineering

Measuring and managing performance for single organizational units within an enterprise introduces a seminal problem: to observe the *specific responsibility principle*—the idea that each organizational unit should be "isolated" from the rest of the enterprise. Given that companies function as an integrated whole, this measurement need inevitably leads to some simplifications.

The goal of the four sections of this chapter is to provide guidelines for dealing with this issue:

- The first section illustrates how to identify organizational units to be measured within the company.
- The second and third sections analyze two different organizational layers: business units and responsibility centers.
- The last section discusses the possibility of enlarging management control systems beyond the boundaries of the company.

8.1 BOUNDARIES AND LEVEL OF ANALYSIS

The levels for which performances are measured identify the *depth* of management control systems. Theoretically, the system can be limited to measure performance for the company as a whole, or detailed indicators for the different levels—business units, functional units, and operational centers—can be introduced. In this latter configuration, a scorecard of indicators can be associated with each level and unit. The higher the depth of the management control system, the higher the cost of the system but also its capability to monitor units' performances, tracking their specific responsibilities.

The depth choice must be consistent with the style of management of the company—more specifically, with the degree of autonomy granted to each unit. In this way, management control systems:

- Provide information relevant to their decisions to each unit and perform operable organizational decentralization
- Ensure accountability for each organizational unit.

Consequently, the depth of management control systems is reduced when the style of management is centralized; in this case, control is exerted by upper levels, mainly through direct supervision, and the costs for increasing the system depth are not counterbalanced by information benefits.

Requirements for management control systems are valid for each organizational level, although their relative importance is markedly different.

In particular, *timeliness* of information is essential at the operational level, where decisions are made continuously across time. At upper levels, usually decisions are less frequent, although they are characterized by larger spatial–temporal influences. Generally, pressure to have timely information decreases moving to upper levels, although the specific competitive context in which the company operates may lead to variations. This observation is not contrasted with the evidence that, nowadays, companies generally need more timely information than in the past; more simply, we highlight the relative importance of timeliness for different organizational levels, contrasting operational with upper-level needs.

The *measurability* of information also becomes more important when moving from upper to operational levels, particularly for behavioral implications of measurement. First, with measurable indicators, upper management prevents opportunist behavior at the operational level; second, operational management sees in measurable data "protection" against possible arbitrariness of superiors in assessing their performances. Similar considerations are valid for the specific responsibility principle.

Long-term orientation is essential at all levels of the enterprise; this becomes particularly relevant for upper levels, which are more directly responsible for long-term competitiveness.

Also, *completeness* and *precision* of information are extremely important at upper levels. Upper levels influence all the performances of the company; hence, they must control all the critical success factors that can affect them. Furthermore, they need precise information in order to assess the relative importance of different phenomena for value creation.

The more we move to operational levels, the more:

- The number of parameters that can be influenced by a single organizational unit decreases, as well as the set of information required for management and control.
- The impact of wrong decisions on the overall results of the enterprise diminishes; as a result, it is less risky to have less precise indicators.

In order to have scorecards suitable for diverse managerial needs, a mix of different indicators is required for different organizational levels and must be consistent with the characteristics that the various types of indicators have.

At the *corporate level*, management control systems should use value creation as the main indicator using value-based indicators; their long-term orientation and completeness counterbalance the problems of measurability and inadequate timeliness in providing data. To guarantee that crisis situations are discovered in a timely fashion, value-based indicators should be supplemented by specific selected nonfinancial indicators that monitor enterprises' critical performances. If management control systems are used for assessing upper managers, some measures based on financial statements can be adopted; typically, companies use ROE or EVA due to their higher measurability.

At the *business unit (BU) level*, indicators based on financial statements are more frequent and applicable; middle managers are, in fact, assessed by the corporate level, which requires that their performances be mostly evaluated with measureable indicators. The most commonly used indicators are ROI (which is a traditional profitability indicator for operating activities), residual income, or economic value added.

For decision making, this information is integrated with the profitability of single product lines, which are often further divided by client or market. To avoid short-term opportunistic behavior, economic indicators should be complemented with value-based indicators for the BU, although they can be measured less frequently. Furthermore, it is also useful to provide some selected nonfinancial indicators to BU general managers; this ensures the timely monitoring of possible crisis signals.

Finally, fundamental measures for the *operational level* are nonfinancial indicators, which are appropriate for the requirements of this level: timeliness and measurability. The inadequate completeness of nonfinancial indicators is less critical at the operational level due to the reduced number of decisional leverages controlled at this level. In addition, nonfinancial indicators can be supplemented with a few selected measures based on financial statements—particularly costs and revenues—according to the type of operational unit.

8.2 MEASURING PERFORMANCES AT BU LEVEL

A BU is an organizational unit with autonomy in choosing both the mix of products/ services produced and the resources used. To isolate performances of BUs within the company, two problems must be considered:

- Existing transactions with other BUs within the company (intracompany exchanges). To separate performances of BUs, transfer prices can be adopted. In this way, transactions among BUs are valued as if they were exchanges with external companies (*transfer pricing problem*).
- Resources used by BUs but managed at the corporate level. First, companies have to decide whether these resources must be included in the assessment of BU performances. In the case of allocation, the *completeness* of information is favored in place of limitations in tracking *specific responsibilities* (*corporate cost allocation problem*).

These two problems are commonly faced during the calculation of EBIT and cash flow (from which further financial indicators are calculated), while they affect nonfinancial indicator results less. For the latter, it is more convenient to identify nonfinancial indicators that isolate specific responsibilities of each organizational unit; for example, if a company wishes to measure the contribution of a BU to the lead time of a process involving several BUs, the nonfinancial indicator can be defined as the time between the moment in which the BU starts its operational phase until the moment it ends the phase.

8.2.1 Transfer Pricing

The transfer price is a "fictitious" price for evaluating intracompany exchanges: It is the price one division charges for a product or service supplied to another unit. The choice of transfer pricing policy is a critical step in designing a management control system; by changing transfer prices, in fact, the performances of involved organizational units are modified.

There are three main types of transfer prices:

- Transfer prices based on market
- Transfer prices based on cost
- Negotiated transfer prices.

Before entering into the detailed analysis of each type, it is worth noting that the choice of the transfer pricing system (TPS) has a diverse impact according to the divisions of the BUs involved. In particular, if BUs belong to the same group, but they are autonomous juridical entities, the TPS choice has fiscal implications, which are even more relevant when BUs are in different countries. Companies can indeed modify their profits in different countries with variations in transfer prices, "moving profit" from countries with a high level of taxation to countries with a lower tax rate.[1] The fiscal impact is one of the major drivers in choosing the TPS, although managerial implications—decision making and motivation—are considered a priority for performance management. Given the objectives of this book, the rest of this section is focused on the managerial aspects of the TPS choice. It is, however, important to stress that the fiscal issue may be a relevant constraint in the choice, sometimes suggesting a double TPS—one for external use focused on fiscal aspects and one for internal purposes targeted to measure and manage BU performances.

8.2.1.1 TPS Based on Market

This first type of transfer price is determined by identifying the price at which the product/service exchanged in internal transactions can be sold externally on the market. Sometimes this price is adjusted, taking into account the lower transaction costs of internal exchanges (e.g., transportation, invoicing). This policy avoids the risk of the buying unit using an external customer—just for internal rivalry—when the external offer is equivalent to the internal deal, eventually diminishing the result for the enterprise overall.

With homogenous markets, where there is a clear reference price, the market price is the most appropriate price for decision-making purposes. A transfer price that is higher than the market price would lead the buying unit to choose external suppliers; a transfer price lower than the market price would lead the selling unit to sell all its products/services externally. In both cases, the enterprise as a group would lose the margin of one of the two units, worsening its performance.

However, there are cases in which the price based on the market is difficult to apply:

- The case of specific and special goods or for which alternative suppliers have significantly different qualities and price; in those cases, the market price is inapplicable
- The case of products/services that are characterized by a highly variable market
- The case of strategic BUs.

In the absence of a reference market, a common alternative is the use of TPS based on cost, assuming that the cost, increased by a percentage margin, is a good proxy of the price. The other two cases are more problematic. With variable market prices, transfer prices have to be redefined very frequently to prevent market variability from impacting the convenience of internal transactions.

For example, consider a company operating in the oil sector that is divided into two BUs: one devoted to oil purchases (upstream BU) and the second carrying out oil refining (downstream BU). Suppose that the trend of prices decreases every day in January. If the company defines transfer prices monthly, the downstream BU is certain to buy oil in the last days of the month at a lower price than the transfer price (equal to the average price of January). Consequently, it would purchase externally. Similarly, with increasing prices, the upstream unit would sell externally, as the market price is more convenient than the internal transfer price. This problem can be reduced by daily updating prices; even in this case, however, market prices can favor opportunistic behaviors, which at least have to be monitored.

The second critical situation for using market prices is with "strategic" BUs. These are units retained by companies for carrying out specific phases, although these BUs

---

operate with competitive disadvantages compared to external suppliers. These BUs have a great deal of leverage in negotiations because they have specific knowledge of processes and costs for critical phases/processes.

Suppose that there are two BUs—A and B—within the same group, exchanging products. The first BU (A) operates in the upstream phase (research-intensive), where the economy of scale is a crucial success factor. The second BU (B) operates in the downstream phase, where there is a market leader (C) with a market share significantly higher than (B). Due to the characteristics of the market, price varies significantly according to the volumes purchased; at a price of €200, corresponding to the scale at which B operates, the corresponding price for C is €120. If B is an independent company, it should exit the market, yet B is considered a strategic BU for the group (A + B) because it can foresee the trends of the downstream market; furthermore, B is a threat (possible vertical integration) to C, which limits C's leverage.

In this case, fixing the transfer price at €120 would penalize A, which would have no convenience in internal exchanges; similarly, fixing the price at €200 would cause B to exit the market.

An interesting solution is adopting *dual transfer pricing*. The dual policy adopts two different prices for the buyer and the seller. For example, in the aforementioned case, the price for B (buyer) would be €120; the price for A (seller) would be €200.

The difference between the two values is compensated by a corporate account, which emphasizes the choice to favor the internal exchanges for pursuing more general objectives for the group. Summarizing the operation:

- Revenues for A = €200
- Cost for B = €120
- Corporate costs = €80.

The corporate account highlights the cost for the group overall to have a strategic BU and constantly compare this with the benefits generated by the strategic unit itself.

8.2.1.2 TPS Based on Cost
This policy bases transfer prices on the cost for the seller. Usually, prices are based on cost adding a markup in order to provide a positive operational margin to the upstream unit. The use of full cost—both actual and standard—is very widespread, not ultimately because external prices are usually fixed on the basis of the full manufacturing cost increased of a markup granting required profitability to the enterprise.

Nevertheless, the use of transfer prices based on full cost has some disadvantages. In the case of the full actual cost, the transfer price increases with the increase of inefficiencies of selling units, with an amplifying effect due to the presence of a percentage markup. In this way, the inefficiencies of the upstream unit (the seller) are actually translated into improved performances, compensated by worsened performances of the downstream unit (the buyer); this violates the specific responsibility principle. Analytically, the EBIT of the upstream unit (the seller) is equal to:

$$\text{EBIT} = P_t \times Q - (c_v \times Q - C_F)$$

Given that:

$$P_t = \left(c_v + \frac{c_F}{Q}\right) \times (1 + mu)$$

where

P_t, transfer price
c_v, unit variable cost
C_F, fixed costs
Q, quantity transferred from the seller to the buyer
mu, markup.

We obtain:

$$\text{EBIT} = (c_v \times Q - C_F) \times mu$$

As a result, the upstream unit (the seller) improves its performance with the increase of its variable and unit costs; this policy (incorrectly) favors inefficiency.

The problem is avoided if transfer prices are based on full standard costs rather than actual costs. In this case, using the symbol "^" to indicate standard values, the formula becomes:

$$P_t = \left(\hat{c}_{v+} \frac{\widehat{C_F}}{\hat{Q}} \right) \times (1 + mu)$$

$$\text{EBIT} = \left(\hat{c}_{v+} \frac{\widehat{C_F}}{\hat{Q}} \right) \times (1 + mu) \times Q - c_v \times Q - C_F$$

Given that $\hat{c}_v$, $\hat{C}_F$, and $\hat{Q}$ are fixed parameters, the selling BU improves its performances when variable and fixed costs are reduced, contrary to the previous case.

Even in this case, however, there are problems related to decision making. The fixed costs of the upstream unit (the seller) are fixed costs for the company overall, yet they are seen by the downstream unit (the buyer) as variable. This situation may lead the buying unit to operate at a level lower than the optimal level for the company overall. Suppose that the upstream (selling) unit has a variable standard cost equal to c_v (Up) and a full standard cost equal to C_{full} (Up), and suppose that the transfer price is fixed at the full standard cost. The downstream unit has incentive to produce until the difference between its selling price and its variable conversion cost is higher than the transfer price—that is:

$$p - c_v(\text{Down}) - C_{full}(\text{Up}) > 0$$

where

c_v (Down), variable conversion costs of the downstream unit
p, external selling price of the downstream unit.[2]

On the contrary, the increase of the activity level of the downstream unit would lead to a reduction of its EBIT.

For the company overall, the threshold is expressed by

$$p - c_v(\text{Down}) - c_v(\text{Up}) > 0$$

The difference between the two "threshold prices" has a significant impact when there is spare manufacturing capacity: The downstream unit would accept a lower number of orders compared to the case in which the decisions are made by corporate; this leads to a suboptimal saturation of the manufacturing capacity for the company overall.

---

[2]This is under the hypothesis that the product is sold directly on the external market, yet this reasoning can also be made if the downstream unit sells its products internally.

To limit the difference between the objectives of single units and the group, the *variable standard cost* plus a markup is sometimes adopted as a reference for transfer prices. The advantage of this solution is actually more abstract than real. To guarantee a positive EBIT to the (upstream) selling unit, in fact, corporate establishes a very high markup; in this way, the two thresholds—to increase the level of activity for the downstream (buying) unit and the company overall—may still diverge significantly, as shown by Eqs. (8.3) and (8.4).

$$p - c_v(\text{Down}) - c_v(\text{Up}) - \text{mark up} > 0$$
$$p - c_v(\text{Down}) - c_v(\text{Up}) > 0$$

8.2.1.3 Negotiated TPS

The problem of transfer prices based on costs in the case of spare capacity is a specific situation or a greater problem; fixing prices for BU internal transactions creates a rigidity, which reduces the capability of the company to operate in turbulent contexts. If the two BUs are two distinct companies facing pressure in terms of prices, the downstream unit will negotiate reduced prices with its supplier to avoid losing the order, penalizing both itself and the supplier.

To solve this problem, the system based on negotiated transfer prices simulates the existence of a real market between BUs. With this policy, the rules for defining transfer prices are not decided at the corporate level; rather, they stem from a negotiation process in order to grant the maximum adaptability of BUs to change in the context. However, at the same time:

- The power of diverse organizational units assumes a relevant weight, as in any market transaction
- Internal negotiation costs increase
- There is no guarantee of greater integration among BUs.

Consequently, negotiated prices are appropriate in turbulent contexts but are inefficient in more stable conditions.

In practice, a "pure" negotiated transfer price system is rare; more often, the corporation grants partial negotiation power within some centrally defined constraints. For example, a large Japanese enterprise operating in the electronic sector (with several commercial and production units) was characterized in the past by strong integration and centralization of decisions; now, they have instead adopted an intermediate system in which commercial units are obliged to buy internally, but they can choose among the diverse internal production divisions and negotiate prices with them. In this way, they stimulate competition and search for internal efficiency, although there can sometimes be a nonoptimal allocation of resources and production capacity.

Another solution adopted by a Scandinavian multinational is the use of negotiated transfer prices but within centrally defined ranges of variability; in this way, they favor adaptability, avoiding the issue, however, that the contractual power of BUs creates problems for other divisions, with negative consequences for the company overall. When external conditions require that the negotiation goes beyond the fixed range, the corporate level must authorize the agreement.

8.2.1.4 Models for Choosing the TPS

All the aforementioned systems have pros and cons. It is thus necessary to identify solutions that are more consistent with the organizational configuration of the specific

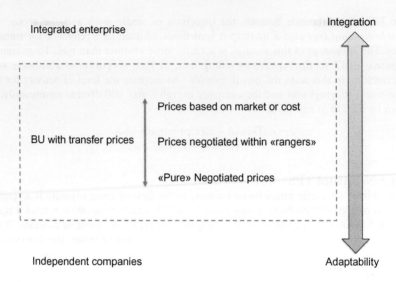

Figure 8.1 TPSs and enterprise characteristics.

enterprise under analysis. More generally, for companies operating in diverse segments of product or markets, the choice to adopt a TPS is an intermediate decision between two extremes: on one hand, the *integrated enterprise*, in which all decisions are made centrally at the corporate level; on the other hand, the *market*, in which each segment of the market/product is governed by independent companies. The divisional solution balances the characteristics of these two extremes. An integrated enterprise is extremely efficient and grants the maximum use of scale effects and synergies (in organizational terms, integration); the market solution favors adapting capability and shorter reaction time to external changes (in organizational terms, adaptability).

Transfer prices are accordingly adopted in management control systems when balancing integration and adaptability is required. As shown in Figure 8.1, the different possible solutions balance these two characteristics. A TPS based on market and cost (which are actually an approximation adopted when the market price is unavailable for the products or services transferred) is based on centralized rules and thus is better able to align BU decisions with the overall company objectives (integration), yet this sometimes lead to suboptimal decisions when the market varies significantly compared to expectations. Negotiated prices essentially create market conditions for BU transactions; this ensures a better ability to adapt to external changes, but they can have high administrative costs, and their outcome highly depends on the interest and contractual power of each BU rather than the company's overall goals. The solution of prices negotiated within a range—which the corporation must authorize—is a compromise.

To summarize, the choice of the TPS is linked to the relative importance between integration and context adaptability, which depends on the turbulence of the external context. As a result, with an increase of external instability, it is appropriate to shift from policies based on market prices to policies based on negotiated prices within ranges and "purely" negotiated

8.2.2 Corporate Cost Allocation

A second important issue related to the measurement of single BU performances is the allocation of corporate costs, which is the possibility to assign to each unit a portion of the overhead resources managed at the corporate level. These costs often include legal offices, research and development, and other administrative expenses. This problem opens up three alternative solutions:

- Adopting a *complete allocation* system, apportioning all the corporate costs among BUs.
- Adopting a *partial allocation* system in which BUs are assigned only the costs that can be directly traced to them with a consumption driver. For example, research and development activities can be divided into two categories: (i) basic research activities of potential use for the entire company and (ii) applied research carried out for a specific BU. With a partial allocation system, only the costs of applied research are allocated among BUs.
- *Avoiding any allocation*, assessing the BUs' performances only on the basis of the cost sustained at their level.

A *complete allocation system* has mainly advantages at the organizational level; the BUs among which corporate costs are allocated actually assume the role of "devil's advocate," preventing the excessive proliferation of corporate expenses and the possible worsening of their performances. The complete allocation makes explicit that corporate resources are not free but that they impact the company's performance. However, there are problems for decision making. The complete allocation system is based on a proportional division, often using basis revenues as allocation. Consequently, BUs are assigned a higher proportion of corporate costs if their revenues increase; also, when their revenues increase, this does not imply an increase in available corporate resources. In extreme cases, an increase in BU revenues could even lead to a decrease of its EBIT and the improvement of performances of other units—violating the specific responsibility principle—and leading to decisions that are inconsistent with the company's overall goals.

Referring again to the specific responsibility principle, the complete allocation system based on full actual costs has an impact on BUs similar to what was illustrated for transfer pricing: inefficiency (corporate level) is transferred to the BUs.

The *absence of corporate cost allocation* has opposing advantages and disadvantages.

Lastly, the sole *allocation of direct costs* is an intermediate solution. This allocation may be carried out in two ways:

- Allocation on the basis of *consumption drivers*
- Definition of *fees*.

To better understand the difference between the two solutions, we consider the case of a corporate finance office with a capacity in a specific period to consult for 200 h and an overall cost of €50,000, which has to be divided among two BUs (METAL and PLASTIC). During the period considered, METAL has used 100 h of legal services and PLASTIC has used 60 h (hence, with an overall usage of the legal office equal to 80%).

With a system based on consumption drivers, the allocation is:

- Cost apportioned to METAL = €50,000 × 100/(100 + 60) = €31,250
- Cost apportioned to PLASTIC = €50,000 × 60/(100 + 60) = €18,750

With a system based on fees, these are calculated before usage in the hypothesis of complete saturation of the legal office. In our example, the hourly fee is €250/h. As a result, the apportioned costs are €25,000 to METAL and €15,000 to PLASTIC. There is a remaining unallocated cost equal to €10,000, which refers to the unused capacity of the human resource office.

The allocation based on *consumption drivers* has a simple problem: the lower the demand for a corporate service, the higher its unit cost. Hence, this system discourages the use of the service when the service is mostly available. On the contrary, the higher the saturation of the resource, the more convenient its use, leading to potential conflicts among BUs for defining priorities in corporate service use.

The fee system prevents this problem, given that the unit cost of the service is not influenced by the demand. Furthermore, if a corporate resource is underused, there is an underallocation of its cost, which remains at the corporate level; this underallocation is like an opportunity cost—an indicator of the potential savings of corporate costs for the enterprise.

The fee system therefore reduces corporate costs when they are underused; however, it is important to highlight that this reduction should not be automatic, particularly:

- When the use of corporate resources is highly variable in time. With a reduction of activity in 1 year compared to the previous one, the lower request of corporate services from BUs can lead to a reduction of these services and their dedicated resources, creating the risk that they will be unable to cope with the renewed level of activity in future years.
- For resources such as marketing or research, which have a higher impact in the long run than in the short term. In this case, the misalignment of the decision-making horizon between BUs, which are more short-term oriented, and the corporate level can influence the use of these activities, especially when the allocation is through direct costs. In this situation, BUs can use these services when they have an actual need in order to maintain the long-term competitiveness of the company.

In practice, corporate costs are often completely allocated to single organizational units, whereas partial allocation becomes relevant for administrative resources only.

8.3 MEASURING PERFORMANCES OF RESPONSIBILITY CENTERS

Responsibility centers are organizational units that are not responsible for revenues and costs (contrary to BUs). These centers are required to identify indicators capable of monitoring only the performances that each responsibility center can influence. As in the case of BUs, the problem is more relevant for financial indicators, which are adopted at the responsibility center level to provide an overview of the results obtained.

There are three diverse types of responsibility centers:

- *Cost centers*, which are organizational units for which a relation between output and required resources can be observed, but they do not have a direct link to the external market.
- *Revenue centers*, which are organizational units that directly interact with the external market.

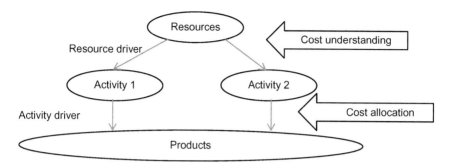

Figure 8.2 Activity-based systems.

- *Expense centers*, which are organizational units that do not directly interact with the external market and for which it is not possible to set a standard relation between input and output.

For all three centers, before designing the specific system of performance indicators, it is necessary to identify activities by adopting an activity-based approach. The identification of activities has several advantages:

- The activity itself is usually homogenous; a responsibility center can carry out heterogeneous activities. Finding a unique indicator for the whole center is hence very difficult. Making a preliminary analysis of activities allows for a better definition of relevant performance indicators for each of them; by assembling these indicators, a scorecard can be easily obtained for the whole responsibility center.
- Boundaries and tasks attributed to organizational units vary very frequently. These changes rarely modify the set of activities carried out by the company. If the management control systems are linked to activities, they become more stable. In the case of organizational changes, performance indicators can be "moved" together with the change of responsibility for activities.
- The activity analysis allows for the separation of value-added activities from nonvalue-added activities.[3] This division improves the design of the performance measurement system. For nonvalue-added activities, the main objective should be the reduction of devoted resources in order to reduce company costs without affecting the value as perceived by clients. The design of the indicator should focus on value-added activities.

8.3.1 Preliminary Analysis of Activities: Activity-Based Management

Activity-based management (ABM) is actually an evolution of activity-based costing (ABC).[4] Conceptually, there are two main phases in ABC (Figure 8.2):

- A phase of *cost understanding*, which identifies the activities for which company resources are used, the overall cost of these activities, and specific indicators that explain the consumption of resources for each activity (*activity driver*).

---

[3]Usually, activities are considered nonvalue-added when there is not a client (internal or external) or when clients do not attribute specific benefits to those activities.
[4]Refer Annex 3 in http://booksite.elsevier.com/9780128019023/.

- A phase of *cost allocation* to determine the cost of products in which costs are attributed to products through activity drivers.

ABM systems are focused on the first phase of this scheme; they represent activities as "microenterprises." The following are attributed to these microenterprises:

- Resources, including personnel, services, technologies, and materials used for carrying out the activity
- Clients, internal or external to the company
- Suppliers, internal or external to the company.

To operationally identify activities, five steps can be followed: (i) process mapping, (ii) constructing the ABC curve, (iii) selecting the driver for primary activities, (iv) merging main activities, and (v) aggregating secondary activities.

The first phase, mapping company processes, analyzes:

- The activities carried out by each organizational unit
- The resources actually devoted to these activities (Figure 8.3).

To correlate resources to activities, a table can be used (refer to Figure 8.4), where for each person the percentage devoted to each activity is called out; similar tables can be used for other types of resources such as machinery (usually, the costs related to machinery include depreciation and support materials).

Information thus obtained is synthesized in an ABC curve (Figure 8.4), where:

- The horizontal axis refers to activities in decreasing order
- The vertical axis indicates the cumulated percentage of the activity costs.

Activities can then be divided into two groups:

- Primary activities: These are activities that consume 80% of overall costs. In the case of high fragmentation of costs, it is preferable to limit the number of activities to 40−50%.
- Secondary activities: All other activities.

	Students tax management	Other incomes management	Expenses management	Fiscal management	Budget	Annual financial report	Cost accounting, monitoring and reporting	Special entities management (e.g., consortium)	Gestione obiettori	Other activities	Extra activities	
Internal personnel	%	%	%	%	%	%	%	%	%	%	%	Check 100%
1			60%		10%		30%					100%
2			20%	70%				30%				120%
3 10%	10%	10%				40%		20%	10%		10%	100%
Sutotal	10%	10%	80%	70%	10%	40%	30%	50%	10%	0%	10%	320%
External resources												
External consultants	%	%	%	%	%	%	%	%	%	%	%	Check 100%
4		85%									15%	100%
5			100%									100%
Sutotal	0%	85%	100%	0%	0%	0%	0%	0%	0%	0%	65%	200%

Figure 8.3 A correlation table between resource (employees in this case) and activities.

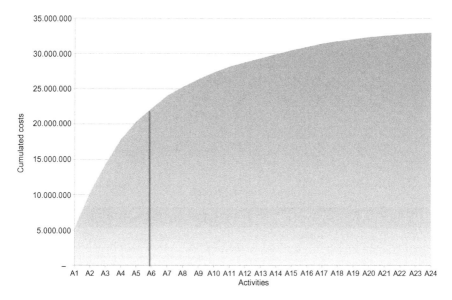

Figure 8.4 Curve of mapped activities.

We will first discuss primary activities. For each of these, the most appropriate driver is identified. Then, activities with the same driver are merged. In the case of activities with similar drivers, the following simulation is suggested:

- Two representative products must be identified—usually a standard product and a customized product.
- Product costs must be calculated under two different hypotheses: (i) merging activities with similar drivers and (ii) keeping activities separated.
- If the costs calculated under the two different hypotheses do not significantly vary, activities are merged; if they do vary, they remain separated.

Finally, secondary activities are examined and then merged with the more similar primary activity.

8.3.2 Cost Centers

Cost centers are organizational units that are responsible for the use of resources (input) but do not determine the level of output. Usually, cost centers include manufacturing and physical transformation units.

Traditionally, performances of cost centers are measured on the basis of variance between standard (budgeted) values and actual incurred costs. The variance framework is divided into three levels, as shown in Figure 8.5.

The first level refers to the difference between the total budgeted cost and the total actual cost. This variance is then divided into two components: the first one (volume variance) is external to the cost center and is linked to output variations and the second one (efficiency variance) is in the responsibility center and is related to the variation of efficiency in the transformation process.

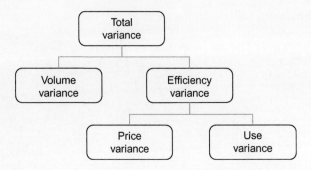

Figure 8.5 Cost variance tree.

Table 8.1 Cost Center Flexible Budget			
	Variable Unit Costs	**Total Fixed Costs**	**Volume**
Budget	Budgeted values	Budgeted values	Budgeted values
Flexible budget	Budgeted values	Budgeted values	Actual values
Actual results	Actual values	Actual values	Actual values

Operationally, the division is carried out introducing a flexible budget, which is a hybrid of the budgeted and actual figures. In cost centers, it is constructed using the actual volume and the standard (budgeted) efficiency to obtain a hybrid cost; in other words, variable and fixed costs are considered equal to the budgeted values (Table 8.1).

The difference between the total actual cost and the flexible budget is thus dependent only on the efficiency because both are calculated using the actual volume produced. This difference is called efficiency variance. The difference between the total budgeted cost and the total cost calculated with the flexible budget is due solely to the variation of the production level (volume), given that both are calculated with the same variable and fixed costs.

The second level examines the efficiency variance in detail, which is—at least partially—controllable by the cost center. The efficiency variance is the result of the variation of two parameters—input prices and input use—that can be controlled differently and by diverse units within the company. The price of inputs is only partially controllable by the enterprise and, internally, it usually depends on the choice made by procurement functions. The use of resources is influenced instead by internal choices—specifically by manufacturing/production units.

To clarify the analytical process, the analysis is herein carried out with reference to the cost of direct materials. To avoid complicating the explanation, we refer to a single product company. This hypothesis can be revised by introducing an altered index that takes different products into account.

The *price variance* monitors the effect of component/material price variations compared to forecasted values; the calculation of this variance assesses how the company acquires resources. Operationally, the price variance is determined as:

$$\Delta_{price} = \sum_{i-1}^{N} q'_{actual}(i) \times [p_{actual}(i) - p_{std}(i)]$$

where N is the number of components/material; p_{actual} is the unit actual price of materials; and q'_{actual} is the quantity of the input (i) actually used.

The *use variance* accounts for the variance, in terms of costs, of the input quantity used to transform a specific level of output. The calculation of the use variance thus assesses the company's efficiency—particularly manufacturing units—with using inputs. Operationally, the use variance is calculated as

$$\Delta_{use} = \sum_{i=1}^{N} p_{std}(i) \times [q_{actual}(i) - q_{std}(i)]$$

where $q_{std}(i)$ is the standard quantity of the input(i) needed to produce a unit of product and $q_{actual}(i)$ is the quantity actually used.

A negative use variance is favorable because it points out the actual use of resources that is lower than the forecasted data (standard).

Once all variances are determined, performances of cost centers can be measured through:

- *Efficiency variance*, under the hypothesis that the cost center is responsible for both prices and the use of inputs.
- *Only the use variance* if the price of inputs is not controlled by the cost center; this is the most common situation, given that the price of material is usually negotiated and controlled by procurement functions and the hourly rate of labor is related to larger contracts involving, at a minimum, the overall corporation and, in some cases, clusters of companies that negotiate with trade unions.

A similar analysis can be performed for direct labor costs—the unit price of direct material must be substituted by the hourly rate of labor and the use of direct material with the time employed for labor activities. For overhead, the variance analysis focuses on the portion of costs allocated to products. Although overhead is important for inventory valuation, it is marginal for management control systems.

The traditional approach is still widespread; however, it has several limitations, especially regarding the specific responsibility principle.

First, the traditional approach assesses cost centers for choices made by other organizational units. As highlighted previously, the possible variation of input prices is usually not decided by manufacturing units; furthermore, the difference between the actual and budgeted use of inputs is only partially controlled by cost centers because it is influenced by:

- The quality of components, which in turn depends on the selected suppliers
- Product manufacturability, which is linked to the quality of design and engineering.

More generally, traditional variance analysis considers as external only variances related to volume variances or input prices, assigning to managers responsibilities all the other variances. Nowadays, the external environment is characterized by a wider set of variables that undermine this assumption and approach.

Costs may vary compared to standards because of changes that are not directly controlled by the cost center, such as a decrease in delivery times, an increase in quality requested by clients, or a larger product range. These changes impact costs, but they are not directly monitored by variables included in the traditional approach, such as volumes, input prices, and input use. Yet given that volumes and prices are unchanged, the traditional analysis would ascribe the cost variance to the cost center efficiency, although the causes are not completely controllable by operational managers.

Second, the traditional approach overlooks some performances that can be influenced by cost centers. The analysis assumes (unrealistically) that cost centers are not able to influence the level of output. The choices and behavior of production centers actually impact the quality of products, delivery time, and demand for after-sales services; consequently, they indirectly influence company revenues.

The lack of a complete, precise connection between measurement and cost centers' responsibilities may lead to opportunistic behaviors. For example, if variances in input use are assigned to production centers and variances in input prices are assigned to procurement functions, it is quite easy for procurement to achieve a favorable variance by buying low-quality materials at a lower price. Similarly, if production centers are not measured by output characteristics, a favorable variance can easily be achieved by reducing quality controls on the output. In this way, costs are reduced for scraps and reworking operations. A traditional management control system would point out the needed improvement in production unit performances, neglecting the decrease in revenues that would be likely caused by the lower quality of products delivered to customers.

To solve these problems, two solutions can be adopted:

- Calculating costs more precisely by adopting an *activity-based logic*
- Constructing a *balanced scorecard* at the cost center level, where further indicators measuring output performances are added to the cost.

The first solution, called *ABB*, changes the logic for constructing flexible budgets; rather than using volume as the base variable, the flexible budget is built with all the drivers that can impact the product cost variability. For example, in the case of activities connected to batch management, the "flexibilization" can be made using the number of batches as a driver. Similarly, for activities related to throughput time, the flexibilization can be made using delivery time.

8.3.3 Expense Centers

Expense centers are organizational units characterized by:

- Output that does not directly financially benefit the enterprise
- A relation between inputs and outputs that is difficult to express using standard coefficients.

Typical expense centers are units that carry out support activities within the enterprise value chain—for example, administrative activities, research and development activities, and human resource management. The term *expense* is used to emphasize that the definition of expense thresholds is usually the only form of control that is implemented; this solution can prevent the surge in expenses but does not comply with the goal of a management control system because it provides no indicators of the coherence between the activities carried out in the expense center and the enterprise objectives.

The limited attention that has traditionally been devoted to expense centers is linked to its historical lower incidence on the overall cost of companies. Nowadays, these support centers have a high incidence in all types of organizations. A possible solution for their measurement is the construction of a balanced scorecard starting with the identification of activities that are carried out. According to the characteristics of the activities of the expense center, different measures can be identified.

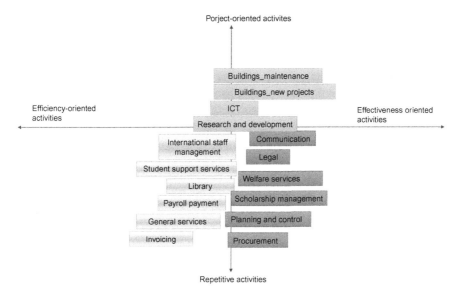

Figure 8.6 Classifying activities in expense centers: administrative services at a university.

A first distinction (Figure 8.6) is between:

- *Repetitive activities*, which are carried out several times during the year (e.g., invoicing or payroll); in this case, it is not necessary to collect information about single outputs of the activities—average data are enough to assess the overall performance of the activity.
- *Project-oriented activities* (e.g., research and development or the design of a new information system). In this case, the activity and its specific output must be controlled.

For repetitive activities, a further distinction is useful between:

- *Efficiency-oriented activities*, wherein the quantitative element is predominant. The output of these activities is standard and defined (e.g., payroll payment). The objective performances of these activities can be satisfactorily measured with efficiency indicators—that is, the ratio between the costs of the resources used divided by the volume of the activity output.
- Activities where the qualitative element is prevalent and thus effectiveness oriented; for these activities, the critical variable is the way in which the output is delivered instead of the volume of output. In terms of indicators, these activities require effectiveness measures such as delivery time or service level.

Project-oriented activities are characterized by the use of significant resources and longer completion times. Hence, each project should be characterized during its definition (budget) by:

- A set of objectives to be achieved (expressed in both qualitative and qualitative terms considering the orientation of the activity toward efficiency or effectiveness)
- A timeline for each objective
- The resources needed and committed for each phase of the project.

The benefit of this approach to performance management depends on the capability to appropriately map and classify activities; otherwise, the system would be incomplete and thus counterproductive.

Finally, the level of precision of the indicators associated with expense centers is usually lower than measures adopted in cost centers. For example, the cost for invoicing compared to the unit cost of production has two possible sources of imprecision:

1. The definition of the quantity of time devoted to invoicing is subjective. This relies on the estimations of employees who actually do the work, whereas production operations can be more easily and objectively measured.
2. Outputs of activities are more heterogeneous (invoices may have a highly different degree of complexity); hence, the concept of "average" is less significant.

These limitations should not be overestimated, however. Given that less attention is usually devoted to expense centers, not even perfectly precise measures can indicate significant improvements.

8.3.4 Revenue Centers

Revenue centers are organizational units responsible for revenues on the market—the most frequent example is commercial units. Traditionally, performances of revenue centers are measured by revenues. When products have significantly different profitability, the *total contribution margin* (*M*) is more appropriate, where *M* is defined as the difference between revenues and variable costs. To maximize revenues in this situation, revenue centers can opportunistically devote greater attention to low-profit products, for which high-volume sales are usually more achievable compared to sales of products with a higher contribution margin.

Because revenues are defined as the product of selling price and sold quantity, assessing a revenue center on the basis of revenues implies assigning them responsibility for variations in prices and quantity sold. Similar to cost centers, the variance between actuals and budgeted figures can be further divided and analyzed using flexible budgets.

Recalling that revenues can be expressed as:

$$\text{Revenue} = \sum_{i=1}^{N} p_i \times V \times q_{vi}$$

where p_i is the price of the product (*i*), V is the total volume of sold goods, and q_{vi} is the percentage of output sold of the product (*i*), the performance of the revenue center depends on:

- Selling price
- Quantity of sold output
- Mix of sales among different products.

These variables are thus possible determinants of revenue variations compared to forecasts. To further disaggregate effects, four different analyses are required:

1. *Budget in standard conditions*, which uses the forecasted data for total sales volume as input data, the mix (i.e., q_{vi} for all products), and the prices of each product. All these data are included in operational budgets.

Table 8.2 Variance Analysis for Revenue Centers

	Price	Mix	Volume
Budget	Budgeted values	Budgeted values	Budgeted values
Flexible budget with standard mixes	Budgeted values	Budgeted values	Actual values
Flexible budget with actual mixes	Budgeted values	Actual values	Actual values
Actuals	Actual values	Actual values	Actual values

2. *Flexible budget with standard mixes*, which calculates revenues that the enterprise could achieve with standard prices and mixes but with the actual total sales volume.
3. *Flexible budget with actual mixes*, which differs from the previous budget due to the inclusion of actual mixes instead of standard values.
4. *Actuals*, where revenues are calculated with actual values for all the variables.

The comparison between revenues obtained by the four levels (refer to Table 8.2 for a summary) explains the variance between actual and budgeted sales, examining the effect of the three determinants. Specifically:

1. The comparison between the budget and the flexible budget with standard mixes shows how the variance in total sales volume impacts revenues (the first two levels, in fact, differ only for this variable). The difference between budgeted revenues and the flexible budget with standard mixes is called *volume variance*.
2. The comparison between the flexible budget with standard mixes and the flexible budget with actual mixes measures the impact on revenues of a diverse product range compared to budget forecasts (the two levels differ only in terms of sales mix). The difference between sales in the flexible budget with standard mixes and sales in the flexible budget with actual mixes is called *mix variance*.
3. The comparison between the flexible budget with actual mixes and actual revenues determines the impact on enterprise revenues of price variations compared to forecasts (the two levels differ only in terms of prices). The difference between revenues in the flexible budget with actual mixes and actual revenues is called *price variance*.

At the second level, variances can be further hierarchically analyzed, assessing the impact of changes in the market share and the total size of the market. The starting point is the relation between revenues, market share (s_m), and total size of the market (Q_m):

$$\text{Revenues} = s_m \times Q_m$$

The implementation of the second-level analysis of variances in revenue centers hence requires the knowledge of two further parameters with high variability and the direct involvement of the marketing department. This analysis is usually carried out only for consumer markets, where market share is a crucial element. Operationally, the second-level analysis requires the introduction of a further hybrid budget called a *budget with actual market share*. At this level, all the variables are kept with reference to the budget with the exception of the enterprise market share, which is calculated using actual values.

The revenue *volume variance* is thus divided into two components: the variance due to market share variation (identified as the difference between budgeted revenues and revenues in the *budget with actual market share*) and the variance due to changes in the total size of the market (determined as the difference between revenues in the budget with actual market share and the flexible budget). The first variance is an indicator of the competitive positioning of the enterprise; the second variance is usually an exogenous phenomenon.

The traditional approach for revenue center analysis has two main problems:

1. Revenue centers influence some variables that are not directly included in sales, at least in the short term. For example, commercial units should also manage client support and assistance activities; instead, sometimes these activities are overlooked to devote higher attention to the selling phase. In the short term, the traditional management control system will highlight a favorable variance in revenues, which would probably be balanced by a more negative image of the enterprise and hence a reduced economic value. This problem can be overcome by developing a balanced scorecard at the revenue center level in which performances are also measured by nonfinancial indicators related to client assistance and revenue growth.

2. Revenue centers often have a high fixed structural cost. In this regard, revenue centers are similar to expense centers; in this case, the center can be analyzed using the approach illustrated in the previous section.

8.4 MEASURING PERFORMANCE BEYOND ORGANIZATIONAL BOUNDARIES: SUPPLY CHAIN AND NETWORK ACCOUNTING

The previous sections analyzed performance management for organizational units formalized within the enterprise organizational structure, yet more and more often, the boundaries of companies are becoming blurred, with an increasing number of activities carried out in collaboration with external organizations. As a result, management control systems should take this trend into account, particularly regarding:

- *Processes*, defined as a chain of activities characterized by supplier—client relationships usually involving more than one organization
- *External entities*, which determine the results of the internal processes of enterprises. The most frequent example is outsourcing.

Network accounting is a particular area of accounting that focuses on the management and control of interorganizational processes—i.e., activities characterized by internal coordination and cooperation. The main challenge from the individual organization is that the economic activity is not dictated by the single enterprise but by a collection of enterprises (at least more than two) that pursue repeated and enduring exchange relationships.

If a process is completely internal, a *process-balanced scorecard* can easily be defined by applying ABM. Once organizational units are mapped, identifying internal suppliers and clients, the supply chain can be easily identified. The balanced scorecards more generally can include:

- Indicators characterizing performances of single activities, similarly to what was illustrated for performances of responsibility centers
- Further synthetic process indicators. For example, the completion time for a process is not necessarily the sum of times for single activities because some activities can be completed simultaneously.

Synthetic measures can be financial and nonfinancial; the choice is related to the level of aggregation of the process. Some enterprises consider a broad set of activities for processes, including procurement, production, distribution, logistics, and sales. Such a process must be monitored by economic-financial measures, given their high level of aggregation, similar to a BU. In other cases, processes refer to more operational and elementary activities (logistical process, new product development process); in this case, information needs are more similar to those of responsibility centers.

In the case of processes linked to external entities, the management control system should be extended beyond the boundary of the company, constructing interorganizational cost management and network accounting (Nilsson, 2005; Wall et al., 2005; Lind and Thrane, 2005). For a management control system to support network management, two main approaches can be identified:

- The control system should be able to support the single organization working within a network—i.e., "management in the network." In this case, the system needs to *account for network effects*. This is the perspective adopted by the single organization to evaluate the convenience of operating inside a network.
- The accounting system should also be able to support the management and control of the entire network, monitoring the ability of the network as a whole to transform input into output. This broader view is acknowledged as "management of the network" and is usually the perspective adopted by the network manager, who should account for the system as a whole. In this second case, the management control system should *account for the network as an entity*.

The next two paragraphs will focus on these two perspectives:

- Performance measures that account for network effects
- Performance measures that account for the network as an entity.

8.4.1 Accounting for Network Effects

Accounting for network effects refers to a management control system that focuses on the management of the single organization *inside* the network (called focal organization to be distinguished from other network enterprises), which is interested in controlling the influence of network partners on its activities. This perspective can be considered an extension of the traditional enterprise management control system, which enlarges the management control system of the individual enterprise with performance of key strategic partners.

Specific key performance indicators (KPIs) can be included in the enterprise measurement system of the enterprise in order to account for the performance of key partners. These indicators can include:

- *Total cost of ownership (TCO)*
- Supply chain measures, such as ABC or EVA
- Risk indicators associated with partners and relationships.

TCO is a measurement that is commonly used in operations management to evaluate supply chain costs of doing business with a particular partner, either a buyer or a distributor. TCO is not associated with a predefined formula, but it quantifies all costs (e.g., acquisition, use, maintenance, or disposal) associated with the purchasing process. This measure supports the focal company's ability to evaluate the financial convenience of maintaining the relationship with key partners, considering not only the price but also other costs involved in the relationship.

Supply chain measures are based on the idea of quantifying costs for the focal company to maintain its relationships with key partners. These measures can include ABC or EVA.

The *supply chain ABC* is a technique that applies the ABC system to a set of relationships in order to quantify the cost associated with each activity and the organizational unit responsible for these costs. This approach is an application of the ABC, which was developed to evaluate activity costs within the single enterprise to a set of relationships. It has the same purpose as TCO—to quantify the convenience of maintaining a relationship—but it consists of a different measurement approach. TCO calculates all costs inherent in a relationship, going beyond the price, whereas ABC allocates all costs of the relationship to activities (e.g., inventory, procurement, transportation, etc.) and then to the organizational unit responsible for those costs.

The *supply chain EVA*, as for the previous measure of ABC, consists of the application of the traditional financial measurement of EVA to the quantification of the entire supply chain value. EVA is expressed as the difference between the net operating profit and the cost of the invested capital. Operationally, the focal company will calculate the determinants of EVA (revenues, costs, and investments) by also including the relationships with its key partners. The application of this measure will lead to a supply chain EVA. The limitations and benefits of this method were previously discussed in Chapter 3.

Finally, *risk indicators* can be adopted to quantify the level of risk associated with the relationship with other partners. Following the perspective of the focal company, risks can be associated with partner selection and relationship management. The first type of risk concerns the possibility of selecting the wrong partner in terms of financial solidity or the quality of product, service, and activities managed. The second type of risk—relational risk—refers to the possibility of having coordination problems successfully working together. Risk indicators can be developed by the enterprise to monitor both partners and relationships. Risk indicators related to partner selection can include the financial data of other partners, their potential level of opportunistic behavior, or the incidence of the item on the service delivered. Relational risk indicators can consider the level of flexibility of the relationship, the level of dependency, the amount of power in the relationship, or the level of miscommunication between the parties.

An alternative approach to account for network effects concerns the direct involvement of key network partners in the management control cycle. This means that strategic buyers or suppliers, considering the example of supply chain networks, are called to jointly develop and feed the control system of the focal organization. The practice of sharing accounting information with key partners is often known as open book accounting. It consists of sharing costs or other financial data upstream and downstream with each key partner in order to make profit data visible to other enterprises within the network. This is a breakthrough with respect to traditional approaches, given that data that would traditionally be kept secret by each party and used in negotiations is here shared between partners. The main advantage of this approach is the possibility for both customers and suppliers to work together to reduce costs, such as product design costs or production process costs.

8.4.2 Accounting for the Network as an Entity

Accounting for the network as an entity refers to a management control system that supports management and control of the network as a whole and its associated activities to realize network output. This perspective of the network is relevant for the network manager, who is accountable for network results, network activities, and the contribution of the single-network actor.

Accounting for the network as an entity requires the development of KPIs, which complement previously discussed measures for the single enterprise with specific indicators to evaluate the network structure and relationships. These relational KPIs can be derived from social network theory and can include the following (a few indicators that are relevant for organizational networks have been included):

- Centrality
- Density
- Multiplexity.

8.4.2.1 Centrality

Centrality indicators generally measure how many connections one node has to other nodes. These indicators are particularly useful for motivational purposes to identify if one enterprise has more influence than the others on network activities. There are several metrics to measure centrality. We focus here on the most appropriate for organizational networks: degree centrality, closeness centrality, and betweenness centrality.

The first indicator is *degree centrality*, which refers to the number of ties (relationships) a node has to other nodes. The higher the ties of a node, the higher the influence of that node. Degree centrality can be measured in terms of the in-degree of centrality, counting the number of incoming ties for each node. The node with the highest level of in-degree centrality is characterized as prominent, given that several other enterprises are willing to establish interactions with this node. Degree centrality can also be measured in terms of out-degree centrality, counting the number of outgoing ties for each node. The node with the highest level of out-degree centrality is very influential because of its ability to establish several exchanges within the network (Figure 8.7).

The second indicator is *closeness centrality*, which measures the degree to which a node is close to all other network nodes. This indicator is useful to evaluate how quickly exchanges occur between an enterprise and other enterprises. Operationally, it is calculated as the sum of geodesic distances from one node to all the others. The formula is as follows:

$$C_c(n) = \frac{1}{\Sigma L(n,m)}$$

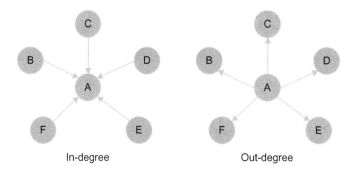

In-degree   Out-degree

Figure 8.7 Degree centrality.

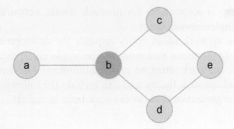

Figure 8.8 Closeness centrality.

where

  $C_c(n)$, the closeness centrality of a generic node (n)
  m, a generic node within the network
  $L(n, m)$, the length of the shortest path between the two nodes n and m.

According to the formula, the value of closeness centrality is between 0 and 1, given that it is calculated as the reciprocal of the shortest distance. The highest level of closeness centrality is 1, which suggests that the reference node (n) is directly connected with all other nodes. On the contrary, a value near 0 suggests a low level of closeness centrality—i.e., few direct connections with other nodes

Looking at the network represented in Figure 8.8, the closeness centrality of Node b will be equal to 0.8. The calculations are as follows:

$$C(b) = 1/(L(b,a) + L(b,c) + L(b,d) + L(b,e))/4 = 4/(1 + 1 + 1 + 2) = 0.8$$

The indicator of *betweenness centrality* measures the ability of an enterprise to be in a gatekeeper position. It provides insights on the degree to which a node serves as a bridge: the higher the value, the higher the influence of the node on the network activity. It is calculated as the number of shortest paths from all vertices to all others that pass through the reference node. Assuming n as a reference node, the formula is as follows:

$$C_b(n) = \sum_{s \neq n \neq t} \frac{\sigma_{st}(n)}{\sigma_{st}}$$

where

  $C_b(n)$, the betweenness centrality of a generic node (n)
  s and t, the nodes within the network different from the reference node n
  σ_{st}, the number of shortest paths to connect s and t
  $\sigma_{st}(n)$, the number of shortest paths to connect s and t, which requires passing from the reference node n.

If we apply this formula to calculate the betweenness centrality of Node b with reference to the network represented in Figure 8.8, we will obtain the following:

$$C_b(b) = ((\sigma_{ac}(b)/\sigma_{ac}) + (\sigma_{ad}(b)/\sigma_{ad}) + (\sigma_{ae}(b)/\sigma_{ae}) + (\sigma_{cd}(b)/\sigma_{cd})$$
$$+ (\sigma_{ce}(b)/\sigma_{ce}) + (\sigma_{de}(b)/\sigma_{de}))/6$$
$$= ((1/1) + (1/1) + (2/2) + (1/2) + 0 + 0)/6 = 3.5/6 \approx 0.583$$

8.4.2.2 Density

The indicator of density measures how well connected a network is. It is calculated as the ratio between the numbers of ties (relationships) that exist in a network out of all possible ties.

$$\frac{\text{actual connections}}{\text{maximum number of connections}}$$

A density of 1 implies that each enterprise within the network is connected to every other. A density of 0 implies that no relationships exist within the network, which can correspond to the moment of network inception. This indicator is intended to provide evidence of how well nodes are interconnected with each other, and therefore it can represent a proxy to evaluate the ability of nodes to communicate with each other.

There is usually a direct relationship between the number of nodes within a network and the measure of density. When the network is composed of few enterprises, the density will be high because it will be easier since all nodes are connected to each other. The higher the number of nodes in a network, the more difficult it will be for each node to establish relationships with all the others.

8.4.2.3 Multiplexity

Network multiplexity is a proxy of the strength of relationships between two nodes within a network. It refers to the extent to which two enterprises are linked together by more than one type of relationship in the network. The type of relationship is different, ranging from economic exchange, social exchange, resource exchange, or information exchange. The higher the amount of different types of relationships between two nodes, the higher the strength of the relationship itself and the ability for nodes to maintain the relationship over time; if one type of tie between them dissolves, other types of ties remain to connect them. For example, the existence of both economic and social exchanges can be related to enterprises that collaborated with each other before the inception of the network. On the contrary, the existence of *uniplexity*, such as economic exchanges only, can refer to enterprises that have been forced to work within a mandated network.

This measure of multiplexity can be particularly useful for motivational purposes to understand the willingness of actors to work together and supports the identification of weak ties.

CHAPTER 9

Performance Control for Projects

Tommaso Buganza

Politecnico di Milano, Department of Management, Economics & Industrial Engineering

The chapter illustrates how to use performance indicators to control project activities. According to the Project Management Institute (www.pmi.org), a project is a "temporary endeavor undertaken to create a unique product or service. Temporary means that every project has a definite end. Unique means that the product or service is different in some distinguishing way from all similar products or services."[1] Because they are unique, projects cannot be controlled like normal processes that are identically repeated hundreds or even millions of times. Each project goes through a standard lifecycle composed of five main phases: initiating, planning, executing, controlling, and closing. Thus, each time we face a project, we need to develop a new project plan in terms of scope, activities, resources, time, and risk. This plan will then become the reference point for the controlling activities. During the executing phase, the actual project development will be constantly compared with the plan, generating performance indicators, analyses of variance and, finally, replanning.

What should be done to accomplish the project scope is technically included in the work breakdown structure (WBS): "a deliverable-oriented hierarchical decomposition of the work to be executed by the project team to accomplish the project objectives and create the required deliverables."[2] The typical WBS is shaped as in Figure 9.1.

In the WBS, the project is progressively divided into more detailed activities at each level until it reaches the work package (WP) level. WPs are small groups of activities detailed enough to be defined in terms of duration, cost, and responsibilities. In relatively simple projects, these are also the basic elements of project control. In big and complex projects, there could be too many WPs to provide a manageable view of the current project performance. In these cases, we normally identify an intermediate level called the control account (CA). CAs can be thought of as small subprojects with their own responsible party called the control account manager (CAM). Hereafter, we will consider the case of a complex project with many CAs managed by different CAMs, as this is the typical case in which the entire performance control methodology presented in the following paragraphs will be beneficial.

Starting from the activities identified in the WBS, many methodologies and tools must be leveraged to properly plan the project (network diagrams, organizational breakdown structure, responsibility assignment matrix, network diagrams, Gantt charts, etc.). It is not our intention to cover these topics but to focus on the project

---

[1] "Project management body of knowledge (pmbok® guide)"—Project Management Institute, 2013.
[2] Idem.

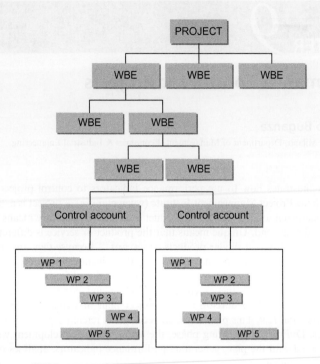

Figure 9.1 Elements of WBS.

controlling phases[3]; hence, we will assume that we have already developed the project management plan and know the total budget and duration of the project. With these data, a last crucial planning step is still needed: the development of the time-phased budget, also known as the budgeted cost of work scheduled (BCWS). This document describes how, according to the plan, the total budget is going to be spent along the project's duration. It can be created at the project level and at the CA level. We will consider this second option. An example of how to create a BCWS of a CA is reported in Box 9.1.

9.1 EARNED VALUE MANAGEMENT

Once the planning phase is over and the BCWS is defined, the project can move into the executing phase. The company's accounting system will keep track of all the resources (both internal and external) used to perform the WP and will provide (virtually at any moment) the total current cost spent on the CA. These data track a second crucial curve for project controlling: the actual cost of work performed (ACWP).

It is not possible to infer any information on the progress of the CA by comparing the BCWS and ACWP. In other words, if there is a difference between the budgeted and actual cost (and the CA is still in progress), it is not possible to understand the cause of this variance.

---

[3]For a detailed analysis of project planning processes, tools, and methodologies, please refer to "Project management body of knowledge (pmbok® guide)"—Project Management Institute, 2013.

Box 9.1 How to Build a BCWS

Let's consider the case of a simple CA composed of five activities. For each activity, we have the following data from the plan: logical predecessors (e.g., Activity B cannot start before the end of Activity A), time, and cost. Even though this can be, in many cases, oversimplistic, let's assume that the total cost of each activity is linearly distributed along the activity time (e.g., Activity A lasts 3 months and costs 30,000€; thus, the monthly cost will be assumed to be constant and equal to 10,000€ per month).

It is now easy to define the period cost of the CA. For example, in Month 4, we plan to be performing Activities B, C, and D with a total monthly cost of 50,000€. The BCWS can now be drawn as the cumulated cost curve along the time planned.

Activity	Pred.	Time (months)	Cost (K€)	Monthly cost
A	-	3	30	10
B	A	2	30	15
C	A	3	60	20
D	A	4	60	15
E	B	3	30	10

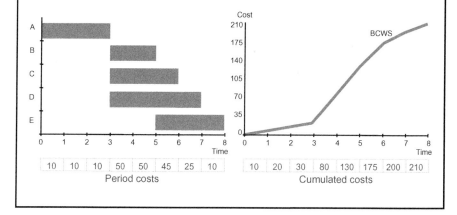

Figure 9.2 shows the case of a CA where, at Time Now, the actual cost is higher than the planned cost ($ACWP_{TN} > BCWS_{TN}$[4]). This difference can be due to two different reasons. The first one is the inefficient use of resources: The scheduled work has been performed, but it required the consumption of more resources than planned (e.g., more man-hours to perform a task). In this case, we would have an extra cost for the work performed. However, the same difference could be given by the anticipation of some activities: the actual work performed is higher than planned

---

[4]$BCWS_{TN}$ and $ACWP_{TN}$ are, respectively, BCWS and ACWP at Time Now.

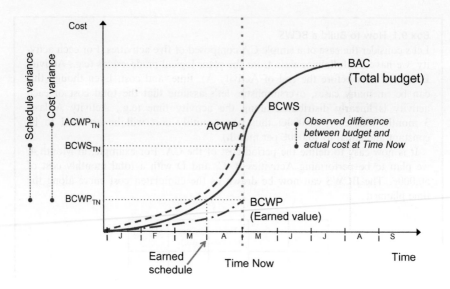

Figure 9.2 Basic elements of the earned value control system.

(e.g., a supplier delivered earlier and we could start a WP before). In this case, we would not have an extra cost, as we just anticipated activities (and costs) we planned to have later.

A discrepancy between planned and actual costs at Time Now can be the result of infinite possible combinations of (1) cost variance (CV); and (2) schedule variance (SV). Thus, we cannot be sure of the project performance by simply comparing the BCWS and ACWP.

In order to understand what the real performance of the CA is, it is necessary to introduce a third curve called the budgeted cost of work performed (BCWP) (also known as earned value), which expresses the physical progress of the activities of the CA at budgeted costs. By comparing this third curve with each of the previous curves, it is now possible to understand the CA's status. For example, in Figure 9.2, we can compare $BCWP_{TN}$ and $BCWS_{TN}$. Both curves show the value of the work at budgeted costs (BCs); therefore, any difference between them can only derive from the difference between the work scheduled (WS) and the work performed (WP) at Time Now. In this case, $BCWP_{TN} < BCWS_{TN}$, which means that the amount of work performed is lower than the WS: The CA is behind schedule.

As less work has been performed, one could expect that the actual cost of the CA at Time Now would be lower than the planned cost ($ACWP_{TN} < BCWS_{TN}$), but we observe the opposite in Figure 9.2. This means that the delay effect was completely counterbalanced by a second effect. To understand why we spent more than planned, even if we performed less work than scheduled, we can now compare $BCWP_{TN}$ with $ACWP_{TN}$. Both curves consider the WP but first consider the budgeted cost (BC), whereas the latter considers its actual cost (AC). Therefore, any difference between them can only derive from efficiency/inefficiency (I spent less/more than planned for the work I did). In our case, $BCWP_{TN} < ACWP_{TN}$; therefore, the CA is over budget.

To summarize, we can say that the CA represented in Figure 9.2 shows a cost higher than planned at Time Now; the reason for this is twofold: It is behind schedule and significantly over budget.

9.2 SYNTHETIC PERFORMANCE INDICATORS FOR PROJECT ADVANCEMENT

The considerations we have made so far are commonly captured by two sets of synthetic indexes: relative performance indexes and absolute performance indexes.

9.2.1 Relative Performance Indexes

These indexes express the cost/schedule performance as ratios:

$$\text{Cost Performance Index (CPI)} = \frac{\text{BCWP}}{\text{ACWP}}$$

If greater than 1, this index indicates that the CA is under budget.

$$\text{Schedule Performance Index (SPI)} = \frac{\text{BCWP}}{\text{BCWS}}$$

If greater than 1, this index indicates that the CA is ahead of schedule.

9.2.2 Absolute Performance Indexes

These indexes make it possible to express the accounting adjustment of the difference between budgeted and actual costs (BCWS and ACWP); for this reason, they are calculated in monetary units:

$$\text{Cost Variance (CV)} = \text{BCWP} - \text{ACWP}$$

If greater than zero, this index indicates that the CA is under budget.

$$\text{Schedule Variance (SV)} = \text{BCWP} - \text{BCWS}$$

If greater than zero, this index indicates that the CA is ahead of schedule.

Finally, it is important to note that the earned value is a cost-based control system and, in some cases, this may impair the interpretation of schedule progress. Let's consider the SV for instance: It expresses the delay in terms of money and not in terms of time. For this reason, a further absolute measurement is often added.

$$\text{Time Based Schedule Variance (SV}_t) = \text{Earned Schedule} - \text{Time Now}$$

where the earned schedule represents the moment when the BCWS was planned to have the same value as the BCWP at Time Now:

$$\text{BCWS(Earned Schedule)} = \text{BCWP(Time Now)}$$

SV_t expresses the SV in time units and, if it is greater than zero, it indicates that the CA is ahead of schedule.

Box 9.2 lists some examples of the practical use of these indexes.

All the indexes we have discussed show the project performance by comparing the current situation to the initial planning (or its revisions). In other words, with particularly positive (or negative) indexes, it will never be easy to define whether the error effectively lies in the project execution or in its planning.

Box 9.2 Reading Earned Value Performance Indexes

The definition of synthetic indexes facilitates a rapid and precise interpretation of the status of the project. For example, in the following figure, it is possible to observe two typical reports that, starting from the subdivision of the project into various CAs, make it possible to show the performance in terms of schedule and cost.

It is easy to identify CA 4 as the biggest issue on this project, as it clearly shows major problems with time (current performance is 29% lower than expected) and with cost (current performance is 52% lower than expected).

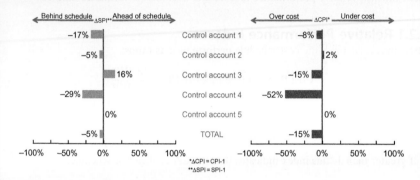

Correct reporting on project progress cannot, however, be based only on the values of the relative indexes (Cost Performance Index (CPI) and Schedule Performance Index (SPI)). These indexes show the performance as a percentage of the planned work, but do not assess the real economic impact of these performances. For this reason, it is always advisable to look at the values of the curves (BCWS, ACWP, and BCWP) and, above all, the values of the absolute indexes (CV and SV). The following table clearly shows that CA 1 is underperforming as well, even if it performs relatively better than CA 4 (both CPI and SPI are below 1 but higher than the CA 4 values). Still, the actual economic impact of the delay and inefficiency of CA 1 (given by CV + SV) is comparable to the one caused by CA 4. This is due to the size of the activities. CA 4 is performing worse than CA 1, but its BCWS planned so far is four times smaller. Therefore, we can say that this is more serious damage applied to a much smaller quantity.

x1000	BCWS	BCWP	ACWP	CV	SV	CPI	SPI
Control account 1	€22,181	€18,400	€19,900	−€1,500	−€3,781	0.92	0.83
Control account 2	€8,926	€8,496	€8,323	€173	−€430	1.02	0.95
Control account 3	€17,250	€19,960	€23,387	−€3,427	€2,710	0.85	1.16
Control account 4	€5,000	€3,575	€7,483	−€3,908	−€1,425	0.48	0.72
Control account 5	Not started	Not started	Not started	Not started	Not started	Not started	Not started
TOTAL	€53,357	€50,431	€59,093	−€8,662	−€2,926	0.85	0.95

Lastly, it is important to note that all the indexes discussed so far are calculated in Time Now. Therefore, by definition, as time passes, these indexes will change. To correctly control the project, it is important to know not only the value of the indexes at Time Now but also their trends. Let's assume that at Time Now, the CA is performing almost as scheduled (SPI = 1). Is this good news? How have we performed so far? Were we behind schedule last month and now we have recovered, or were we well ahead of schedule and are now slowing down?

To answer these questions, we need to consider indicators such as CPI and SPI along a time span. This can be done using the following graph, where we can see how the project CPI is decreasing constantly (going from 1.3 to 0.85), but this is counterbalanced by a constant increase of time performances (SPI goes from 0.80 to 0.95). In such a case, we can make the hypothesis that the delay on the project was destroying value (e.g., penalties, delays in invoicing, and lower customer satisfaction), and the project manager decided to speed up the project, even spending more than planned.

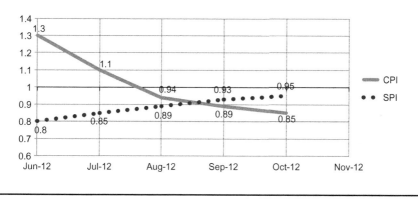

9.3 PERCENTAGE OF COMPLETENESS AND THE CALCULATION OF THE EARNED VALUE (BCWP)

Applying earned value to project control is complicated by the need to calculate the values of BCWS, ACWP, and BCWP.

Drawing the BCWS correctly requires the capacity to correctly plan the project, particularly when allocating the resources and defining the allocation drivers to apportion the costs of internal resources.

Drawing the ACWP correctly entails the measurement of both external costs (purchases, services, etc.) and internal costs (human resources and asset consumption). While allocating the external costs to the CA is, on the whole, simple, doing the same with internal costs can be more difficult. In order to have a precise allocation of internal costs to the CA, it is necessary to measure the consumption of internal resources by controlling their actual workloads. It is therefore essential to have time reports: tools that, at fixed intervals (weekly or monthly) accurately measure the quantity of resources spent on a specific CA.

Even if calculating the BCWS and ACWP may require significant effort, rigorous processes, and adequate managerial tools, calculating the BCWP is by far the most difficult task to be performed to apply the earned value methodology. The formula to calculate the BCWP is the following:

$$BCWP = BAC \times POC$$

The budget at completion (BAC) represents the total planned value for the controlled item (single CA or whole project). The BAC must already be estimated to close the planning phase, and it is already included in the BCWS (it represents its final point). Thus, the critical value to be estimated in order to properly calculate the BCWP is percentage of completeness (POC). In some cases, measuring the POC is easy—mostly when the activity releases physical and measurable outputs (e.g., units produced by an assembly line). In other cases, measuring the POC is very complex, especially if it is difficult to estimate the total amount of resources needed to carry out the activity since the planning phase (e.g., the project management activity).

Six main methods can be identified to measure the POC:

1. Weighted milestones: Main milestones along the activity are identified, and each of them is assigned a weight given by the ratio between the budgets estimated to reach the milestone over the total cost of the activity.
2. 50/50 or 0/100: These are particular cases of milestones where the weight is fixed. In 50/50, the POC is 50% once the activity has started and until its end, when it becomes 100%. In 0/100, the POC is always 0% until the end of the activity, when it becomes 100%. These methodologies may seem less precise than weighted milestones, but for relatively short and small activities, they work well and require considerably less significant planning and controlling effort.
3. Units complete: This is suitable for WPs where multiples are being done. Each unit is assigned a standard cost so as to allow earned value to be calculated from the sum of the standard costs of units completed to date.
4. Management assessment: This is also called percent complete. Earned value is estimated by the WP manager, who sets the POC based on his or her knowledge, experience, and perception.
5. Apportioned effort: This method is used for work that is not easily measured but that is proportional to a measurable effort whose POC is applied to both activities.
6. Level of effort (LoE): The POC of an activity is proportional to the time elapsed. Here, earned value to date is always the same as what is budgeted (BCWP = BCWS).

Some methods are, by their very nature, more objective than others (e.g., 1, 2, and 3) and therefore more suitable for controlling projects. Methods 4 and 5 are more subjective or based on nonphysical parameters and should be used as little as possible. The last method (LoE) deserves a more detailed analysis. By definition, it is not consistent with the earned value methodology, as it assumes that actual work will be performed as planned (BCWP = BCWS). Nevertheless, it is trivial to implement and is appropriate for measuring tasks such as program management, which are very difficult to assess and are normally too small to introduce significant distortions into data.

Box 9.3 lists an example of the application of different measurement methods.

Box 9.3 Earned Value: Example of Application

As an example, we will look at the application of the earned value method to a project named "New Vessel." The project is composed of different CAs (Module 1 … Module n, Integration). We will focus our attention on the first CA, which requires the performance of eight WPs. The planning of the CA is summarized in the following figure, along with the time-phased budget (BCWS) and the control methods that will be used during the executing phase.

	BCWS$_1$	BCWS$_2$	BCWS$_3$	BCWS$_4$	BCWS$_5$	BCWS$_6$	BCWS$_7$	BCWS$_8$	BCWS$_9$	BCWS$_{10}$	BAC
WP 1	100 K€	100 K€	200 K€	300 K€	300 K€						1000 K€
WP 2			150 K€	300 K€	450 K€	630 K€	630 K€	630 K€	630 K€	600 K€	4020 K€
WP 3			15 K€	30 K€	45 K€	63 K€	63 K€	63 K€	63 K€	60 K€	402 K€
WP 4				71 K€							71 K€
WP 5					71 K€						71 K€
WP 6							71 K€				71 K€
WP 7									71 K€		71 K€
WP 8	30 K€	30 K€	30 K€	30 K€	30 K€	30 K€	30 K€	30 K€	30 K€	30 K€	300 K€
CA	130 K€	130 K€	395 K€	731 K€	825 K€	794 K€	723 K€	794 K€	723 K€	761 K€	6006 K€

Time Now = 4

WP 1 is a typical design and engineering activity where we can identify three main milestones. The weight of the milestones is directly proportional to the budget. WP 2 is a production activity that will release a total amount of 134 units; for this reason, the control method selected is Units Complete. WP 3 is a control activity related to the previous activity. We cannot define what activities will be performed and when, but based on historical data, we know that it normally costs 10% of the production activity. For this reason, we distribute the time-phased budget in the same way as WP 2 and will control it using the same POC (apportioned effort). WPs 4–7 are four tests on manufactured units and will be controlled using a simple 0/100 method. Finally, WP 8 is project management and will be controlled using LoE.

Let's now assume that we wish to control the CA performances at Time Now = 4. The value of the BCWS for the CA at Time Now will be obtained by summing the CA's monthly BCWS from Months 1 to 4:

$$BCWS_4 = 130 + 130 + 395 + 731 = 1386 \text{ K€}$$

The ACWP will be provided directly by the accounting department, which will obtain it from the company Enterprise Resource Planning (ERP):

$$ACWP_4 = 1100 \text{ K€}$$

To calculate the BCWP (earned value), we must check the physical progress of each activity by talking with each WP responsible. The results of these interviews are reported in the following table, along with information regarding the selected control method and the BAC. Finally, the table reports the calculated POC per each WP, its BCWP, and the BCWP of the whole CA.

	Control method	Status	POC	BAC	BCWP (BAC*POC)
WP 1	Milestones (20%-50%-30%)	1st Milestone met	20%	1000 K€	200 K€
WP 2	Units complete (std cost 30K€)	8 Units produced (134)	5,97%	4020 K€	240 K€
WP 3	Apportioned effort	In progress	5,97%	402 K€	24 K€
WP 4	0/100	Test done	100%	71 K€	71 K€
WP 5	0/100	Not started	0%	71 K€	-
WP 6	0/100	Not started	0%	71 K€	-
WP 7	0/100	Not started	0%	71 K€	-
WP 8	LoE	In progress	n.a.	300 K€	120 K€
CA					655 K€

At this point, it is possible to calculate the synthetic performance indexes for the CA:

$$CPI = BCWP/ACWP = 655/1100 = 0,60 \text{ (over budget)}$$
$$SPI = BCWP/BCWS = 655/1386 = 0,47 \text{ (behind schedule)}$$
$$CV = BCWP - ACWP = 655 - 1100 = -445 \text{ K€ (over budget)}$$
$$SV = BCWP - BCWS = 655 - 1386 = -731 \text{ K€ (behind schedule)}$$
$$SVt = ES - TN = 3 - 4 = -1 \text{ month (behind schedule)}$$

Note in $BCWP_{TN} = BCWS_{ES}$

The earned value indicators clearly show that the CA is far behind schedule and over budget. Data should still be analyzed with care. It is undoubtedly true that WP 2 is behind schedule, as only eight units have been produced instead of 15. WP 1 appears to be even more behind schedule: The second milestone has a weight of 50% and has not been met, which means that the activity is definitely behind schedule. Nevertheless, we cannot be sure that the activity progress is really 20%. We could be very close to meeting the second milestone, which would considerably increase the BCWP from 655,000€ to 1,155,000€ and modify the performance indicators (e.g. CPI would become 1.05 and SPI would become 0.83). This example clearly shows how data coming from the earned value management system must always be interpreted by project managers. In this case, the best course of action would be to acknowledge a delay in the production activity (WP 2) and ask the person in charge of the design and engineering activity (WP 1) how far he or she is from the next milestone.

9.4 ESTIMATE AT COMPLETION

Knowing the status of a CA is the first step of the control process, but it still is not enough to make managerial decisions about the CA. Before making decisions that might change the CA, such as de-scoping, increasing effort, or accepting delays, we must learn what would happen if we did not make any change at all. In other words, before making any decisions, we need to forecast what would likely be the final cost and time of the CA if we go on as planned. Only in this way will it be possible to conduct a differential analysis to understand whether to implement any corrective action and which actions should be taken.

The earned value methodology can support the calculation of the estimate at completion (EAC). In order to see how, we will refer to the example in Box 9.3 for the calculation of the earned value performance indicators.

We already know that the CA is largely behind schedule and over budget. Therefore, we can assume that, if no corrective action is taken, both the CA budget and the duration of the project must be increased.

The main question, however, is: How much more will this cost and how much longer will the project take?

To calculate the new estimates, we must ask ourselves a question about the nature of the deviations from planning. In some cases, deviations are due to contingent causes—causes that have already impacted the project and are not supposed to affect it anymore (e.g., the effect of a trade union dispute that has already been resolved). In other cases, however, the causes that affected the CA are structural, and their effects will continue influencing it in the future (e.g., stress on the raw materials market due to a macroeconomic cycle that is expected to last longer than the CA itself). In these two cases, the mechanism for calculating the EAC will be different.

If the causes of the variation are contingent, we will use the CV, which measures the cost performance, to update the BAC and the SV_t, which measure the time performance, to update the duration according to the following formulas:

$$EAC_\epsilon = BAC - CV$$
$$EAC_t = Duration - SV_t$$

Therefore, assuming that the error is contingent, the new time and cost estimates for the CA in Box 9.3 would be:

$$EAC_\epsilon = 6006 \ K\epsilon - (-455 \ K\epsilon) = 6451 \ K\epsilon$$
$$EAC_t = 10 \ m - (-1 \ m) = 11 \ m$$

If, however, the causes are structural, we need to make assumptions about the future performance indicators as well.

Normally, it is assumed that the performances at Time Now (CPI and SPI) will remain unchanged from Time Now until the end of the CA.

Under this assumption, EAC_ϵ will be equal to the actual cost of the work performed so far (ACWP) plus the actual cost of work remaining (also called the estimate to complete [ETC])

$$EAC_\epsilon = ACWP + actual \ cost \ of \ work \ remaining$$

Additionally, we can express the budgeted cost of work remaining as the difference between the BAC (budgeted cost of 100% of the estimated work) and BCWP (budgeted cost of the percentage of work performed so far).

$$budget \ cost \ of \ work \ remaining = (BAC - BCWP)$$

Because we have assumed that the future efficiency will be equal to that of the past, we can use CPI to transform it into the actual cost of work remaining:

$$actual \ cost \ of \ work \ remaining = \frac{budget \ cost \ of \ work \ remaining}{CPI}$$

In conclusion, then:

$$EAC_€ = ACWP + \frac{(BAC - BCWP)}{CPI}$$

In the same way, it is possible to calculate:

$$EAC_t = Time\ Now + \frac{(duration - earned\ schedule)}{SPI}$$

Therefore, assuming a structural error, the new time and cost estimates for the CA in Box 9.3 would be:

$$EAC_€ = 1100\ K€ + \frac{(6006\ K€ - 655\ K€)}{0.60} = 10.086, 33\ K€$$

$$EAC_t = 4\ m + \frac{(10\ m - 3\ m)}{0.47} = 18.89\ m$$

The new estimates greatly differ in the case of contingent or structural errors. In general, it can be said that, with the same performance indexes, the assumption of a structural error amplifies (either positively or negatively) the effects on the estimates. This effect diminishes with the progress of the activity. In fact, if we consider structural $EAC_€$ as an example, when the work performed (BCWP) increases, the difference between BAC and BCWP trends to zero and EAC trends to ACWP.

$$\lim_{POC \to 100\%} EAC_{structural} = ACWP$$

9.5 COMPLETING COST/SCHEDULE PERFORMANCE INDEXES (TCPI/TSPI)

Using the earned value techniques to define the EAC requires many approximations—the most important of which are related to the method chosen to measure the physical progress of the activities (POC) and to the assumption that in the future we'll maintain the performances we have had so far. Therefore, it is obvious that estimates obtained in this way cannot be considered perfectly reliable or incontrovertible. When it is necessary to update the plan of an ongoing CA, the appraisal made by the CAM and the team may be more reliable than the pure and aseptic EAC calculated on a spreadsheet.

However, in some cases, these appraisals can also be biased by contingent factors. It is a known problem that the person working on a task is often too optimistic and emotionally involved to run the estimates with pure objectivity.

Fortunately, though, even when the new budget and time are forecasted by experts, the earned value management techniques can provide important support to the decision-making process by assessing the feasibility of new estimates for the CA.

The basic idea is very simple. Let's assume that the CAM provides new estimates for the cost and duration of his or her ongoing CA. Knowing the performances at Time Now, it is possible to calculate how we need to perform going forward to meet these new estimates. In other words, the earned value technique "translates" the new estimates expressed in terms of cost and time into estimates expressed in terms of performance indicators to be reached. More specifically, we'll call the to-complete cost performance index (TCPI) the cost performance to be maintained from now on in order to match the new estimates provided by the CAM and his or her team.

The formula to calculate TCPI comes directly from the one in the previous chapter to calculate the structural EAC_{ϵ}. In that case, the EAC_{ϵ} was the dependent variable and CPI was an input variable: We assumed that we would perform the same in the future as we have in the past. This assumption is precisely the main reason why, in many cases, the EAC_{ϵ} is not reliable. Another possibility is to consider the final cost as a known value (provided by the CAM and his or her team) and calculate the cost performance (TCPI) that should be maintained going forward to meet it.

We can replace variable EAC_{ϵ} with the new estimate provided (new cost) in the formula, and then we will calculate the TCPI:

$$EAC_{\epsilon} = ACWP + \frac{(BAC - BCWP)}{CPI} \to TCPI = \frac{(BAC - BCWP)}{(new\ cost - ACWP)}$$

In the same way, the to-complete schedule performance index (TSPI) can also be calculated, starting from the new time declared by the CAM and his or her team.

$$TSPI = \frac{(duration - earned\ schedule)}{(new\ time - time\ now)}$$

To see a practical application of both TCPI and TSPI, we can use the example in Box 9.3 again.

We know that the CA is behind schedule and over budget. Let's assume that, despite these performances, the CAM declares that the activity will be concluded on time and on budget. In other words, new time = 10 months and new cost = 6,006,000€.

These targets will force us to work with performances well above 1 to recover the delay and the inefficiency accumulated so far. Applying the formulas, these new estimates can be translated into the new performance target.

$$TCPI = \frac{(6006\ K€ - 655\ K€)}{(6006\ K€ - 1100\ K€)} = 1.09$$

$$TSPI = \frac{(10\ m - 3\ m)}{(10\ m - 4\ m)} = 1.17$$

These figures must be analyzed carefully. For example, the TCPI seems to be reasonable. It is only a bit higher than the planned performance (CPI = 1). Nevertheless, we cannot avoid considering that the cost performance so far has been considerably lower (CPI = 0.60). Increasing the index from 0.60 to 1.09 means increasing the performance by 82%. This is not impossible, but it is evidently a challenging target, and specific recovery plans should support such a statement to make it reliable. Similar considerations might be done for the TSPI, which should increase by 149%.

As any other indicator within the earned value management methodology, the TCPI (TSPI) is correlated with the POC. It is simple to imagine that, if an activity is over budget and it has just started (POC = 1%), we still have plenty of work to perform. Thus, a slight improvement in performance might be enough to close the activity on budget. However, if the same activity is over budget and it is almost over (POC = 99%), the improvement of performance should be enormous in order to recover in the last 1% of work what has been lost in the previous 99%.

CHAPTER 10

Forms and Techniques for Financing

10.1 MARKETS AND FINANCIAL NEEDS COVERAGE

In order to achieve the goal of value creation, the management of financial resources is extremely important. Management equilibrium requires the use and collection of financial resources to be characterized in such a way that the value creation goal is pursued. The investment structure—which is representative of how money is invested (i.e., in the short term or in fixed assets)—and the financing structure—which is representative of how money is raised (i.e., through debt or equity)—have to be aligned, adhering to at least three conditions.

First, the investment structure must be consistent in terms of the time horizon with the structure of the resources with which investments are financed. Capital uses that generate cash in the short term also require financial methods that are characterized by short-term returns and reimbursement. Likewise, those structures of capital use with medium- to long-term returns will need reimbursement that covers types of long-term financing.

Second, in building the structure of financing sources, attention should be paid to punctuated cash management and balance. Commitments with the various sponsor categories must be consistent with the firm's capability to generate cash from its core businesses in each period of time (t),[1] as the following equation shows:

$$FCFF_t/CASHOUTFLOW_t \geq 1 \qquad (10.1)$$

where $FCFF_t$ is the cash flow the firm business generates in each period and $CASHOUTFLOW_t$ is the cash flow associated with the obligations to financial stakeholders (debtholders—i.e., bondholders, banks, or other financial institutions). The equilibrium should have a financing source structure that absorbs cash exactly when the firm produces it. The indicator is required to be at least 1; however, it should be higher than 1 due to the possible volatility of the $FCFF_t$ produced over time.

Third, enterprises should seek equilibrium between returns and the cost of capital. Investments must generate a return that should be able to remunerate the cost of capital. The cost of capital is related to the financial structure choices and thus to the composition of the financial sources. Therefore, it is an expression of the expectations of all those who finance the firm. Hence, the collection and management of financial resources require a great deal of attention and could contribute to the firm's value creation.

As a result, it is essential to comprehend how and where firms can obtain financial resources.

---

[1]Period t can be days, months, or quarters according to the needs of the company.

Firms could comply with these necessities by resorting to self-financing—i.e., the resources generated through their own management—and/or to external sources—i.e., the resources collected through external operations. Cases in which companies are able to fulfill their obligations with self-financing are the least frequent. Hence, the most widespread solution is the recourse to external sources.

Before looking for the most suitable solutions to collect financial resources, it is important to understand how to quantify and qualify the financial requirement to be fulfilled.

10.1.1 How to Measure Financial Needs

Financial need should be quantified and qualified. Some steps can be taken to attain the right measurement.

> First, it must be defined the overall amount of resources needed for the company to function.
>
> Afterward, resources must be related to ordinary needs (e.g., inventory, raw material, operating costs) and other circumstances related to the running of the company (e.g., investments, debt reimbursement).
>
> Finally, it has to be timed the financial need, which means tracing the temporal distribution of cash flows.

Some of the steps are not related to the amount of the financial need; they may refer only to the features of the requirement.

To clarify, think of a firm that needs to finance its own inventory, for which some costs to buy raw materials and transform them through labor have been anticipated. However, the firm is waiting to sell this inventory, which means then invoicing and collecting compensation. For this reason, the company really needs to cover its temporary requirement with resources that can be reimbursed and remunerated as soon as the inventory will be converted to cash flow (sales)—i.e., in the short term.

A second case is when firms need to finance an investment for buying new equipment to improve efficiency. This will lead to the reduction of production costs in the short and medium term. In that case, the firm will need to cover a significant initial financial requirement, which will then give gradual returns. Hence, it has to cover a long-lasting requirement with resources that can be remunerated and reimbursed gradually over time in concert with the materialization of the cost savings.

A third example is firms that need to finance an investment in a new product, starting from the initial stages of research and development until effective commercialization. In this case, the firm will need to finance a large amount for a long period of time and can afford to pay it back only when the new product is able to generate cash flow.

These three cases are representative of what can happen during the decision-making and planning phases and demonstrate how the financial requirement not only must be quantified but also qualified in order to find the best solution. This must be consistent with the company's overall needs, not only in quantitative terms but also in terms of the remuneration and reimbursement dynamic.

Therefore, during company planning, it is important to question the amount of financial resources that are required and where these will come from—i.e., through which possible solutions it is possible to collect them.

It is possible to proceed with either a direct or an indirect method.

The direct method leads to the definition of requirements through a thorough list of all the company's necessities. For example, the list could include the acquisition of new technology, the acquisition of a company branch, debt reimbursement—all cases that could lead to the identification of the requirement through an estimation of the related commitment in each situation.

The indirect method esteems the capital requirement linking it to the company size. It is the most consistent with a gradual and incremental dynamic of the company management.

For example, suppose that a company has revenue in time t_0 equal to 120 million euros, its net working capital equals 18 million euros, and its net fixed assets equal approximately 42 million euros. Let's suppose that the capability in terms of fixed investments has not been saturated yet and that the company could grow without new investments in net fixed assets.

If the company has a goal to grow by approximately 20% during the period t_1, under the hypothesis of no saturation of the productive capacity, it should ask to finance its incremental net working capital. Surpassing 120 million euros in revenue to 144 million euros, therefore, its net working capital will increase from 18 million euros to 21.6 million euros, with a net financing requirement of approximately 3.6 million euros. To take this path, the company should be certain in advance to have sufficient financial coverage. The indirect method passes through the definition of the company dimensional goals with a gradual logic during time and, as a consequence, it brings to the definition of the financial requirement.

In more general terms, it can be calculated as follows:

$$(\text{Sales}_{t+1} - \text{Sales}_t) \times \text{IC}_t = \text{FinancialRequirement}_t \qquad (10.2)$$

where

Sales_{t+1}, expected sales
Sales_t, actual sales
IC_t, intensity of the invested capital (net working and/or fixed assets)
$\text{FinancialRequirement}_t$, consequent financial requirement to be covered.

The determination of the financial requirement from a quantitative point of view and its qualification in terms of features open up the search for resources on different possible frontlines. If they are not available internally or the internal resources are used in a different way, companies should seek additional options to find financing externally.

10.1.2 How to Cover Financial Needs

The resource collection to model the financial structure could take place on two principal financial markets:

- The equity market
- The debt market.

The *equity market* helps companies obtain financing through the issuance of shares and in general terms of equity. Companies can issue several types of shares:

- Common shares: They carry voting rights and dividend rights just like residual claimholders—that is, when all other financial stakeholders and preferred shareholders have already been remunerated.
- Preferred shares: They typically do not carry voting rights but are entitled to receive a certain level of remuneration as dividends before common shareholders.

Companies issue shares and, in this way, they are able to collect financial resources. The collection of financial resources through shares is, overall, the most stable form of collection. Companies issue shares, and underwriters buy them. Through this operation, companies collect capital, and investors acquire two different types of rights.

First, investors acquire the right to be remunerated, which remains a residual right. In fact, shareholders have the right to be remunerated only after all the remaining stakeholders have been remunerated. Therefore, shareholders are also called *residual claimholders* and underwrite risk capital—i.e., the most risky form of investment in the firm but also the most stable form of financing for companies. This financing is more stable because companies do not have time constraints and are not limited in the way with which they remunerate or reimburse this capital.

The second type of right is related to the *governance* system of companies. The ownership of equity capital gives shareholders the right to vote within social bodies in which the owners are represented. Shareholders are the owners of the firm and, consequently, they have the right to nominate directors and the right to have a say in fundamental business decisions, such as the approval of the company's balance sheet. Obviously, these voting rights, as well as ownership rights, are proportional to the quota owned.

The equity market can then be divided into:

- The *public equity* market. When the collection of resources takes place on a public market, this is called *public equity*. A typical situation is the listing on the stock exchange. Companies must be admitted to the listing in the stock exchange—i.e., on an official and regulated market—through the issuance of shares in the community of investors. In this way, companies collect financial resources by selling their own shares on the market. The market can, in turn, trade those shares without taking away the related resources to the companies that have collected them. The choice of the listing is particularly relevant for company growth and has very serious implications in terms of costs and benefits. The company must pay fees to be listed on the exchange; the company must also adhere to the requirements for public companies and may also have to change its strategy in terms of transparency, governance, and company information.
- The *private equity* market. The collection of equity resources can also take place on a private market, where it is possible to have private partners or institutional investors (e.g., private equity funds) who acquire shareholdings in companies, underwriting issued shares and consequently financing them as investors of risk capital.

The *debt market* is a market where financers lend money to a company, which is then obligated to remunerate them and reimburse them according to an established method and schedule. In this way, the debt market and the equity market are contradictory. In the equity market, investors have a residual remuneration for which they have relevant governance rights, whereas in the debt market, financers have the right to be remunerated and reimbursed according to an established contract.

The debt could be collected issuing bonds (or, in general, debt securities) or through banking loans (or, in general, financial companies, loans). In the first case, the company is moving within the bond market, while in the second instance, it is moving within the banking debt market.

The equity, bond, and banking markets represent three fundamental branches of capital markets wherein companies can obtain financing depending on their specific needs. Hence, within these branches, the most favorable technical solutions will be identified in order to give companies financial equilibrium consistent with the goal of creating value.

10.2 FORMS AND TECHNIQUES FOR SHORT-TERM FINANCING

Short-term financial decisions affect current assets and current liabilities, and managers should raise money to cover working capital needs. In fact, short-term financial decisions focus on cash inflows and outflows from within a year or less.

To choose the best short-term option, it is important to compare the different possibilities according to their cost, which means including and analyzing not only the interest to be paid to the lender but also the fees the lender requires. In addition, the many borrowing options are characterized by different schedules and flexibility.

The access and flexibility to financing is nation specific—e.g., the Italian Law nr. 108/1996 introduced a cap on interest rates for each different lending form in order to define a threshold beyond which the rate becomes usurious. Table 10.1 lists data provided by the Bank of Italy in 2014 that show examples of the different rate levels depending on the type of loan.

Companies have different financing choices in order to meet short-term debt obligations such as lines of credit, commercial papers, and factoring, which will be described in the following sections.

10.2.1 Lines of Credit

A line of credit is an available amount of money that a firm can borrow. It is a very flexible option of financing. It should be used for covering short-term cash imbalances

Table 10.1 Examples of Different Rate Levels		
Type of Debt	**Threshold**	**Rate**
Lines of credit	Up to EUR 5000	11.48%
	Over EUR 5000	10.06%
Unsecure overdraft	Up to EUR 1500	16.25%
	Over EUR 1500	15.01%
Anticipation and bank discount	Up to EUR 5000	8.90%
	From EUR 5000 to EUR 100,000	8.06%
	Over EUR 100,000	5.49%
Factoring	Up to EUR 50,000	7.43%
	Over EUR 50,000	4.67%
Vehicle leasing	Up to EUR 25,000	7.92%
	Over EUR 25,000	7.52%
Real estate leasing	Fixed rate	6.52%
	Floating rate	4.87%
Revolving credit	Up to EUR 5000	16.97%
	Over EUR 5000	12.31%
Mortgage loan	Fixed rate	5.17%
	Floating rate	3.73%
Source: Bank of Italy, press release, March 25, 2014.		

due to the mismatching of operating cycle inflows and outflows; otherwise, it will become a very onerous obligation, as the rate in Table 10.1 shows.

The bank or the financial institution that gives a line of credit to a client is risking improper use by the client firm (outline of the bank credit use), financial instability, and economic loss.

The main costs the client is subjected to are the following:

- Interest payables, whose interest rates are defined by exogenous circumstances, pricing policy and bank features, client risk profile and relative bargaining power, and operation features.
- A commitment fee, which is calculated as a fixed percentage on the loan amount that covers the possible unused credit.
- An arrangement fee, which covers all the administrative processes, including the transaction implementation.
- An agency fee, which covers the management of the credit relationship.

10.2.2 Commercial Papers

Commercial papers are securities issued by companies—in particular, large enterprises—to raise resources for their financial needs. They are tradable on the money market, and their maturity is generally between 1 and 9 months.

When issuing commercial papers, banks, finance companies, and corporations are promising to pay the face value on the note maturity date. In fact, this is an unsecured form of credit, as no collateral is required. For this reason, only firms with a great credit rating are able to sell their commercial papers at a reasonable price.

Commercial papers have low marketability, as there is not a secondary market, even though the issuer could repurchase the note prior to maturity. Generally, being issued commercial papers is cheaper than getting a loan from a bank.

The U.S. Federal Reserve System (FED) publishes data on the commercial paper rates supplied by the Depository Trust & Clearing Corporation. Table 10.2 lists the commercial papers' annual average rates. They include calculation programs with at least one "1" or "1 + " rating in the AA[2] financial and AA nonfinancial commercial paper interest rate, but no ratings other than "1" for the short-term credit rating and programs with at least one "AA" rating, including split-rated issuers for the long-term credit rating. The A2/P2 nonfinancial category includes programs with at least one

Table 10.2 Commercial Paper Rates for Different Categories as of March 31, 2014

	AA Financial				AA Nonfinancial				A2/P2 Nonfinancial			
	1-day	15-day	30-day	90-day	1-day	15-day	30-day	90-day	1-day	15-day	30-day	90-day
2012	0.09	0.11	0.12	0.20	0.11	0.12	0.13	0.19	0.38	0.42	0.46	0.53
2013	0.07	0.07	0.09	0.14	0.06	0.07	0.08	0.11	0.25	0.27	0.30	0.33
2014[a]	0.05	0.05	0.07	0.13	0.05	0.05	0.05	0.10	0.20	0.21	0.25	0.28

[a]Data through March 28.
Source: www.federalreserve.gov.

[2]Refers to the rating evaluation.

"2" rating, but no ratings other than "2" in relation to the short-term credit rating and programs with at least one "A" or "BBB"/"BAA" rating, including split-rated issuers, but none with any ratings outside the "A"–"BBB"/"BAA" range for the long-term credit rating.

10.2.3 Factoring

Factoring is a credit service that concerns the acquisition of commercial credit by an intermediary (factor) in order to receive advance payments. In fact, the factor pays a percentage (approximately 80%) to the counterparty as soon as it receives an assignment or the receivable.

An example could be a firm that has a credit of 1000€ on March 31 to be paid 90 days later. The creditor could sell this credit to a factor, which will anticipate an amount (let's suppose 800€—i.e., 80% of the face value) and which will cash in 1000€ on June 30 (the day the debtor is supposed to pay). Figure 10.1 shows this situation graphically.

The factoring agreement could be:

- *with recourse*, which means that the credit risk is on the creditor firm under reserve—i.e., the factor requires the return of anticipated amounts to the party who sells the credit in case the debtor does not fulfill its duties at maturity;
- *without recourse*, here, the factor assumes the insolvency risk. In this case, the factoring cost for the creditor is comprehensive of this risk analysis, and in the case of insolvency, the factor cannot recoup costs from the client who gives the credit. This functions as a protection against bad debt quality, even if it is not costless.

In order to address company needs, the EU Federation for the Factoring and Commercial Finance Industry[3] identifies different types of factoring that can be found in the market.

Full factoring requires the commercial credits of a firm to be ceded to the factor that collects and manages them; this is the typical factoring contract. *Reverse factoring* implies that the factor contacts the supplier of a buyer firm, offering it a factoring contract regarding the discount of its invoices to the buyer. *Maturity factoring* means that the supplier receives the receivables payment on a due date. In addition, a factoring contract could be related to a receivable that could be in a foreign currency; thus, there is an exchange rate risk.

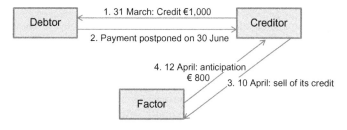

Figure 10.1 Factoring actors and process.

---

[3]The EUF is the representative body for the factoring and commercial finance industry in the EU. It comprises national and international industry associations that are active in the region.

In a typical factoring contract, some of the following items could be included:

- Interest payment on the advanced amounts
- Management and credit administration service fee
- Invoice fee (for each invoice transferred)
- Account and proceeds fee, as the relationship with the factor is generally regulated on a current account
- Percentage commission based on the face value of the receivables.

In addition, some other costs could arise, depending on the type of factoring. In the case of without recourse factoring, the factor could require an additional amount to be protected in case the debtor does not fulfill its duty while in a with recourse factoring the client could be charged of a preliminary investigation fee as the factor wants to assess the reimbursement faculty of the firm which sells the credit.

According to the EU Federation for the Factoring and Commercial Finance Industry, the global total business volume of the factoring industry increased from EUR 760 billion in 2003 to EUR 1325 billion in 2008, achieving a remarkable EUR 2120 billion in 2012. The European market increased from EUR 827 billion in 2009 (67% of global volume) to EUR 1200 billion in 2012 (60% of global volume).

10.3 FORMS AND TECHNIQUES FOR LONG-TERM FINANCING

Managers should be aware that a good mix between long-term financing and short-term financing supports the company in terms of timing, flexibility, and cash flows.

Long-term financing includes equity financing and debt financing. In fact, an issuance of new shares will increase the equity of the company, whereas the issuance of new debt (e.g., corporate bonds or a new bank loan) is a liability.

The following sections will discuss the meaning of IPOs and analyze bonds, syndicated loans, and leasing, which allows a company to use an asset in return for periodical payments.

10.3.1 IPOs

An initial public offering (IPO) is the process through which a company becomes listed on a stock exchange. Going public requires the company to meet the minimum listing requirements for the exchange and to fulfill a process with specific regulatory issues. Figure 10.2 shows the timetable that a company interested in admission on the London Stock Exchange—AIM should expect.

Due to the abundance of tasks to be performed, generally a company picks intermediaries with a great deal of expertise. There could be an accounting consultant, a legal advisor, and one or more investment banks. In the case of more than one investment bank that supports the company, a syndicate is formed whose tasks encompass the preparation of due diligence, the preparation of the red herring (i.e., the preliminary prospectus for the authority and investors), the final prospectus, the assessment of the market, the organization of road shows, and the collection of expressions of interest. In addition, there could be an underwriter (an investment bank) with a greenshoe or overallotment option that gives it the right to sell additional shares than were initially available.

There are some potential advantages for a company to offer its securities on the market. In fact, through an IPO, the company raises money to expand its operations, acquire other companies, and provide liquidity to shareholders. However, the decision

Pre flotation preparation

24–36 months before admission

* Develop a robust business plan
* Ensure contracts are in place with customers and suppliers
* Review management information systems and operational and compliance controls
* Consider ownership and tax issues

12–24 months before admission

* Read the Exchange's flotation pack
* Attend one of our flotation seminars
* Contact us for a one-to-one meeting
* Adopt "best practice" corporate governance standards
* Complete any planned strategic intiatives such as acquisitions

6–12 months before admission

* Review and plan your investor relations (IR) strategy
* Ensure you have independently-audited financial accounts, if applicable, for a 3-year period
* Consider commissioning an independent expert's report on you business
* Make any necessary changes to the executive board
* Appoint nonexecutive directors
* Ensure your company is incorporated under the relevant laws
* Consider whether to conduct pre flotation fundraising
* Decide on the method of flotation
* Hold a beauty parade of advisers

The admission process

12–24 weeks before admission

* Appoint your advisers
* Instruct all advisers
* Agree the timetable to admission

6–12 weeks before admission

* Review any problem areas that have emerged
* Produce the draft prospectus/admission document
* Produce the first draft of the other required documents
* Conduct the initial review of pricing issues
* Review PR presentations
* Host analyst presentations

1–6 weeks before admission

* Continue drafting meetings
* Carry out and complete due diligence
* Hold PR meetings and roadshow
* Register the prospectus with the UKLA
* Submit 10-day announcement to Exchange of intention to join AIM

1 week before admission

* All documents completed and approved
* Pricing and allocation of the offer
* Register the prospectus
* Sign subscription agreement
* Bulk print final prospectus

Admission week

* Pay exchange fees
* Submit documents
* Admission to AIM granted
* Trading begins

Figure 10.2 London stock exchange–AIM admission timetable. http://www.londonstockexchange.com/companies-and-advisors/aim/for-companies/joining/admission-timetable.pdf.

to go public increases the company's costs, as it has to pay underwriting fees, legal and accounting advisors fees, and fees required by the stock exchange. In addition, there could be a change of control as new shareholders replace previous ones; in this case, the company should disclose more information to the market. In addition, investor relations should be appointed, and the company should handle corporate governance issues.

10.3.2 Bonds

A bond is a security that requires the issuer to pay specified interests (coupons) and make principal payments to the bondholders at maturity or even on specified dates. The requirements for issuing bonds are regulated country by country. Normally, limited companies can issue bonds and just with a maximum amount as a percentage of capitalization.

The repayment of the capital could be one-shot at maturity or amortized during the bond life, while the coupon may not be provided (zero-coupon bond) or it could be present and have a monthly, quarterly, semi-annual, or annual frequency (coupon bond) calculated at a fixed or floating rate.

Generally, the coupon is expressed in a percentage on the face value (FV) of the bond. For example, an annual coupon of 4% on a bond whose FV is 1000€ means a coupon amount of 40€ per year.

In the case of a fixed rate coupon, the amount of the coupon will be constant over time, whereas in the case of a floating rate coupon, the formula through which the coupon will be calculated is constant over time—e.g., coupon = base rate + spread, where the base rate could be the Euribor or the Libor rate in the European market, and the spread is contractually defined. The coupon rate could also step up (so it increases over time up to maturity) or step down, which means that it decreases over time up to maturity.

Bonds are issued not only by companies (corporate bonds) but also by governments (government bonds) and municipalities (municipality bonds).

In addition, there is a particular class of bonds—i.e., hybrid bonds—that has specific features and whose seniority is lower than the one of ordinary bonds (Figure 10.3).

It is possible to value a bond knowing its coupon amount $c\%$ and frequency t (if any), its face value FV, and its maturity T. In addition, an analyst needs to identify an appropriate discount rate for that security.

With this information, the value of a bond is the present value of the coupon and the FV that the holders will receive:

$$\text{bond value} = \sum_{t=0}^{T} \frac{c_t\% \times FV}{(1+k_t)^t} + \frac{FV}{(1+k_t)^T}$$

Obviously, in the case of a zero-coupon bond, the formula is much simpler:

$$\text{bond value} = \frac{FV}{(1+k_T)^T}$$

One of the most relevant issues is the identification of the most appropriate discount rates, one for each period in which the coupon is stripped. In the case of a risk-free bond, the discount rates could be directly inferred from the term structure of interest rates. The term structure of the interest rate curve denotes the relationship between the yield on risk-free zero-coupon bonds at different maturity dates. Figure 10.4 shows the term structure of interest rates based on US treasuries.

When valuing a nonrisk-free bond, the discount rate should consider an additional premium for the riskiness of the security. In this way, the discount rate is inferred from the term structure of interest rates plus an additional spread that

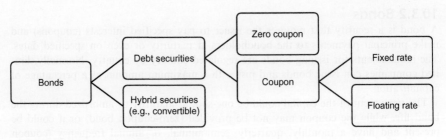

Figure 10.3 Different features of bonds.

considers the company risk as measured by its default spread. In fact, rating agencies publish the default probability of a company at least annually given its rating and the additional spread required by nonrisk-free companies (refer to Figure 10.5 and Table 10.3).

Often, the yield to maturity (YTM) is calculated and reported in the bond information. This is the yield that equals the discounted coupons and the face value to the bond value, whose value should be known through the previous formulas. In order to mathematically obtain this value, mathematical software or a trial-and-error approach

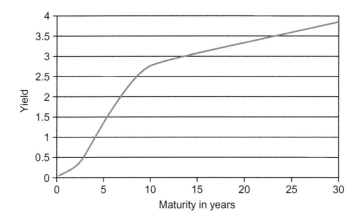

Figure 10.4 US term structure of interest rates as of November 25, 2013. http://fxstreet.com.

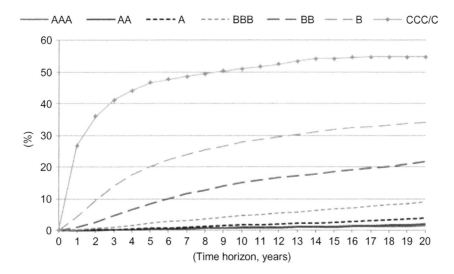

Figure 10.5 Global corporate average cumulative default rates by rating (1981–2012). S&P's Global Fixed Income Research and S&P's CreditPro® 2013.

Table 10.3 Ratings and Default Spread

Rating	AAA	AA	A	BBB	BB	B	CCC	CC	C	D
Spread	0.40%	0.70%	1.00%	2.00%	4.00%	6.50%	8.75%	9.50%	10.50%	12.00%

Source: Damodaran website as of January 2014.

can be used. In fact, this requires solving an f-power equation, where f is the frequency with which coupons are given. Find the YTM so that:

$$\text{bond value} = \sum_{t=0}^{T} \frac{c_t \% \times \text{FV}}{(1+\text{YTM})^t} + \frac{\text{FV}}{(1+\text{YTM})^T}$$

Another relevant parameter of a bond is its duration D. The duration, expressed in years, considers the discounted sum of cash flows and times compared to the dirty price.

$$D = \frac{1}{P}\left(\sum_{t=0}^{T} \frac{c_t \% \times \text{FV}}{(1+k_t)^t} \times t + \frac{\text{FV}}{(1+k_t)^T} \times T\right)$$

The Macaulay duration is calculated substituting the discount rates with the YTM as found previously.

$$D^{\text{MAC}} = \frac{1}{P}\left(\sum_{t=0}^{T} \frac{c_t \% \times \text{FV}}{(1+\text{YTM})^t} \times t + \frac{\text{FV}}{(1+\text{YTM})^T} \times T\right)$$

Its relevance comes from its linkage to the bond volatility—i.e., the bond's sensitivity to interest rate changes. In fact, it gives an idea of the increase (decrease) of the bond price in case of a Δk decrease (increase) of each discount rate.

$$\text{Volatility } \sigma = \frac{\Delta P}{P} = -\frac{D^{\text{MAC}}}{1+\text{YTM}} \times \Delta k$$

The bond value is called the *dirty price* in the financial market in contrast with the *clean price*, which is the difference between the dirty price and accrued interests. Accrued interests are those accumulated since the previous coupon payment. This can be calculated as follows:

$$\text{clean price} = \text{dity price} - \text{accrued interests} = \text{dirty price} - c \times \frac{m}{M}$$

where m is the time bucket since the previous coupon payment and M is the time bucket between two consecutive coupon payments. Be sure that the time buckets of the numerator and dominator are the same—e.g., both days, months, or years.

Bonds are classified even for the ratio between the face value and the clean price. In particular:

If clean price $<$ FV, then the bond is said to quote below par.
If clean price $=$ FV, then the bond is said to quote at par.
If clean price $>$ FV, then the bond is said to quote above par.

As shown previously, zero-coupon bonds always quote below par, so they are always sold at a discount on the face value. The difference between the bond price and its face value is the only remuneration the bondholder receives. Table 10.4 lists some available data about a bond.

Table 10.4 Bond IT0004503717 Description	
Description	ENI 06/2014 FX 4% EUR
ISIN	IT0004503717
Last price	104.02
Minimum price	104.01
Maximum price	104.089
Issue date	June 26, 2009
Issuer	ENI
Time to maturity (days)	448
Maturity	June 29, 2015
Coupon type	Fixed rate
Coupon date	June 29, 2014
Quotation type	Clean price
Accrued interests (act/360)	3.0466
Duration	1.073
Currency	EUR
Listing market	Italian MOT
Issue price	99.9
Coupon rate	4%
Coupon frequency	Annual
Face value	1.000
Security class	Corporate
Country of register	Italy
Source: www.milanofinanza.it/quotazioni.	

10.3.3 Leasing

A *lease* is a contractual agreement between a lessee (user) and a lessor (the owner of the asset). It gives the right to the lessee to use an asset for a period, making periodic payments (e.g., monthly, semiannually, or annually) to the lessor.

The lessor could be the asset manufacturer or an independent leasing company that buys the asset from the manufacturer and leases it out.

From an accounting point of view, leasing could be *off-balance sheet financing*, as a firm could use an asset through a lease and not necessarily disclose the existence of the lease contract on the balance sheet. In the IFRS accounting standards, the IAS 17—last amended in 2010—regulates leasing accounting.

Generally, we can distinguish between operating leases and finance leases. According to the IAS 17.4, "a lease is classified as a finance lease if it transfers substantially all the risks and rewards incident to ownership. All other leases are classified as operating leases." Thus, it suggests focusing on the substance of the transaction rather than the form.

An operating lease is related to more standardized items. It is generally shorter term in comparison with finance leasing but even more so than the economic life of the asset. The lessee could ask to renew the asset, give it back, or even cancel the leasing prior to the expiration date.

A financial lease is generally longer term, and at the end of the leasing period, the asset ownership should be transferred or the lessee should be given the opportunity to redeem the asset.

It is crucial to know who is responsible for the asset insurance, maintenance, and taxes. In an operating lease, the lessor transfers the related costs to the lessee, including them in the lease payments. In finance leasing, the lessee is the responsible party.

Companies often face the choice between leasing an asset rather than buying it. In fact, leasing an asset is less capital intensive and lets the company deduct the entire amount of the lease payments it makes.

Even in comparison with a loan, the company achieves a tax shield. In fact, the loan gives the company the opportunity to deduct only the interest payments. In addition, a loan generally does not permit the company to finance the entire amount of an asset value—only a maximum of 50–65% (before the financial crisis, this was up to 80–100%).

According to the analyses by Assilea and Aritma,[4] the Italian lease market shows a 15.9% decline on contract numbers and a 34.6% decline in contract value at approximately 16.7 billion euros. There has been a strong decrease in real estate leasing at 3.6 billion euros (− 48.9%, while it was −13% at a European level[5]) and −50.8% on the contract value and −67.6% on contract numbers in leasing for the railway, aeronautics, and naval industries. In addition, 75% of Italian leasing contracts are addressed to SME. While the Italian vehicle leasing segment decreased by 25.1% in value, at a European level, it grew by 5.2% compared to 2012.[6]

10.3.4 Syndicated Loans

A syndicated loan is provided by a group of lenders. It is structured, arranged, and administered by one or several commercial or investment banks known as arrangers (refer to Figure 10.6). The aim is to lend money to a borrower with a unique contract. This allows the partition of credit that a stand-alone bank could not disburse.

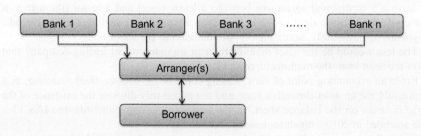

Figure 10.6 General structure of a syndicated loan.

[4]Assilea and Aritma, Leasing Annual Report, 2012.
[5]European data are reported in a Leaseurope press release available at http://www.leaseurope.org/uploads/documents/press-releases/pr140314-Preliminary%20Survey.pdf.
[6]Please refer to Footnote 5.

Figure 10.7 reports the volume of global syndicated loans, categorized by the amount lent in each quarter and the total number of issues per year. It is important to pay attention to the decrease of the issues in 2013, as this number does not include the 2013 4Q data. Table 10.5 summarizes the 2013 3Q proceeds and issues according to geographical distribution, while Table 10.6 lists the most relevant global syndicated loans given in 2013 up to 3Q.

Syndicated loans are a way to have access to credit if a company needs a large amount of money, with the advantage of signing a unique contract and communicating with a unique administrator (the arranger bank). In addition, this method allows the company to opt for a flexible and customized solution.

Another financing option is bond placement, as discussed in Section 10.3.2. While this lets the company issue securities with customized but standardized features and turn to a more extensive and liquid market, this is not as effective for large sums, as only certain companies can afford this option—i.e., investment-grade enterprises or those with a sound reputation.

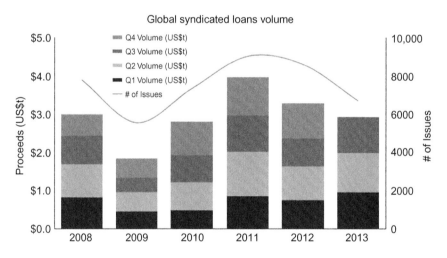

Figure 10.7 Global syndicated loan volume. Thompson Reuters, Global Syndicate Loans Review, 3Q 2013.

Table 10.5 2013 3Q Data on Syndicated Loans		
	January 1, 2013 to March 9, 2013	
	Proceeds (US$)	Number of Issues
Americas	1,752,080.9	3300
Europe	580,803.2	879
Africa/Middle East/Central Asia	62,699.3	101
Asia-Pacific	314,112.9	955
Japan	223,225.9	1497
Global	2,932,922.2	6707
Source: Thompson Reuters, Global Syndicate Loans Review, 3Q 2013.		

Table 10.6 Top 10 Global Syndicated Loans. January 1, 2013 to March 9, 2013.				
Closing Date	Borrower	Target Market	Package Amt (US$m)	Primary UOP
September 13, 2013	SoftBank Corp	Japan	19,930.7	Refn/Ret Bank Debt
June 5, 2013	Wal-Mart Stores Inc.	United States	17,353.0	Refn/Ret Bank Debt
June 13, 2013	Glencore Xstrata PLC	Switzerland	17,340.0	Refn/Ret Bank Debt
May 14, 2013	DTCC	United States	14,621.0	Refn/Ret Bank Debt
February 13, 2013	NK Rosneft	Russian Fed	14,212.0	Acquisition Fin.
May 31, 2013	Thermo Fisher Scientific Inc.	United States	14,000.0	Future Acquisitions
September 30, 2013	Nestle SA	Switzerland	13,488.0	Refn/Ret Bank Debt
June 6, 2013	HJ Heinz Co.	United States	13,100.0	Leveraged Buyout
February 8, 2013	Enel SpA	Italy	12,618.6	Refn/Ret Bank Debt
September 26, 2013	Daimler AG	Germany	12,142.5	Refn/Ret Bank Debt
Source: Thompson Reuters, Global Syndicate Loans Review, 3Q 2013.				

Annexure 1: Consolidated Financial Statement

Deborah Agostino

Politecnico di Milano, Department of Management, Economics & Industrial Engineering

Consolidated financial statements are financial reports that show the financial results of a group of companies as if individual entities were a single economic entity. The group consists of a parent company and all its controlled entities. The parent is the enterprise that controls one or more enterprises. Each controlled company maintains its set of financial statements that are independent of the entity that owns the company itself. The parent instead prepares the consolidated financial statement of the group that comprises the same documents prepared by the single enterprise. These documents have two main purposes:

- To provide information on the situation of the *resources of a group* of companies, detailing the item "equity investments"
- To provide information on the *incomes of the group* without considering revenues and costs related to intragroup operations.

The parent company must prepare consolidated financial statements when it has control over another company. Following IAS principles,[1] control exists when:

- The parent holds more than one-half of the voting power in another company or
- The parent holds <50% of voting power in another company, but it exerts a significant influence over the other enterprise (i.e., controls the board of directors).

Box A1.1 Exemption to Financial Statement Consolidation

A parent company is required to prepare consolidated financial statements if control over another company exists. However, some exemptions exist. Following IAS principles, a parent is not required to (but may) present consolidated financial statements if the following four conditions are met (paragraph 4 of IFRS 10):

1. The parent is itself a wholly owned subsidiary or is a partially owned subsidiary of another entity and its other owners, including those not otherwise entitled to vote, have been informed about, and do not object to, the parent not presenting consolidated financial statements
2. The parent's debt or equity instruments are not traded in a public market
3. The parent did not file, nor is it in the process of filing, its financial statements with a securities commission or other regulatory organisation for the purpose of issuing any class of instruments in a public market
4. The ultimate or any intermediate parent of the parent produces consolidated financial statements available for public use that comply with International Financial Reporting Standards.

---

[1] US GAAP, for example, requires consolidated financial statements when ownership is >50%.

This chapter presents the principles of consolidation by first introducing the concept of a "group" and the type of control between companies. Then, theories to represent groups will be described and, finally, the principles of consolidation will be analyzed.

A1.1 THE CONCEPT OF A "GROUP"

A "group" can be defined as a collection of companies constituted by a parent (the controlling entity) and one or more controlled entities. Each company of the group represents an independent legal entity, which is considered a unique economic entity through the consolidated financial statement.

The parent company—also defined as the holding company—holds administrative and decisional power over the other companies within the group. Depending on the type of activity of the holding, it can be:

- A *pure holding company*, when it does not produce goods or services, but its activity consists of owning and managing participations in other controlled entities.
- A *mixed holding company*, when it controls other entities while at the same time providing goods and services.

Depending on the degree of influence exerted by the parent company, the controlled entity can be a subsidiary, an associate, or a joint venture.

A *subsidiary* is a controlled company in which the parent exerts a dominant influence (IAS 27). This means that the parent owns more than 50% of voting rights. Even if the parent does not hold more than one-half of the voting right, a dominant influence exists if the parent has the power:

- To govern the financial and operating policies of the entity under a statute or an agreement
- To appoint or remove the majority of the members of the board of directors or
- To cast the majority of votes at a meeting of the board of directors.

This means that if Company A owns 46% of voting rights of Company B and the remaining shares are owned by thousands of small shareholders, then Company A has a dominant influence, even without controlling more than one-half of Company B.

An *associate company* is a controlled company in which the parent exerts a significant influence. The parent holds less than 50% of voting rights but more than 20%. This control provides the parent with the possibility to be represented in the board of directors and participates in the decision-making process, even without having the majority of voting rights.

A *joint venture* occurs when two or more entities undertake an economic activity under joint control (IAS 31). The joint control implies that the control of economic activities is shared among the entities belonging to the joint venture, which requires unanimous consensus of the involved entities to make strategic decisions. Following IAS 31, joint ventures are considered as part of a group, but in some countries, such as the United States, they are considered external.

A parent and its controlled entities—subsidiaries, associates, or joint ventures—can therefore constitute the group. The portion of the controlled entity that is not controlled by the parent is owned by other shareholders, which represent the *minority interest* in the group. This minority interest represents claims on the group resources by shareholders outside the group. Information on the minority interest can be found in the consolidated financial statement depending on the method of consolidation that is adopted, as we will see in the next section.

A1.2 THEORIES OF CONSOLIDATION

The group can be analyzed following different perspectives—called theories of consolidation—which influence the consolidation of financial statements in different ways. Three different theories of consolidation can be identified:

- Proprietary theory
- Entity theory
- Parent company theory.

Each of these theories emphasizes different elements of the group (Figure A1.1), which in turn are associated with different methods of consolidation.

The differences in consolidation are related to the following elements:

- The accounting of the differences derived by the consolidation procedures
- The accounting of capital gains and losses related to assets or liabilities
- The definition or registration of minority interests when the percentage of control is lower than 100%.

Proprietary theory focuses on the parent company. Controlled companies are considered an investment by the parent. Therefore, the central element is not the group, but the parent company itself. According to this perspective, the consolidated financial statement represents an enlarged financial statement of the parent company, which contains detailed information on investments made by the parent in the controlled entities. Given this structure, the consolidated financial statement presents some informative gaps, given that it does not contain details on the invested capital within the group, and minority interests are not shown.

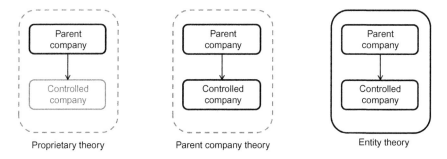

Figure A1.1 Representation of theories of consolidation.

Entity theory considers the group as a third entity that is autonomous from the plurality of the individual enterprises. In this case, the central element is the group as a whole. Following this perspective, the consolidated financial statement is complete. It provides information on the group as a whole, and minority interests are detailed. This structure can satisfy the information needs of stakeholders that interact with the group for different reasons.

Parent company theory is positioned between proprietary theory and entity theory. It considers the group an independent entity according to the entity theory. However, it focuses on the parent company and its interests following the proprietary theory perspective.

A1.3 METHODS OF CONSOLIDATION

This section discusses the methods of consolidation, which vary according to the theory adopted to conceptualize the group (proprietary theory, entity theory, or parent company theory). Three different methods of consolidation can be adopted:

- Proportionate method
- Line-by-line method
- Equity method.

Irrespective of the specific method adopted, the following steps should be taken when consolidating financial statements.

A1.3.1 First Step of Consolidation

To harmonize accounting principles between companies of the group. Each independent company can adopt different accounting criteria. The first step of the consolidation procedure is to verify that accounting principles are homogeneous among companies in the group. For example, all financial documents used in the consolidation should be drawn up to the same reporting date. Accounting principles related to inventories or amortization criteria should also be aligned among the different enterprises.

A1.3.2 Second Step of Consolidation

To delete equity investments. The consolidated financial statement presents the financial situation of a group of companies and therefore information on intragroup equity investments is not provided. When starting the consolidation procedure, equity investments should be deleted from the consolidated assets; at the same time, the same amount of the parent's portion of equity of each controlled entity should also be deleted. The difference between equity investments (the purchasing price) and the total fair market value of the difference between assets and liabilities of the controlled company is called goodwill and is recognized as an asset in the consolidated balance sheet. The goodwill is recognized only when the difference between the equity investment and the market value of the assets of the controlled company is positive. If the difference is negative, this negative value should be listed in the profit and loss account.

Box A1.2 Goodwill Recognition

Consider Company A, which acquires the whole share capital of Company B at a price of 100,000 € as of March 31. The balance sheets of the respective companies at this date are shown herein.

	A	B
Property, plant, and equipment	60,000	30,000
Equity investments	100,000	
Other noncurrent assets	20,000	5000
Current assets	30,000	10,000
Total assets	**210,000**	**45,000**
Capital	140,000	35,000
Reserves	70,000	10,000
Total liabilities	**210,000**	**45,000**

At the same date, the market value of Company B's assets was as follows:

	B
Property, plant, and equipment	35,000
Other noncurrent assets	7000
Current assets	13,000
Total assets	**55,000**

The difference between the equity investment of 100,000 € and the fair value of assets of Company B (55,000 €) will give a goodwill of 45,000 €.

In order to define the consolidated balance sheet, the equity investment will be deleted and replaced by the assets and liabilities of Company B. Accordingly, the consolidated asset values will be equal to the assets of Company A summed with the fair value of the assets of Company B.

The consolidated balance sheet is shown herein:

	Consolidated Balance Sheet
Property, plant, and equipment	95,000
Goodwill	45,000
Other noncurrent assets	27,000
Current assets	43,000
Total assets	**210,000**
Capital	140,000
Reserves	70,000
Total liabilities	**210,000**

A1.3.3 Third Step of Consolidation

To eliminate intragroup exchanges. Following the same logic to delete equity investments to provide information related to the group as an independent entity, intragroup exchanges within the group should also not be considered in consolidation in order to avoid the double-counting of any items (IAS 27). If the parent company and its subsidiaries do business together, intragroup payables or receivables and intragroup sales, costs, and profits are removed from consolidated financial statements.

Box A1.3   Intragroup Exchanges

Assume that Subsidiary Y sells 100 € of products to parent Company X and that this sale is on credit. Each individual enterprise will register these events on its records: Company Y will recognize a sale of 100 € and an account receivable of the same amount. Company X will register an increase of inventory of 100 € and an account payable of the same amount.

However, from a group perspective, no transaction has occurred. Products (and the associated payables and receivables) have just moved from one company to another, but no exchanges have occurred outside the group. Therefore, this transaction should be eliminated from consolidated financial statements but should be detailed in the records of each company in the group.

These three steps are adopted to consolidate financial statements independent of the method of consolidation. Each method is discussed in detail in the following sections.

A1.3.4 Proportionate Method

The proportionate method is related to proprietary theory. Following this method, the consolidated financial statement is defined considering the fair value of assets and liabilities of the controlled company multiplied by the percentage of control from the parent. The emphasis is on the parent company and its investments on controlled entities. Information on minority interests is not provided in the consolidated statement.

Assume that parent Company X acquires 60% of Company Y at a purchasing price of 5000 €. The balance sheets of the two companies are presented in Table A1.1 (for simplicity, we assume that the book values of Company Y correspond to market values).

The consolidated financial statement of the group composed of Company X plus Company Y must be defined.

Assuming that the accounting principles between the companies are homogeneous, the first step to consolidation is deleting equity investments. This operation must be counterbalanced by the omission of the shareholder equity of the controlled company. The result will be as follows in Table A1.2.

The second step of consolidation requires the calculation of the goodwill associated with the difference between the market value of the acquisition and the book value of

Table A1.1 Balance Sheets of Company X and Company Y		
	X	Y
Property, plant, and equipment	4000	9000
Equity investments	5000	
Current assets	4500	7000
Total assets	**13,500**	**16,000**
Subscribed capital	3000	2000
Reserves	2000	2000
Liabilities	8500	12,000
Total liabilities	**13,500**	**16,000**

Table A1.2 Omission of Equity Investments				
	X	Y	X + Y	Variation
Property, plant, and equipment	4000	9000	13,000	
Goodwill			–	
Equity investments	5000		5000	−5000
Current assets	4500	7000	11,500	
Total assets	**13,500**	**16,000**	**29,500**	
Subscribed capital	3000	2000	5000	−2000
Reserves	2000	2000	4000	−2000
Liabilities	8500	12,000	20,500	
Total liabilities	**13,500**	**16,000**	**29,500**	

the controlled company. The proportionate method calculates this value by focusing only on the percentage of control by the parent:

$$Goodwill = market\ value(\%\ control) - book\ value(\%\ control)$$

With reference to the example, the goodwill will be equal to 2600 €, calculated as the difference between the market value of the percentage of the company acquired for 5000 € and the book value of the controlled portion of 2400 €.

The third step consists of defining the value of the remaining assets and liabilities. They are defined considering the fair value of all items of assets and liabilities multiplied by the percentage of control. Considering the example, the value of property, plant, and equipment will be equal to the value of Company X (4000 €), adding the value of property, plant, and equipment of Company Y for the only percentage controlled by the parent (9000 × 0.6 = 9400).

Table A1.3 shows the result of the consolidation detailed in the last column.

The final consolidated statement does not provide any information on minority interests and still focuses on the parent company. For this reason, the usefulness of the information for third parties is quite limited.

Table A1.3 Consolidated Financial Statement Following the Proportionate Method				
	X	Y	X + Y	Consolidation
Property, plant, and equipment	4000	9000	13,000	9400
Goodwill			–	2600
Equity investments	5000		5000	–
Current assets	4500	7000	11,500	8700
Total assets	13,500	16,000	29,500	20,700
Subscribed capital	3000	2000	5000	3000
Reserves	2000	2000	4000	2000
Liabilities	8500	12,000	20,500	15,700
Total liabilities	13,500	16,000	29,500	20,700

A1.3.5 Line-by-Line Method (Related to Equity Theory)

The line-by-line method can be applied to both equity theory and proprietary theory. This paragraph focuses on the application of the line-by-line method with reference to equity theory.

Given that the group is considered a separated and stand-alone entity, the consolidated financial statement is defined considering the fair value of all assets and liabilities of all the companies of the group. Hence, line by line, all the items are summed considering the overall amount, arriving at the consolidated value. Furthermore, the consolidated statement provides information on minority interests included as part of the consolidated shareholders' value.

Consider the same previous example: parent Company X acquires 60% of Company Y at a purchasing price of 5000 €. The consolidated financial statement must be defined adopting the line-by-line method. The steps of consolidation do not vary and consist of the omission of equity participation, calculation of goodwill, and definition of the remaining items.

The first step requires deleting equity participation and the corresponding value of the shareholders' equity of the controlled company. The result is analogous to the previous example with the proportionate method (refer to Table A1.2).

The second step implies the calculation of the goodwill. The formula will change as follows:

$$\text{Goodwill} = \text{total market value} - \text{total book value}$$

With reference to the example, the goodwill will be equal to 4333 € calculated as the difference between the total market value of 8333 € and the total book value of 4000 €. This approach is consistent with the principle behind the entity theory to consider the group as a third independent entity.

The third step consists of defining the value of the remaining assets and liabilities. They are calculated by summing, line by line, the value of each company involved. In the example, the consolidated value of property, plant, and equipment will be equal to the value of Company X (4000 €), adding the total value of property, plant, and equipment of Company Y (9000 €).

Table A1.4 shows the result of the consolidation detailed in the last column.

Table A1.4 Consolidated Financial Statement Following the Line-by-Line Method (Entity Theory)

	X	Y	X + Y	Consolidation
Property, plant, and equipment	4000	9000	13,000	13,000
Goodwill			–	4333
Equity investments	5000		5000	–
Current assets	4500	7000	11,500	11,500
Total assets	**13,500**	**16,000**	**29,500**	**28,833**
Subscribed capital	3000	2000	5000	3000
Reserves	2000	2000	4000	2000
Minority interests				3333
Liabilities	8500	12,000	20,500	20,500
Total liabilities	**13,500**	**16,000**	**29,500**	**28,833**

Table A1.5 Consolidated Financial Statement Following the Line-by-Line Method (Parent Company Theory)

	X	Y	X + Y	Consolidation
Property, plant, and equipment	4000	9000	13,000	13,000
Goodwill			–	2600
Equity investments	5000		5000	–
Current assets	4500	7000	11,500	11,500
Total assets	**13,500**	**16,000**	**29,500**	**27,100**
Subscribed capital	3000	2000	5000	3000
Reserves	2000	2000	4000	2000
Minority interests				1600
Liabilities	8500	12,000	20,500	20,500
Total liabilities	**13,500**	**16,000**	**29,500**	**27,100**

A1.3.6 Line-by-Line Method (Related to Parent Company Theory)

The line-by-line method can also be applied with reference to parent company theory. In this case, the only difference from the previous application is in the calculation of goodwill, which is based on the portion of shares owned by the parent rather than on the whole market value of the controlled entity. The formula is analogous to the one applied for the proportionate method and will provide the same value of goodwill of 2600 €. The remaining calculations are equal to the line-by-line method related to entity theory.

Applying the calculation to the previous example, the consolidated financial statement will result as follows.

As you can see from Table A1.5, this approach mixes the calculation of goodwill of the proportionate method with the sum of the total value of items of the line-by-line method.

If we compare the results of the three approaches, we can see that the line-by-line method generates a higher value of the group (assets equal to 28,833 €) when compared with the proportionate method (assets equal to 20,700 €). These differences are aligned with the theories behind these approaches: equity theory, which considers the group a stand-alone entity, and proprietary theory, which considers the group an extension of investments by the parent.

A1.3.7 Equity Method

The equity method is a synthetic method to consolidate financial statements that does not show the details of the group but simply includes the excess of profits of the controlled entities in the value of the investment of the parent. The value of the controlled company corresponds to the book value of the company itself. The value of the acquisition for the parent company is calculated as follows:

$$\text{Book value}(t) = \text{book value}(t-1) + \text{profits}(t) - \text{dividends}(t)$$

where

t = year
Book value = value of the controlled company
Book value $(t-1)$ = value of the controlled company at year $(t-1)$
Profits = profits gained by the controlled company
Dividends = dividends distributed by the controlled company.

Assume that a parent buys an entity for 50 million € (for simplicity, we assume no goodwill) in a given year. In the first year after the acquisition, the controlled company makes a profit of 10 million € and distributes dividends for 1 million €. The application of the equity method would show a revised value of the acquisition for the parent company of 59 million €. No other information on the group is provided.

As you can see from the example, this is a very synthetic approach that does not provide detailed information on the assets and liabilities of the group. It is usually applied when the parent company exerts a significant influence and owns less than half of voting rights.

A summary of the methods of consolidation, distinguished according to the type of equity participation, is provided in Table A1.6.

Table A1.6 Consolidation Methods and Their Application		
Equity Participation	**Type of Control**	**Consolidation Method**
Subsidiary (IAS 27)	Significant influence	Line-by-line method
Associate (IAS 28)	Dominant influence	Equity method or proportionate method
Joint venture (IAS 31)	Joint control	Equity method or proportionate method

REFERENCES

Aaker, D.A., 1996. Measuring brand equity across products and markets. Calif. Manage. Rev. 38, 3.

Abdel-Maksoud, A.B., 2004. Manufacturing in the UK: contemporary characteristics and performance indicators. J. Manuf. Technol. Manag. 15, 155–171.

Agostino, D., Arnaboldi, M., 2012. Design issues in Balanced Scorecards: the "what" and "how" of control. Eur. Manag. J. 30 (4), 327–339.

Agyemang, G., 2009. Responsibility and accountability without direct control? Local education authorities and the seeking of influence in the UK schools sector. Account. Audit. Account. J. 22 (5), 762–788.

Akehurst, G., Afonso, C., Goncalves, H.M., 2012. Re-examining green purchase behaviour and the green consumer profile: new evidences. Manag. Decis. 50 (5), 972–988.

Albright, T., Stan, D., 2004. An investigation of the effect of Balanced Scorecard implementation on financial performance. Manag. Account. Res. 15, 135–163.

Amram, M., Kulatilaka, N., 1999. *Real Options: Managing Investment in an Uncertain World.* Harvard Business School Press, Cambridge, Massachusett.

Arena, M., Arnaboldi, M., 2013a. Risk and budget in an uncertain world. Int. J. Bus. Perform. Manag. 14 (2), 166–180.

Arena, M., Arnaboldi, M., 2013b. Risk and performance management: are they easy partners? Manag. Res. Rev. 37 (2), 152–166.

Arena, M., Azzone, G., 2005. ABC, Balanced Scorecard, EVATM: an empirical study on the adoption of innovative management accounting techniques. Int. J. Account. Audit. Perform. Eval. 2 (3), 206–225.

Arena, M., Arnaboldi, M., Azzone, G., 2010a. Student perception and central administrative services: the case of higher education in Italy. Stud. High. Educ. 35 (8), 941–959.

Arena, M., Arnaboldi, M., Azzone, G., 2010b. The organizational dynamics of enterprise risk management. Account. Organ. Soc. 35 (7), 659–675.

Arena, M., Arnaboldi, M., Azzone, G., 2011. Is enterprise risk management real? J. Risk Res. 14, 7.

Armstrong, P., 2002. The costs of activity-based management. Account. Organ. Soc. 27, 99–120.

Aseeri, A., Bagajewicz, M.J., 2004. New measures and procedures to manage financial risk with applications to the planning of gas commercialization in Asia. Comput. Chem. Eng. 28 (12), 2791–2821.

Assilea and Aritma, 2012. Rapporto sul leasing 2012.

Baird, K.M., Harrison, G.L., Reeve, R.C., 2004. Adoption of activity management practices: a note on the extent of adoption and the influence of organizational cultural factors. Manag. Account. Res. 15, 383–399.

Barretta, A., Busco, C., 2011. Technologies of government in public sector's networks: In search of cooperation through management control innovations. Manag. Account. Res. 22 (4), 211–219.

Beasley, M.S., Clune, R., Hermanson, D.R., 2005. Enterprise risk management: an empirical analysis of factors associated with the extent of implementation. J. Account. Public Policy 24, 521–531.

Belhadjali, M., Halperin, M., Lusk, E.J., Matzner, D., 2005. DSS utilization: a comparative study for major firms in Germany and the USA: an examination of the Implementation Paradox. Prob. Perspect. Manag. 2, 40–44.

Berland, N., Sponem, S., 2005. Interactive budgetary control and management by objectives: evidence from a case study. European Accounting Association Congress, Goteborg, May.

Bickley, J.H., 1959. The nature of business risk. J. Insur. 25 (4), 32–42.

Bischof, J., Speckbacher, G., Peiffer, T., 2003. A descriptive analysis on the implementation of Balanced Scorecards an German-speaking countries. Manag. Account. Res. 14, 361–387.

Black, F., Scholes, M., 1973. The pricing of options and corporate liabilities. J. Polit. Econ. 81, 637–659.

Bourguignon, A., Horreklit, H., Malleret, V., 2004. The American Balanced scorecard versus the French tableau de bord: the ideological dimension. Manag. Account. Res. 15, 107–134.

Brickley, J.A., Zimmerman, J.L., 2010. Corporate governance myths: comments on Armstrong, Guay, and Weber. J. Account. Econ. 50 (2), 235–245.

Bromwich, M., Walker, M., 1998. Residual income past and future. Manag. Account. Res. 9, 391–419.

Brooking, A., 1997. Intellectual Capital. International Thomson Business Press, London.

Bruggerman, W., Everaert, P., Levant, Y., 2005. A Case Study in a Distribution Company. European Accounting Association Congress, Goteborg, May 2005

Calandro, J., Lane, S., 2006. Insights from the Balanced Scorecard An introduction to the Enterprise Risk Scorecard. Meas. Bus. Excell. 10 (3), 31–40.

Carlsson Walle, M., Kraus, K., Lind, J., 2011. The interdependencies of intra- and inter-organizational controls and work practices – The case of domestic care of the elderly. Manag. Account. Res. 22 (4), 313–329.

Chapman C.S., Kihn L.A., May 2005. Reassessing the role of budgets in strategic management. European Accounting Association Congress, Goteborg.

Chenhall, R.H., 2005. Integrative strategic performance measurement system, strategic alignment of manufacturing, learning and strategic outcomes: an exploratory study. Account. Organ. Soc. 30, 395–422.

Chenhall, R.H., Langfield-Smith, K., 1998. Adoption and benefits of management accounting practices: an Australian study. Manag. Account. Res. 9, 1–19.

Chenhall, R.H., Hall, M., Smith, D., 2010. Social capital and management control systems: a study of a non-government organization. Account. Organ. Soc 35 (8), 737–756.

Clarkson, M.E., 1995. A stakeholder framework for analyzing and evaluating corporate social performance. Acad. Manag. Rev. 20 (1), 92–117.

Collier, P.M., Berry, A.J., 2002. Risk in the process of budgeting. Manag. Account. Res. 13 (3), 273–297.

Consob, 2013. Rapporto sulla corporate governance delle società quotate italiane 2013.

Copeland, T.E., Koller, T., Murrin, J., 1990. Valuation: Measuring and Managing the Value of Companies. John Wiley & Sons.

Costigan, M.L., Lovata, L.M., 2002. Empirical analysis of adopters of economic value added. Manag. Account. Res. 13, 215–228.

Cuganesan, S., Dumay, J.C., 2009. Reflecting on the production of intellectual capital visualisations. Account. Auditing Account. J. 22 (8), 1161–1186.

Damodaran, Aswath, 2010. Applied Corporate Finance. John Wiley & Sons Inc.

David, F., 1996. Cash Flow Performance Measurement: Managing for Value. *Financial Executives Research Foundation*, Inc., Morristown, NJ, 6.

Davis, S., Albright, T., 2004. An investigation of the effect of Balanced Scorecard implementation on financial performance. Manag. Account. Res. 15, 135–153.

Edvinsson, L., 1997. Developing intellectual capital at Skandia. Long Range Plann. 30, 366–373, Elsevier Science Ltd.

Edvinsson, L., Malone, M.S., 1997. Intellectual Capital. Piatkus, London.

Epstein, M., Manzoni, J.F., 1998. Implementing corporate strategy: from Tableaux. Eur. Manage. J. 16, 190–203.

EU Commission, 2010. Green Paper.

EU Federation for the Factoring and Commercial Finance Industry, EUF Brochure, September 2010.

EU Federation for the Factoring and Commercial Finance Industry, EUF Brochure, April 2013.

EU Federation for the Factoring and Commercial Finance Industry, EUF Brochure, August 2013.

Evans, R.E., 2004. An exploratory study of performance measurement systems and relationship with performance results. J. Oper. Manage. 22, 219–232.

Fama, Eugene F., French, Kenneth R., 1996. Multifactor explanations of asset pricing anomalies. The journal of finance 51.1, 55–84.

Fiss, P.C., Zajac, E.J., 2004. The diffusion of ideas over contested terrain: the (non)adoption of a shareholder value orientation among German firms. Adm. Sci. Q. 49, 501–534.

Fraser, I., Henry, W., 2007. Embedding risk management: structures and approaches. Managerial Audit. J. 22 (4), 392–409.

Gosselin, M., 1997. The effect of strategy and organizational structure on the adoption and implementation of activity-based costing. Account. Organ. Soc. 2, 105–122.

Greer, H.C., 1954. Managerial Accounting-Twenty Years from Now. Account. Rev. 29 (2), 175–185.

Gunasekaran, A., McGaughey, R.E., Williams, H.J., 2005. Performance measurement and costing system in new enterprise. Technovation 25, 523–533.

Guthrie, J., Petty, R., 2000. Intellectual capital: Australian annual reporting practices. J. Intellect. Capital 1 (3), 241–251.

Hansen, S.C., Otley, D.T., Van der Stede, W.A., 2003. Practice developments in budgeting: an overview and research perspective. J. Manag. Account. Res. 15, 95–116.

Ikaheimo, S., Malmi, T., 2003. Value based management practices—some evidence from the field. Manag. Account. Res. 14, 235–254.

Jorion, P., 2007. Value at risk: The New Benchmark for Managing Financial Risk. McGraw-Hill.

Kalu, T.C.U., 1999. Capital budgeting under uncertainty: an extended goal programming approach. Int. J. Prod. Econ. 58, 235–251.

Kaplan, R.S., Anderson, S.R., 2004. Time-driven activity-based costing. Harv. Bus. Rev., 131–138.

Kaplan, R.S., Norton, D.P., 1992. The Balanced Scorecard—Measures That Drive Performance. Harv. Bus. Rev. 70, 71−79.

Keller, K.L., 1993. Conceptualizing, Measuring, and Managing Customer-Based Brand Equity. J. Mark. 57 (1), 1−22.

Kester, W.C., 1984. Today's options for tomorrow's growth. Harv. Bus. Rev. 62 (2), 153−160.

Langer, H., Schröder, R., Wall, F., May 2005. Accounting along the value chain: empirical motivation, theoretical framework, and case study in the service sector. European Accounting Association Congress, Goteborg.

Lawrie, G., Cobbold, I., 2004. Third-generation balanced scorecard: evolution of an effective strategic control tool. Int. J. Prod. Manag. 53 (7), 611−623.

Lebas, M. in Bhimani, 1996. Management Accounting, European Perspectives. Oxford University Press, Oxford, pp. 84−85.

Lewis, V.B., 1952. Toward a theory of budgeting. Public Adm. Rev. 12 (1), 42−54.

Lind, J., Thrane, S., 2005. Accounting in Scandinavia—The Northern Lights. CBS Press, Copenhagen.

Mabert, V.A., Soni, A., Venkataramanan, M.A., 2003. The impact of organization size on enterprise resource planning (ERP) implementations in the US manufacturing sector. Omega 31, 235−246.

Malmi, T., Brown, D.A., 2008. Management control systems as a package—Opportunities, challenges and research directions. Manage. Account. Res. 19 (4), 287−300.

McDonald, R., Siegel, D., 1986. "The Value of Waiting to Invest". Q. J. Econ. 101 (4), 707−727.

McNulty, James J., et al., 2002. What's your real cost of capital. Harv. Bus. Rev. 80 (10), 114−121.

Modigliani, F., Miller, M., 1958. The cost of capital, corporate finance, and the theory of investment. Am. Econ. Rev. 3 (48), 261−297.

Moody's Investors Service, 2013. Suggest Future Risks for Investors, Quest for yield could leave creditors vulnerable in a downturn, <http://online.wsj.com/public/resources/documents/CovenantQualityMay2013.pdf>.

Mouritsen, J., 1998. Driving growth: economic value added vs. intellectual capital. Manage. Account. Res. 9, 461−482.

Nielsen, S., Sørensen, R., 2004. Motives, diffusion and utilisation of the balanced scorecard in Denmark. Int. J. Account. Auditing Perform. Eval. 1, 103−124.

Nilsson, U., Suppliers' costing system for supporting supply chain management and interorganizational cost management, Sabanci University

Player, S., 2003. Why some organizations go beyond budgeting. J. Corp. Account. Finance 14, 3−9.

Power, M., 2007. Organized Uncertainty Designing a World of Risk Management. Oxford University Press.

Preinreich, G.A.D., 1938. Annual Study of Economic Theory: The Theory of Depreciation. Econometrica 6, 219−241.

Provan, K.G., Sydow, J., 2008. Evaluating Inter-organizational Relationships. In: Cropper, S., Ebers, M., Huxham, C., Smith Ring, P. (Eds.), The Oxford Handbook of Inter-organizational Relations. Oxford University Press, Oxford, pp. 691−710.

Ross, Stephen A., 1976. The arbitrage theory of capital asset pricing. J. Econ. Theory 13 (3), 341−360.

Scherrer, G., in Bhimani, 1996. Management Accounting, European Perspectives. Oxford University Press, Oxford, 103.

Selim, G., Yiannakas, A., 2000. Outsourcing the internal audit function: a survey of the UK public and private sectors. Int. J. Audit. 4, 213–226.

Sharpe, William F., 1964. Capital asset prices: A theory of market equilibrium under conditions of risk. J. Finance 19 (3), 425–442.

Speckbacher, G., Bischof, J., Pfeiffer, T., 2003. A Descriptive Analysis on the Implementation of Balanced Scorecards in German-Speaking Countries. Manage. Account. Res. 14, 361–387.

Spira, L.F., Page, M., 2003. Risk management: the reinvention of internal control and the changing role of internal audit. Account. Audit. Account. J. 16 (4), 640–661.

Stewart, G.B., 1991. The Quest for value. Harper Collins, New York, NY.

Stewart, T.A., 1997. Intellectual Capital. Nicholas Brealey Publishing, London.

Sveiby, K.E., 1997. *The New Organizational Wealth: Managing and Measuring Knowledge Based Assets*. Barret-Koeheler, San Francisco, CA.

Sveiby, K.E., 2007. Methods for measuring intangible assets. Available at: www.sveiby.com.

Thrane, S., 2007. The complexity of management accounting change: bifurcation and oscillation in schizophrenic inter-organizational systems. Manage. Account. Res. 18 (2), 248–272.

Tierny, J., Smithson, C., 2003. Implementing Economic Capital in an industrial company: the case of Michelin. J. Appl. Corp. Finance 15 (4), 81–94.

Triantis, A., 2005. Realizing the potential of real options: does theory meet practice? J. Appl. Corp. Finance 17 (2), 8–16.

Van Eeverdingen, Y.M., Waarts, E., 2003. The effect of national culture on the adoption of innovations. Mark. Lett. 14 (3), 217–232.

Verbeeten, F.H.M., 2006. Do organizations adopt sophisticated capital budgeting practices to deal with uncertainty in the investment decision? A research note. Manage. Account. Res. 17, 106–120.

Wieder, B., Booth, B., Matolcsy, Z., 2000. ERP-systems and functional integration in Australia's industry. 4th Annual SAP Asia Pacific, Institute of Higher Learning Forum.

Wilcox King, A., Zeithaml, C.P., 2003. Measuring organizational knowledge: a conceptual and methodological framework. Strateg. Manage. J. 24, 763–772.

Printed and bound by CPI Group (UK) Ltd, Croydon, CR0 4YY

08/05/2025

01864800-0003